Against Epistemology: A Metacritique

THEODOR W. ADORNO

Against Epistemology: A Metacritique

Studies in Husserl and the
Phenomenological Antinomies

Translated by Willis Domingo

Originally published as *Zur Metakritik der Erkenntnistheorie* © Suhrkamp Verlag, Frankfurt am Main 1970

English translation © Basil Blackwell Publisher Limited 1982
First published in English 1982
This edition first published in 2013 by Polity Press

Polity Press
65 Bridge Street
Cambridge CB2 1UR, UK

Polity Press
350 Main Street
Malden, MA 02148, USA

ISBN-13: 978-0-7456-6537-5
ISBN-13: 978-0-7456-6538-2(pb)

A catalogue record for this book is available from the British Library.

Printed and bound in Great Britain by MPG Books Group Limited, Bodmin, Cornwall

Every effort has been made to trace all copyright holders, but if any have been inadvertently overlooked the publisher will be pleased to include any necessary credits in any subsequent reprint or edition.

For further information on Polity, visit our website: www.politybooks.com

Contents

For Max

Preface

Portions of an extensive manuscript produced in Oxford during my first years of emigration, 1934–37, have been selected and reworked. For I felt their scope and significance kept them above simple academic dispute. Without sacrificing contact with the subject matter and thus the obligation to argue effectively against a method designed to forego the need for argument, the question I shall broach – by means of a concrete model – is the possibility and truth of epistemology in principle. Husserl's philosophy is the occasion and not the point of this book. Thus it is not to be presented as a completed whole and then subject to some sort of comparison. As is appropriate for a thought which does not submit to the idea of a system, I seek to organize what is thought around its focal points. The result was a discontinuous and yet most closely connected, mutually supporting set of individual studies. Overlapping was unavoidable.

This book inclines toward substantive philosophy. The critique of Husserl aims across his work at the tendency, which was of such emphatic concern to him and which he felt German philosophizing appropriated much more fundamentally than is currently admitted. The book is, nevertheless, not systematic in the sense of the traditional contrast to history. If it challenges the very concept of system, it also seeks to grasp an historical core inside the substantive question. For the historical/systematic distinction also falls under the critique of this book.

Nowhere do I pretend it is philological or hermeneutic. Secondary literature is ignored. A number of Husserl's own texts, especially in the second volume of the *Logical Investigations*, are a densely complex thicket and certainly even ambiguous. Should my interpretation occasionally be in error, I would be the last to defend it. On the other hand, I could not respect programmatic declarations, and had to abide by what the texts themselves appeared to me to say. Thus I did not allow myself to be intimidated by Husserl's assurance that pure phenomenology is not epistemology, and that the region of pure consciousness has nothing to do with the concept of the structure of the given in the immanence of consciousness (*Bewußtseinsimmanenz*) as it was known to pre-Husserlian criticism. How exactly Husserl distinguishes himself from this criticism is just as much a matter of discussion as whether that distinction is binding or not.

My analysis is confined to what Husserl himself published, with preference for the authentic phenomenological writing – on which the restoration of ontology was based – over the later works, in which Husserl's phenomenology betrayed itself and reverted into a subtly modified neo-Kantianism. Yet, since the revision of pure phenomenology came not from the convictions of its creator, but was rather imposed by its object, I thus felt free to turn to the *Formal and Transcendental Logic* and the *Cartesian Meditations*, whenever the drift of the discussion demanded it. All the pre-phenomenological writings have been ignored, in particular the *Philosophy of Arithmetic*, as well as the posthumous publications. Comprehensiveness was never my aim. The analyses Husserl actually carried through and to which he himself devoted his energy provoked my attention more than the total edifice.

Yet my intention was certainly not the mere critique of details. Instead of disputing individual epistemological issues, micrological procedure should stringently demonstrate how such questions surpass themselves and indeed their entire sphere. The themes which compose such a movement are summarized in the Introduction. The four studies alone, however, are responsible for the cogency of what I have developed.

Three of the chapters have appeared in *Archiv für Philosophie*. Chapter 4 was published separately as early as 1938 under the title 'Zur Philosophie Husserls' (Band 3, Heft 4). Chapters 1 and 2 came out in 1953 (Band 5, Heft 2 and Band 6, Heft 1/2). The final chapter in particular has been thoroughly revised since its first appearance.

Frankfurt
Easter 1956

Θνατὰ χρὴ τὸν Θνατόν, οὐκ α'Θάνατα τὸν Θνατὸν φρονεῖν.

A mortal must think mortal and not immortal thoughts.

Epicharmus, Fragment 20*

Procedure and Object

The attempt to discuss Husserl's pure phenomenology in the spirit of the dialectic risks the initial suspicion of caprice. Husserl's programme deals with a 'sphere of being of absolute origins',[1] safe from that 'regulated, methodically cultivated spirit of contradiction', which Hegel once called his procedure in conversations with Goethe.[2] The dialectic, as Hegel conceived it and which was later turned against him, is, however congenial, qualitatively different from the positive philosophies, among which in the name of the system his is included. Though Hegel's logic, like Kant's, may be 'fastened' to the transcendental subject, and be completed (*vollkommener*) Idealism, yet it refers beyond itself – as does everything complete according to Goethe's dialectical dictum. The power of the uncontradictable, which Hegel wields like no other – and whose force later bourgeois

* [Fragment *263 (123ᵇ Ahr), p. 140, *Poetarum Graecorum Fragmenta*, ed. U. von Wilamowitz-Moellendorf, vol. VI, fasc. prior.; *Comicorum Graecorum Fragmenta*, ed. Georg Kaibel, *Doriensum Comoedia Mimi Phlyaces*, vol. 1, fasc. prior. (Weidmann, Berlin, 1899). Source of fragment, Arist. *Rhet.* II, p. 1394b 25. Trans.]

[1] *Ideen*, I, p. 107; cf. *Ideas*, p. 154.
[2] *Goethes Gespräche mit Eckermann* (Insel, Leipzig, 1925), p. 375, 18 October 1827; cf. R.O. Moon, tr., *Eckermann's Conversations with Goethe* (Morgan, Laird and Co., London, no date), p. 527.

philosophy, including Husserl's, only gropingly and in fragments rediscovered for itself – is the power of contradiction. This power turns against itself and against the idea of absolute knowledge. Thought, by actively beholding, rediscovers itself in every entity, without tolerating any restrictions. It breaches, as just such a restriction, the requirement to establish a fixed ultimate to all its determinations. It thus also undermines the primacy of the system and its own content.

The Hegelian system must indeed presuppose subject–object identity, and thus the very primacy of spirit which it seeks to prove. But as it unfolds concretely, it confutes the identity which it attributes to the whole. What is antithetically developed, however, is not, as one would no doubt currently have it, the
13 structure of being in itself, but rather antagonistic society. For it is no coincidence that all the stages of the *Phenomenology of Spirit* – which appears as self-movement on the part of the concept – refer to the stages of antagonistic society. What is compelling about both the dialectic and the system and is inseparable from their character of immanence or 'logicality', is made to approximate real compulsion by their own principle of identity. Thought submits to the real compulsion of societal debt relations and, deluded, claims this compulsion as its own. Its closed circle brings about the unbroken illusion of the natural and, in the end, the metaphysical illusion of being. Dialectic, however, constantly brings this appearance back to nothing.

In the face of this, Husserl appealed to the end, in the name of his serried complete presentation of phenomenology, to that Cartesian illusion which applies to the absolute foundations of philosophy. He would like to revive *prima philosophia* by means of reflection on a spirit divested of every trace of the entity pure and simple. The metaphysical conception which characterized the beginning of the era appeared in the end as most exceedingly sublimated and disabused. As a result, however, it just appeared all the more unavoidable and consistent, naked and bare: The development of a doctrine of being under the conditions of nominalism and the reduction of concepts to the thinking subject. But this phenomenological conception just rejects dialectical analysis and Hegel's negativity as the enemy. The doctrine that everything is mediated, even supporting immediacy, is irreconcilable with the urge to 'reduction'[3] and is stigmatized as logical

[3] Cf. *Ideen*, passim, esp. pp. 59 and 94 ff; and *Ideas*, pp. 103 and 140 ff.

nonsense. Hegel's scepticism about the choice of an absolutely first (*absolut Ersten*), as the doubt-free and certain point of departure for philosophy, is supposed to amount to casting philosophy into the abyss. In the schools deriving from Husserl this theme quickly enough turned against all labour and effort of the concept, and thus bore the brunt of inhibiting thought in the middle of thinking.

Whoever does not let himself be intimidated by this, seems from the outset to miss his measure. He seems to pander to the fruitless transcendent critique which repays the empty claim to an overarching 'standpoint' with being non-binding and with the fact that it never did enter into the controversy, but prejudged it 'from above', as Husserl would have said.

Immanent Critique 14

Yet Husserl's methodological objection remains far too formal in regard to the dialectic, which utterly refuses to be committed to the distinction between matter and method. Dialectic's very procedure is immanent critique. It does not so much oppose phenomenology with a position or 'model' external and alien to phenomenology, as it pushes the phenomenological model, with the latter's own force, to where the latter cannot afford to go. Dialectic exacts the truth from it through the confession of its own untruth.

Genuine refutation must penetrate the power of the opponent and meet him on the ground of his strength; the case is not won by attacking him somewhere else and defeating him where he is not.[4]

The contradiction in the idea of an ontology gained from an historically irrevocable nominalism is evident to a consciousness armed against academic consensus. This contradiction is that there should be found, openly or disguised, a doctrine of being disposed before all subjectivity and lifted above its critique, but

[4] G.W.F. Hegel, *Sämtliche Werke*, ed. Hermann Glockner, vol. 5, *Wissenschaft der Logik, zweiter Teil, Die Subjektive Logik oder Lehre vom Begriff*, 4th ed., Jubiläumsausgabe (Fromann, Stuttgart – Bad Cannstatt, 1964), p. 11; cf. *Hegel's Science of Logic*, tr. A.V. Miller (George Allen and Unwin, London, Humanities Press, New York, 1969), p. 581.

with reference back to that very subjectivity which had denied the doctrine of being as dogmatic. The thought of dialectic, however, does not leave this contradiction abstract, but uses it as the motor of conceptual movement to the binding decision concerning what has been phenomenologically asserted. No stratum can be uncovered as the authentic first with the hammer of original being from under the constituents of pure phenomenology. And the phenomenological claim cannot thereby be somewhere surpassed. Rather, ostensible originary concepts – in particular those of epistemology, as they are presented in Husserl – are totally and necessarily mediated in themselves, or – to use the accepted scientific term – 'laden with presuppositions'.

The concept of the absolutely first must itself come under critique. Were it to turn out that the givenness with which epistemology deals, postulates the mechanism of reification, while in philosophy of immanence, to which that term belongs, reified existence refers back to the structure of the given, it does not reciprocally follow that the reified has primacy over the given. Indeed the hierarchical schema of supporting first and what is derived from it rather loses validity. Any attempt to pass justification on to a privileged category gets entangled in anti-15 nomy. This is expressed in immanent method by the analysis of the reified running into the given and vice versa. That, however, is no objection to a procedure which does not appropriate the norm of reducibility, just against the method which obeys the canon of such reducibility. If critique of the first does not seek to set off in quest of the absolutely first (*Allerersten*), then it must not plead against phenomenology what the latter and many of its successors have in mind, namely providing an immanent philosophical foundation for transcendent being. The issue is the very concept and legitimacy of such a foundation and not the content thesis, however constantly it may change, of what the final ground may be. The character of philosophical compulsion must be broken by taking it strictly and calling it by name. No other newer and yet older constraint (*Bann*) should be devised in its place.

Mediating the First

An emphatic use of the concept of the first itself is implied in the fact that the content of what is asserted as first is less essential than the question of the first as such, and that perchance the conflict over dialectical or ontological beginnings – whether to begin with a first principle at all, that of being or spirit – remains irrelevant before the critique of representation. That use lies in the identity hypothesis. Everything should just arise out of the principle which is taken as the philosophically first, regardless of whether this principle is called being or thought, subject or object, essence or facticity. The first of the philosophers makes a total claim: It is unmediated and immediate. In order to satisfy their own concept, mediations would always just be accounted for as practically addenda to thought and peeled off the first which is irreducible in itself.

But every principle which philosophy can reflect upon as its first must be universal, unless philosophy wants to be exposed to its contingency. And every universal principle of a first, even that of facticity in radical empiricism, contains abstraction within it. Even empiricism could not claim an individual entity here and now or fact as first, but rather only the principle of the factical in general. The first and immediate is always, as a concept, mediated and thus not the first. Nothing immediate or factical, in which the philosophical thought seeks to escape mediation through itself, is allotted to thinking reflection in any other way than through thoughts.

This was both noted and explained by the pre-Socratic metaphysics of being in Parmenides' verse that thought and being are the same. And thus certainly the genuinely Eleatic doctrine of being as absolute was already denied. With the principle of *νοεῖν*, that reflection was thrust into the process which had to destroy the pure identity of *εἶναι* though remaining confined to it as the most abstract concept, the ineradicable opposite of the most abstract thought.

The criteria which have been bestowed on the 'true being' of things are the criteria of non-being, of nothingness; the 'true world' has been constructed out of contradiction into the actual world: indeed an apparent world, insofar as it is merely a moral–optical illusion.[5]

All ontology ever since was idealistic.[6] It was idealistic at first unknowingly, then for itself as well, and finally against the despairing will of theoretical reflection, which wants as an in-itself to break out of the self-established realm of spirit into the in-itself. In contrast, the distinctions, which sustain the official history of philosophy, including that of the psychological and the transcendental, pale into irrelevance.

Husserl's sincerity conceded that in the *Cartesian Meditations.* Yet he constantly reiterates that even pure descriptive psychology is in no sense transcendental phenomenology, despite the strict parallelism between the two disciplines.

To be sure, pure psychology of consciousness is a precise parallel to transcendental phenomenology of consciousness. Nevertheless the two must at first be kept strictly separate, since failure to distinguish them, which is characteristic of transcendental psychologism, makes a genuine philosophy impossible.[7]

But what is at issue are the nuances. This admission weighs all the heavier in that Husserl himself must furnish the criterion that allowed the contrast between the pure ego which in the end he promoted, the homeland of the transcendental, and the immanence of consciousness in traditional scientific style. In the latter the data of consciousness could be a part of the world – existence (*Dasein*) – but not in the former. But to the question as to what else 17 they may be, he imparts the information 'actuality phenomena'.[8] Non-existent (*ohne Dasein*) phenomena can, however, hardly be in question.

---

[5] *Nietzsche Werke, kritische Gesamtausgabe*, eds.Giorgio Colli and Mazzino Montinari, part VI, vol. 3, *Götzendämmerung* (de Gruyter, Berlin, 1969), p. 72; cf. *The Portable Nietzsche*, ed. and tr. Walter Kaufmann, *Twilight of the Idols* (Viking, New York, 1968), p. 484.

[6] Ibid. p. 71; Kaufmann, p. 483.

[7] *CM*, pp. 33–4; cf. Cairns ⟨70⟩.

[8] Ibid. p. 34; Cairns ⟨71⟩, '*Wirklichkeitsphänomenon*'.

property

Mathematicization

Since the philosophical first must always already contain every-thing, spirit confiscates what is unlike itself and makes it the same, its property. Spirit inventories it. Nothing may slip through the net. The principle must guarantee completeness.

The accountability of the stock becomes axiomatic. Availability establishes the bond between philosophy and mathematics that has lasted ever since Plato amalgamated both the Eleatic and the Heraclitean tradition with that of the Pythagoreans. His later doctrine that Ideas are numbers is no simple orgy of exotic speculation. One may almost always read off what is central from the eccentricities in thought. The metaphysics of numbers exemp-larily effects the hypostasis of order with which spirit so thor-oughly weaves a cover over dominated things, until it seems as though the fabric were itself what is concealed. Socrates in Plato's middle period already feels it 'necessary to take refuge in concepts, and use them in trying to investigate the true essence of things'.[9]

But the thicker the veil before spirit, the more reified spirit, as master, itself becomes – as occurs with numbers. In the concept of the first already belongs in the number series. Wherever a πρῶτον and becomes thematic in the concept of being in Aristotelian metaphysics, number and computability are also thought. In itself the first already belongs in the number series. Wherever a πρῶτον is discussed, a δεύτερον must present itself and let itself be counted. Even the Eleatic concept of the supposedly isolated One is comprehensible only in its relation to the Many that it negates. We object to the second part of Parmenides' poem on account of its incompatibility with the thesis of the One. Yet without the Idea of the Many, that of the One could never be specified. In numbers is reflected the opposition of organizing and retentive spirit to what it faces. First spirit reduces it to indeterminacy, in order to make it the same as itself, and then determines it as the Many. Of course, spirit does not yet say it is identical with or reducible back to itself. But the two are already similar. As a set of unities the Many forfeits its particular qualities till it reveals itself as the *18* abstract repetition of the abstract centre.

[9] Plato, *Phaedo*, p. 99; cf. also ibid., p. 100.

18 The difficulty of defining the concept of number arises from
the fact that its peculiar essence is the mechanism of concept construction, which must then help in defining number.
Concepts themselves involve subsumption and thus contain
numerical ratio. Numbers are an arrangement for making the
non-identical, dubbed 'the Many', commensurable with the
subject, the model of unity. They bring the manifold of experience to its abstraction. The Many mediates between logical
consciousness as unity and the chaos which the world becomes as
soon as the former confronts the latter. If, however, unity is
already contained in the Many in itself as the element without
which the Many cannot be considered, then conversely the One
demands the idea of counting and plurality. Surely the thought of
plurality has not yet restored what the subject faces to unity
through synthesis. The idea of the unity of the world belongs to a
later stage, that of the philosophy of identity. The continuity of
the number series, however, remained since Plato the model of all
continuous systems and of their claim to completeness. The
Cartesian rule, respected by all philosophy which presents itself
as science, not to skip intermediate steps, can already be inferred
from it. In dogmatic anticipation of later philosophical identity
claims, it already imprints a uniformity on what is to be thought,
though it is uncertain whether continuity actually belongs there.
The identity of spirit with itself and the subsequent synthetic
unity of apperception, is projected on things by the method
alone, and thus becomes more ruthless as it tries to be more sober
and stringent.

That is the original sin of *prima philosophia.* Just in order to
enforce continuity and completeness, it must eliminate everything which does not fit from whatever it judges. The poverty of
philosophical systematics which in the end reduces philosophical
systems to a bogey, is not at first a sign of their decay, but is
rather teleologically posited by the procedure itself, which in
Plato already demanded without opposition that virtue must be
demonstrable through reduction to its schema, like a geometrical
figure.[10]

[10] Cf. Plato, *Meno*, passim, esp. pp. 86–7.

Concept of Method

Plato's authority, as well as the inculcation of mathematical habits of thought as the only kind which are binding, hardly permit one to become fully conscious of the monstrousness of the fact that a concrete social category, like that of virtue – which was expressly located by Gorgias in a social context, namely that of lordship[11] – should in such a way be reduced to its skeleton as if that were its essence. In the triumph of mathematics as in every triumph resounds, as in the oracles' decree, something of mythical mockery: Whoever heeds it has already forgotten the best. Mathematics is tautology also by the limitation of its total dominance to what it itself has already prepared and formed. In the *Meno* Socrates' desideratum that virtue be reduced to its unchangeable but also abstract features, extracted from Gorgias' context, is expressed as self-evident and thus unfounded and dogmatic – indeed without opposition. And this is perhaps not without reason, for the monstrousness can thus be obfuscated.

But this desideratum, which can still be detected behind every analysis of meaning in pure phenomenology, is already the methodological desideratum in the pregnant sense of a mode of procedure of spirit, which can always be reliably and constantly used because it divests itself of any relation to things, i.e. the object of knowledge – a relation which Plato still wanted to be held in respect.[12] Such a concept of method is one of self-implication and of recourse to the self-mastering subject, the as yet unconscious preliminary form of epistemology. It was hardly ever more than reflection of method. Yet it completes a pattern which belongs constitutively to the concept of a πρώτη φιλοσοφία. Since this cannot be represented as other than methodical, so method, the regulated 'way', is always the law-like consequence of a successor to something earlier. Methodical thinking also demands a first, so that the way does not break off and end up being arbitrary. For it was devised against that. The procedure was so planned from the beginning that nothing outside its sequence of stages could disturb it. Hence the imperviousness of method to everything from Cartesian doubt right up to

[11] Ibid. p. 73.
[12] Cf. Plato, *Phaedrus*, pp. 265–6.

Heidegger's respectful destruction of the philosophical legacy.
20 Only specific and never absolute doubt has ever become dangerous to the ideologists. Absolute doubt joins of itself in the parade
through the goal of method, which is once again to be produced
out of method itself. This corresponds in Husserl's epistemology
to the distinction between the ἐποχή and sophistry or scepticism.[13] Doubt simply shifts judgement to preparing for assuming
the vindication of pre-critical consciousness scientifically in secret
sympathy with conventional sensibility (*Menschenverstand*).

At the same time, however, method must constantly do
violence to unfamiliar things, though it exists only so that they
may be known. It must model the other after itself. This is the
original contradiction in the construction of freedom from contradiction in the philosophy of origins. The τέλος of cognition
which, as methodical, is protected from aberration, autarchic and
takes itself to be unconditioned, is pure logical identity. But it
thereby substitutes itself for things as the absolute. Without the
act of violence of method, society and spirit, substructure and
superstructure would have hardly been possible. And that
subsequently grants it the irresistibility which metaphysics
reflects back as trans-subjective being. The philosophy of origins,
which as method first matured the very idea of truth, was also,
however, originally a ψεῦδος. Its thought paused for breath only
in moments of historical hiatus such as that between the
relaxation of the force of scholasticism and the beginning of the
new bourgeois–scientific impulse. In Montaigne, e.g., the timid
freedom of the thinking subject is bound to scepticism about the
omnipotence of method, namely science.[14]

Socially, however, the split of method from things in its
constitution appears as the split between mental (*geistiger*) and
physical labour. In the work process the universality of the
advance of method was the fruit of specialization. Spirit, which
has been narrowed to a special function, misunderstands itself as
absolute, for the sake of its peculiar privilege.

The break in Parmenides' poem is already a sign of the
discrepancy between method and matter (*Sache*), although a
concept of method is still missing. The absurdity of two sorts of

[13] Cf. *Ideen* [56] and *Ideas*, p. 99.
[14] Cf. in Montaigne, *Essais* (Rat, Paris) o.J. II, chap. XII ('Apologie de Raimon
Sebond'), pp. 113. ff.

truth, which enter unmediated beside one another, though one of them is supposed to be mere appearance, flagrantly expresses the absurdity of the earliest manifestations of 'rationalization'. Truth, 21 being and unity, the highest Eleatic terms, are pure determinations of thought and Parmenides recognizes them as such. They are also, however – as he and his successors still conceal – instructions as to how to think, viz. 'method'. Natorp's a-historical neo-Kantianism had a better grasp of this aspect of ancient philosophy than the far too respectful immersion in its archaic venerability. Things confront both methodical procedure and Parmenides' original utterances as just disturbing content. They are a simple fraud which method rejects. Parmenides' δόξα is the surplus of the world of sense over thought; only thought is true being. It is not so much that the pre-Socratics authentically pose original questions which have grown dumb through the guilt of later desecration. Rather, in them and even Plato the break and alienation are expressed purely and undisguisedly. That is their value, one of thoughts which have not yet veiled the unholy to which they give witness. The advancing *ratio*, however, has as an advancing mediation ever more ingeniously hidden that break without ever coming to master it. Thus it continually strengthened the untruth of the origin. Plato's doctrine of χωρισμός already thought both spheres together, as opposed to the yawning and conceptually unrestricted contradiction of the Eleatics, though in their glaring contradiction. This was a first mediation before all μέθεξις, and Plato's later work, like all of Aristotle's, strives strenuously to fill the gap. For while this is built into philosophies of origin as their proper condition, yet they cannot possibly tolerate it. It admonishes them of their impossibility in that their objectivity is derived from subjective arbitrariness. Their inclusiveness *is* the break.

Hence the fanatical intolerance of the method and its total arbitrariness, against any arbitrariness as deviation. Its subjectivity sets up the law of objectivity. The lordship of spirit believes only itself to be without bounds. As regained unity, however, it merely assures disunion. It is truly an absolute, the appearance of reconciliation, disattached from that to which it was to be reconciled, and in such absoluteness all the more an image of the hopeless debit structure. Indeed the continuous texture, 22 which spirit nevertheless cannot do without, inflicts disaster on philosophies of origin, and also takes the condition of their freedom from them. The process of demythologization, which spirit merging into second mythology undergoes, reveals the untruth of the very idea of the first. The first must become ever more abstract to the philosophy of origin. The more abstract it becomes, the less it comes to explain and the less fitting it is as a foundation. To be completely consistent, the first immediately approaches analytic judgements into which it would like to transform the world. It approaches tautology and says in the end nothing at all. The idea of the first consumes itself in its development, and that is its truth, which would not have been gained without the philosophy of the first.

Promoting the Subject

By furnishing the principle from which all being proceeds, the subject promotes itself. Thus little has changed from Husserl back to the market cries and self-publicity of those pre-Socratics who, like unemployed medicine men, roam around and whose dishonesty echoes in Plato's rage against the Sophists. Husserl's writings are full of wonder for the 'prodigious expanses'[15] which open up to him. In the *Cartesian Meditations* he says, 'A science whose peculiar nature is unprecedented comes into our field of vision'[16] or

Once we have laid hold of the phenomenological task of describing consciousness concretely, veritable infinities of facts – never explored prior to phenomenology – become disclosed.[17]

Heidegger strikes the same note in his pronunciamento that being is 'the most unique of all'.[18] Since long ago the spokesman for *prima philosophia* has beat his breast as he who has everything in the bag and knows all. He makes a claim to sovereignty over the many (which he binds to himself through scorn) such as Plato

---

[15] *Logik* [21], cf. also [225 ff]; and Cairns ⟨157⟩ and ⟨217 ff⟩.

[16] *CM*, p. 31; cf. Cairns ⟨68⟩.

[17] Ibid. p. 43; cf. Cairns ⟨79⟩.

[18] Martin Heidegger, *Einführung in die Metaphysik* (Niemeyer, Tübingen, 1953), p. 60; cf. tr. Ralph Manheim, *Introduction to Metaphysics* (Yale, New Haven and London, 1968), p. 79.

still acknowledged as part of a demand for philosopher kings. Even at its highest level, viz. Hegel's doctrine of absolute knowledge, *prima philosophia* has not been cured of this. Hegel just let slip what otherwise poor sages mostly kept to themselves, i.e. that philosophy itself is true being. Plato, on the other hand, was contented, outside of utopia, with reserving a favourable place for philosophers in immortality.[19] The open or secret pomp and the totally unobvious need for absolute spiritual security – for why, indeed, should the playful luck of spirit be diminished by the risk of error? – are the reflex to real powerlessness and insecurity. They are the self-deafening roar through positivity of those who neither contribute to the real reproduction of life nor actually participate in its real mastery. As middlemen, they only commend and sell to the master his means of lordship, spirit objectified (*versachlicht*) into method. What they do not have they want at least in the mirage of their own domain, that of spirit. Irrefutability replaces mastery for them and merges with the service which they in fact carry out, their contribution to the mastery of nature. Punishment immediately overtakes their subjectivism, deluded from the very beginning, for its restrictiveness. For the sake of mastery, subjectivism must master and negate itself. Just to avoid mistake – since that is how they promote themselves – they abase themselves and at best would like to eliminate themselves. They use their subjectivity to subtract the subject from truth and their idea of objectivity is as a residue. All *prima philosophia* up to Heidegger's claims about 'destruction'[20] was essentially a theory of residue. Truth is supposed to be the leftover, the dregs, the most thoroughly insipid. The content of even Husserl's phenomenological residuum is utterly meagre and empty and is convicted of that as soon as philosophy, as in the sociological excurses of the *Cartesian Meditations*,[21] ventures the slightest step to free itself from the prison of the residuum and return to free life.

For *philosophia perennis* behaves towards undiminished experience as do Unitarians towards religion, and culture to what it

---

[19] Plato, *Phaedo*, passim, esp. p. 82.
[20] Cf. Martin Heidegger, *Sein und Zeit* (Niemeyer, Tübingen, 1972), pp. 19 ff; and tr. John MacQuarrie and Edward Robinson *Being and Time* (Harper and Row, New York and Evanston, 1962), ibid.
[21] *CM in §58, pp. 135 ff; Cairns ⟨159 ff⟩*.

neutralized concept administers. Huxley is ironically correct when he passes thinkers in review and picks out his *philosophia perennis* from what they have in common. The resulting flimsy quintessence extracts what had already been implied, where true being was pathetically awarded for the first time to the general concept. Only in freedom is spirit capable of filling and reconciling itself with what it let go. An element of uncertainty comes over spirit whenever it does not descend to mere protestation. Freedom itself is never given and constantly menaced. The absolutely certain as such, however, is always unfreedom. The requirement to indulge in certainty works, like all compulsion, at its own destruction. Under the banner of doubt-free certainty the scientific spirit obliterates all doubt-free certainty.

But that does not upset the leading idea of something left over. The absolutist Husserl, who wishes to methodically extract the 'phenomenological residuum',[22] shares that idea and even its terminology with raging nominalists and relativists like Pareto, who contrasts residues and derivatives.[23]

The most divergent tendencies of traditional theory[24] are agreed that, in accord with the practice of natural science, whatever conceals pure things, viz. 'interfering factors', should be eliminated. Such factors, however, are a constant subjective supplement in things. But the more fundamentally the operation is carried through, the more compellingly it leads to pure thoughts and thus to the very humans it strives to eliminate. The path to freedom from anthropomorphism, which first philosophy enters under the standard of demythologization, leads to the apotheosis of ἄνθρωπος as a second mythology. Not least because it was reminiscent of psychology, did proud philosophy since Husserl reject psychology. Dread of psychology leads philosophy in quest of the residuum to sacrifice everything for which it exists. What innocent parsons in distant provinces may still preach – namely that infinity is worth no more than a penny – is implied in

---

[22] Cf. *Ideen* [91 ff]; *Ideas*, p. 136 ff.

[23] Vilfredo Pareto, *Traité de la sociologie générale* (Paris, 1932), pp. 56 and 459; cf. *The Mind and Society; a Treatise on General Sociology*, ed.Arthur Livingston, tr. Andrew Bongiorno and Arthur Livingston (Dover, New York, 1963).

[24] Cf. Max Horkheimer, 'Traditionelle und kritische Theorie', *Zeitschrift für Sozialforschung* 6 (1937), p. 245 ff; and *Critical Theory, Selected Essays*, tr. Matthew J. O'Connell, *et al.* (Herder and Herder, New York, 1972).

Property

all *prima philosophia*, not least of all that of Max Scheler who so thoroughly despised the petite bourgeoisie. But, since Plato hypostatized eternal ideas, the fact that the temporal has ensconced from metaphysics, and the residua of the temporal been reified, is due to metaphysics thriving in deficiency, the continual fear of forfeiting the insignificant. Metaphysics disconcertedly constructs its infinity along the lines of the temporal, viz. property relations constructed by men and which, alienated, rule over them. Husserl's programme of philosophy as a rigorous science and its idea of absolute security are no exception. His Cartesianism builds fences around whatever *prima philosophia* believes it holds the title deeds of the invariable and *a priori* for, 25 i.e. around what (in the French of the *Cartesian Meditations*) 'm'est spécifiquement propre, à moi ego'.[25] Thus *prima philosophia* itself becomes property. Accordingly, *prima philosophia* is unaware of the function of invariants for cognition and whether it is dealing with something essential or indifferent. Thus Husserl expects a healthy reform of psychology in the construction of an intentional, i.e. pure *a priori* psychology, without discussing whether, in the richness of its insight, empirical and certainly not unvarying psychology furnishes much more than the other which can be fearless because it risks nothing.

Persistence as Truth

With the imposition of the persisting (*das Bleibende*) as the true, the onset of truth becomes the onset of deception. It is a fallacy that what persists is truer than what perishes. The order, which remodels the world into disposable property, is passed off as the world itself. The invariance of the concept, which would not be unless the temporal determinacy of what is grasped under concepts were ignored, is confused with the unchangeability of being in itself.

The grotesque manœuvre of that phenomenological practitioner* who deals with what is called the problem of immortality in his jargon, by unblushingly acknowledging the destruction of

* [Max Scheler. Trans.]

[25] MC, p. 78; cf. CM, p. 39; and Cairns ⟨78⟩.

every soul, but then consoling himself because the pure concept of every such soul, its individual εἶδος, is incorruptible – this helpless trick brings to light simply through its clumsiness what is hidden in the cavernous depths of great speculation.

Heraclitus, whom Hegel and Nietzsche both praised,[26] had already compared essence and the past. Ever since the first authentic formulation of the theory of Ideas,[27] the past has always been ascribed to appearance, the kingdom of δόξα and illusion. Infinity was reserved for essence. Only Nietzsche protested.

The other idiosyncrasy of the philosophers is no less dangerous; it consists in confusing the last and the first. They place that which comes at the end – unfortunately! for it ought not to come at all! – namely, the 'highest concepts', which means the most general, the emptiest concepts, the last smoke of evaporating reality, in the beginning, as the beginning. This again is nothing but their way of showing reverence: the higher may not grow out of the lower, may not have grown at all. Moral: whatever is of the first rank must be *causa sui*. Origin out of something else is considered an objection, a questioning of value. All the highest concepts, the entity, the unconditional, the good, the true, the perfect – all these cannot have become and must therefore be *causa sui*. All these, moreover, cannot be unlike each other or in contradiction to each other. . . . That which is last, thinnest, and emptiest is put first, as cause in itself, as *ens realissimum*.[28]

But what Nietzsche views as the sacrilege of 'sick web-spinners'[29] that, for the sake of life, never should have 'come about', was perpetrated with the wildness of life itself. The calamity which he explains out of that πρῶτον ψεῦδος as a sickness of spirit, arises from real lordship. Victory was codified by the victor setting himself up as better. After a successful act of violence, the subjugated should believe that what survives has more right on its side than what perishes. The dues the survivor has to pay for this, namely that thought transfigures him into truth, is his own life. He must be dead in order to be consecrated to infinity.

---

[26] Cf. Hegel, *Sämtliche Werke*, vol. 17, *Vorlesungen über die Geschichte der Philosophie* I, pp. 344 ff; cf. Nietzsche, *Götzendämmerung*, p. 69 and Kaufmann, *Twilight of the Idols*, pp. 480–1.
[27] Plato, *Symposium*, pp. 210e ff.
[28] Nietzche, *Götzendämmerung*, p. 70; Kaufmann, *Twilight of the Idols*, pp. 481–2.
[29] Ibid.; ibid. p. 482.

You ask me which of the philosophers' traits are really idiosyncrasies?
For example, their lack of historical sense, their hatred of the very idea of
becoming, their Egypticism. They think that they show their respect for
a subject when they de-historicize it, *sub specie aeterni* – when they turn
it into a mummy. All that philosophers have handled for thousands of
years have been concept-mummies: nothing real escaped their grasp
alive. When these honourable idolaters of concepts worship something,
they kill it and stuff it; they threaten the life of everything they worship.
Death, change, old age, as well as procreation and growth, are to their
minds objections – even refutations. Whatever is does not become;
whatever becomes is not. Now they all believe, desperately even, in the
entity. But since they never grasp it, they seek for reasons why it is kept
from them.[30]

But at the same time Nietzsche undervalued what he saw
through. Thus he stayed in a contradiction out of which the self-
reflection of thought still has to emerge.

Formerly, alteration, change, any becoming at all, were taken as proof of
mere appearance, as an indication that there must be something which
led us astray. Today, conversely, precisely insofar as the prejudice of
reason forces us to posit unity, identity, permanence, substance, cause, 27
thinghood, being, we see ourselves caught in error, compelled into
error. So certain are we, on the basis of rigorous examination, that this is
where the error lies.[31]

The metaphysics of the persisting draws its epistemological
foundation from the constancy of the thing over its appearances.
So the enlightened critique which Nietzsche revives (for it is in
essence Hume's) disintegrated the hypostasis of the thing set up
by that metaphysics. But even that cannot succeed without a
hitch. Opposing the solid to the chaotic and mastering nature
would never succeed without a moment of solidity in the
subjugated. Or else it would constantly expose the subject as a lie.
Just sceptically disputing that moment as a whole and localizing it
in the subject, is no less subjective hubris than the absolutization
of the schemata of conceptual order. In both cases subject and
object are already congealed in ὑποκείμενον. Sheer chaos, from

[30] Ibid. pp. 68–9; ibid. pp. 479–80.
[31] Ibid. p. 71; ibid. p. 482.

which reflective spirit disqualifies the world for the sake of its own total power, is just as much spirit's product as the cosmos which it establishes to revere.

The Elementary

Philosophical concepts represent the solid and supporting as the elementary. It should be simpler than what is supported – something even Descartes never doubted. But since the ὑποκείμενον is truer than that which is raised above it, primitiveness and truth are brought together.

That is perhaps the most disastrous consequence of the assumption of immediacy, with which the subject desperately deceives itself about itself as mediation. A tendency to regression, a hatred of the complicated, is steadily at work in theory of origins, thus guaranteeing its affinity with lordship. Progress and demythologization have neither exposed nor extinguished this tendency, but rather have let it appear even more crassly wherever possible. The enemy, the other, the non-identical is always also what is distinguished and differentiated from the subject's universality. Philosophers have defamed it wherever reflection behaves radically and with obvious vigour, from Plato's curse against ostensibly effeminate musical keys to Heidegger's invective against 'idle talk' (*Gerede*). Ever since they began to question what was at the beginning, the act which cuts the Gordian knot lay on their lips. Even Hegel warded off that tendency of traditional philosophy with the motif of the nullity of the individuated. To its greater glory, the pure concept abuses the more highly developed individual as impure and decay. No progress of scientific and philosophical rationality without such retrenchment.

Totalitarian systems have not contrived that saying out of the historical nowhere, but rather brutally executed what ideology for thousands of years had prepared spiritually as the lordship of spirit. The word 'elementary', however, includes both the scientifically simple and the mythologically original. The equivocation is as little an accident as most. Fascism sought to actualize philosophy of origins. The oldest, what has existed the longest, should immediately and literally rule. Hence the first's inclination

to usurpation lurches glaringly into the light. Blood and earth, the
original forces which the fascists concretized, and which in
industrial society are entirely chimerical, became child's play even
in Hitler's Germany. The identity of originality and lordship came
down to whoever had the power being presumably not just the
first, but also the original. Absolute identity as a political
programme turns into absolute ideology which no one any longer
believes.

The Regressive

First philosophy has in no sense been pure lordship. Its initial
goal is liberation from the context of nature, and rationality has
never entirely given up the memory of autonomy and its
acualization. But as soon as it was absolutized, it almost constantly approached the feared dissolution. The philosophy of
origins – which through self-consistency, the flight before the
conditioned, turns to the subject and pure identity – also fears
that it will lose itself in the determinacy of the purely subjective,
which, as isolated moment, has precisely never reached pure
identity and bears its defect as well as its opposite. Great
philosophy has not escaped this antinomy. Thought, which 29
regards itself as the ground of being, is always on the point of
prohibiting itself as a disturbing factor in being. Even idealistic
speculation has only apparently transgressed this prohibition,
that is, so to speak, desubjectivized the subject. The self-
concealed abstraction mechanism immanently inclines to the
same ontology as it works against. By dint of this tendency,
troubled philosophy of origins has fled from subjective reflection
back into Platonism and must also strive despairingly to reduce
such recidivism to a common denominator with the irrevocable
subjective-critical motif.

That goes back to Kant. He wished to both refute the conclusion of the first as immediacy and to verify the first in the form of
the *constituens*. He liquidated the question of being, and yet
taught *prima philosophia*, 'foundationalism' in every respect. Even
Hegel's heroic struggles against this were ineffective. Subject–
object was still disguised subject.

The problem of being today does *not* stand before us once

again, free from the ruins of millennia, as authentic in the face of such transcendental subjectivity – though the apologists of this question would like that. Rather, its absolute in-itself is merely absolute delusion about its own subjective mediacy, which is immanent to the question of being itself. The movement of thought which aims at knowledge of origins announces its own bankruptcy with its both dogmatic and empty positing of being. It celebrates origin at the expense of knowledge.

The irrationality, in which the philosophically absolutized *ratio* perishes, confesses to the arbitrariness of whatever seeks to eliminate the arbitrary. It does so not just in talk about existential projects but already in Husserl, who decreed that phenomenological reductions should produce his 'sphere of being of absolute origins', as if their execution were arbitrary. This is, in express contradiction to the concept of obligation (*Nötigung*) from Kantian ethics, for example, and Kant's derivation of the Copernican revolution as altogether necessary and needed by reason for mastering those contradictions in which reason is no less necessarily entangled. Today the more total the claim of ontology, which stretches out to mythos over all reflective thought, the
30   more dependent it becomes on mere 'attitude' (*Einstellung*), which in Husserl functions as practically an existential of cognition.

While such philosophizing straightforwardly emulates mathematics in its handling of the so-called constitution problem, since mathematics can proceed arbitrarily, in the name of the most rigorous stringency, and posit and vary manifolds at will, the arbitrariness of the absolute soon fulfils its political function. The form of total philosophy is appropriate to the total state in that it links the arbitrariness of speech, in which the necessity of words vanishes, with the dictatorial command of unprotesting recognition. Authority and usurpation return to being immediately one.

Philosophy of Origins and Epistemology

The philosophy of origins took shape scientifically as epistemology. The latter wished to raise the absolutely first to the absolutely certain by reflecting on the subject – not to be excluded from any concept of the first. But the drive to identity is also strengthened in the course of such reflection. Thoughts – which are no longer, in Husserl's words, 'straightforwardly' (gera-dehin) executed, but rather turned back upon themselves – seal themselves off more and more from whatever does not emanate from them and their jurisdiction, the immanence of the subject. The fact that in immanence the world is produced, or rather the validity of judgements about the world is verified, is to begin with no more problematic than judgement unconcerned with media-tion. So it was only very gradually established as a principle in the progress of reflection.

Arbitrariness, the complement of compulsion, already lurks in the assumption that such a recourse is the sufficient condition of truth, even though it be motivated step by step by scientific contemplation. Epistemology falls into this arbitrariness by its own process. The qualification of the absolutely first in subjective immanence founders because immanence can never completely disentangle the moment of non-identity within itself, and because subjectivity, the organ of reflection, clashes with the idea of an absolutely first as pure immediacy. Though the idea of philos-ophy of origins aims monistically at pure identity, subjective immanence, in which the absolutely first wishes to remain with itself undisturbed, will not let itself be reduced to that pure identity with itself. What Husserl calls the 'original foundation' (Urstiftung) of transcendental subjectivity is also an original lie. Hence immanence itself is constantly being polarized into subjec-tive and objective moments in epistemological analysis. Emil Lask showed quite emphatically how that was so. Husserl's noetico-noematic structure is likewise one of dualistic immanence, though that did not make him conscious of the contradiction thereby perpetuated.

The return of subject and object within subjectivity and the duality of the one is detailed in two types of epistemology, each of which lives on the unrealizability of the other. These fall roughly into the rationalist and empiricist sort. As complement-ary enemies, they are not so radically distinguished in their internal structure and their conclusions as traditional history of philosophy suggests. The metacritique of epistemology should deal with both. Empiricism has never defended as conclusively as rationalism and its idealistic successors the idea of the absolutely first and absolute identity. It seems less entangled and thus abandons itself with far diminished energy to the process which leads through entanglement up to the bounds of the qualifications of immanence itself. Thought capitulates into empiricism too early and with too little resistance. By humbly deferring to sheer existence, thought fails to come to grips with it and thus abandons the moment of freedom and spontaneity.

Logically consistent critical and self-reflective thought grasps, in the very jurisdiction of immanence, incomparably more about essence – viz. about the life process of society – than a procedure that resigns itself to registering facts, and really lays down its arms before even beginning. Though empiricism as an epistemology tracks down the conditions of all knowledge in factical-psychological consciousness which it regards as an underlying principle, this consciousness and what is given in it could always be different, according to empirical ground rules. Such consciousness contradicts the idea of the first which is nevertheless the only motivation for analysis of consciousness, even the empiricist 32 analysis of the 'human understanding',* as philosophical method. The isolated subjective antipode within consciousness, however, or 'spirit', which withdraws from the isolated objective encounterability of the entity or the 'given', thus withdraws from determination just as much as its opposite. Both spirit and its 'actions' defy analysis. It does not let itself be established in the way that epistemology as scientific method should demand, while what can be established itself is already formed according to the model of that facticity to which spirit should present the antipode. But spirit can as little be separated from the given as the given from spirit. Neither is a first. Since both are essentially mediated by one another, both are equally unsuitable as original principles. Were one of them to want to discover the original principle itself in such mediacy (*Vermitteltsein*), then it would confuse a relational with a substantial concept and reclaim the *flatus vocis* as origin.

Mediacy is not a positive assertion about being but rather a directive to cognition not to comfort itself with such positivity. It is really the demand to arbitrate dialectic concretely. Expressed as a universal principle, mediacy, just as in Hegel, always amounts to spirit. If it turns into positivity, it becomes untrue. Mastering

* [In English in the text. Trans.]

such aporia is the perennial effort of epistemologies, though none will succeed. Every one of them stands under Anaximander's curse, whose philosophy of being was one of the earliest but practically prophesied the coming destiny of them all.

The metacritique of epistemology requires constructive reflection upon its structure as one of guilt and punishment (*Schuld und Strafe*), necessary error and futile correction. With growing demythologization, philosophical concepts become ever more spiritual *and* more mythical. The Introduction to Hegel's *Phenomenology of Spirit* and its hitherto unredeemed programme anticipates something of that need. Certainly the immanent critique of epistemology itself is not exempt from the dialectic. While philosophy of immanence – the equivocation between logical and epistemological immanence indicates a central structure – can only be ruptured immanently, i.e. in confrontation with its own untruth, its immanence itself is untruth. Immanent critique must transcendently know of this untruth just to begin. Hegel's *Phenomenology* corresponds 33 to this by both passively following the movement of the concept and actively directing this movement, thus transforming the object.

The concept of immanence sets the limits on immanent critique. If an assertion is measured by its presuppositions, then the procedure is immanent, i.e. it obeys formal-logical rules and thought becomes a criterion of itself. But it is not decided as a necessity of thought in the analysis of the concept of being that not all being is consciousness. The inclusiveness of such an analysis is rather thereby halted. To think non-thinking (*Nichtdenken*) is not a seamless consequence of thought. It simply suspends claims to totality on the part of thought. Immanence, however, in the sense of that equivocation of conscious and logical immanence, is nothing other than such totality. Dialectic negates both together. Epistemology is true as long as it accounts for the impossibility of its own beginning and lets itself be driven at every stage by its inadequacy to the things themselves. It is, however, untrue in the pretension that success is at hand and that states-of-affairs would ever simply correspond to its constructions and aporetic concepts. In other words, it is untrue according to the measure of scientificity which is its own.

That the critique of such untruth may itself remain imprisoned in the abstractions which it undoes, as a superfluous concern of the erudite, cannot be maintained after the materialistic dialectic, whose aim is to stand the philosophy of consciousness on its head, degenerates to the same dogmatics and dispatches philosophy of consciousness by sheer decree, without ever having confronted the logic of the matter. Before that succeeds, idealism will rise easily from the dead.

System and Debit

Despite its static-descriptive tenor and apparent reluctance to speculate, Husserl's epistemology is also roped into a debit structure. Its very system resembles, in modern terms, a credit system. Its concepts form a constellation in which everyone must redeem the liabilities of another, even though the presentation conceals the litigation pending between them. Husserlian expressions like fulfilment (*Erfüllung*) – i.e. of a contract; evidence – judicial exhibits; judgement – of a trial – all unwittingly construe epistemology analogously to a legal contest. In the end, the similarity grows even stronger at every possible locus through archaizing supplements from the language of law, such as 'demesne' (*Domäne*), and 'endowment' (*Stiftung*).*

The most enlightened epistemology still participates in the myth of the first in the figure of a contract which is never fulfilled and therefore in itself endless, self-repeating without respite. Its metacritique presents it with its promissory note and forces from it the external insight, gained from society, that equivalence is not truth and that a fair trade-off is not justice. The real life process of society is not something sociologically smuggled into philosophy through associates. It is rather the core of the contents of logic itself.

Opposing Forces in Epistemology

Epistemology, the quest for the pure realization of the principle of identity through seamless reduction to subjective immanence, turns, despite itself, into the medium of non-identity. As advanc-

* [In Husserl these are usually translated as 'domain' and 'foundation' respectively. Trans.]

ing demythologization, it does not simply consolidate the jurisdiction of the concept, purified of everything heterogeneous, but rather also works at breaking through that jurisdiction. Its posthumous realization and the writing of its inner history is the true awakening. Individual epistemological conditions are thus not absolutely false – they become that only when they seek absolute truth – but neither are they concerned with states-of-affairs. Each of them is necessitated only by the demand for non-contradiction. What must be eliminated is the illusion that this non-contradictoriness, the totality of consciousness, is the world, and not the self-contemplation of knowledge. The last thing the critique of epistemology – whose canon is the mediacy of the concept – is supposed to do is proclaim unmediated objectivism. That is the job of contemporary ontologies or the thought bureaucrats of the Eastern bloc.

Criticizing epistemology also means . . . retaining it. It must be confronted with its own claim to being absolute, be it Kantian and its question of how metaphysics as science is possible, or Husserl's ideal of philosophy as rigorous science. The usurpation of universality which epistemology perpetrates also requires that the universality of thought be satisfied. This implies the disintegration of the privilege on which the philosophical spirit has survived by ascribing universality to itself. Cognition, which 35 measures itself by the ideal of universality, can no longer be monopolized by the medicine men and sages who compel it. Wisdom is just as anachronistic as – according to Valéry's insight – virtue. The more consistent the procedures of epistemology, the less it expands. Thus it prepares the end of the fetishism of knowledge. The fetishizing spirit becomes its own enemy. And this has seldom been as penetrating or prototypical as in Husserl. If philosophy of immanence codifies the ὕβρις of spirit that wants to be everything, then it has precisely already discovered the moment of reflection and mediation. And thus it has also determined both knowledge as labour and the bearer of knowledge, the logical-general subject, as society. Every concept of dialectic would be null without the moment of subjective reflection. What is not reflected in itself does not know contradiction. And the perversion of dialectical materialism into the state religion of Russia and a positive ideology is theoretically based on the defamation of that element as idealistic.

Though philosophy of immanence may, with reason, tend to lapse into dogma, ontology or replica realism, it does also develop the antidote. Idealism was the first to make clear that the reality in which men live is not unvarying and independent of them. Its shape is human and even absolutely extra-human nature is mediated through consciousness. Men cannot break through that. They live in social being, not in nature. Ideology, however, is idealism which merely humanizes reality. In this it is one with naive realism as its reflective justification. It thus immediately revokes what is in 'nature', even transcendental nature.

The Drive for System

The structure of immanence as absolutely self-contained and all-inclusive is necessarily always already system, irrespective of whether it has been expressly deduced from the unity of consciousness or not. Nietzsche's mistrust of *prima philosophia* was thus also essentially directed against system builders. 'I mistrust all systematizers and I avoid them. The will to a system is a lack of integrity.'[32] Just as newer authors infer the thought of the system of right from didactic requirements, such as for a self-contained presentation convincing to hearers,[33] so philosophical systems may indeed be referred to a related need.

The two first system builders in the grand manner were also the first directors of organized schools. As the system leaves nothing out, so behaves the teacher, speaker and demagogue to his listeners. His irrational authority is mediated through *ratio*. The claim to leadership is mediated through logical-argumentative compulsion. Even Plato's Socrates finished off his interlocutors with the far from Attic-elegant proof of their ignorance. The soft echo of discomfort at this reverberates through Alcibiades' panegyric at the end of the *Symposium*. The more problematic wisdom becomes, the more untiringly it must stress its stringency. Therefore, the logic of consistency commends itself since it permits the exercise of the compulsion to thought while ignoring the experience of the object – and thus 'formally' and in-contest-

[32] Ibid. p. 57; ibid. p. 470.
[33] CF. Helmut Coing, *Geschichte und Bedeutung des Systemgedankens in der Rechtswissenschaft*, in *Frankfurter Universitätsreden*, Heft 17, 1956, p. 36.

ably. While Plato's philosophy denounced the rhetoricians, who dealt formally with objects about which they understood nothing, he *also* applied himself to an advocate's formalism, in the method of conditioning concepts, which surpassed sophistic formalism only in logical consistency. In the contest Socrates must almost always be in the right against those designated as his opponents,· even though and because he 'knows nothing'. Not by chance does it remain in suspense in Agathon's speech, or occasionally in the *Phaedrus*, whether Plato is parodying a rhetorical showpiece or presenting a stage of the truth, or, in the end, both. The bombastic character of several pre-Socratic sayings certainly follows from the concomitant exclusiveness of the total knowledge they ascribe to themselves, the inclusiveness of the system.

That is perhaps the darkest secret of first philosophy. Its great discovery, the emphatic distinction between essence and appearance, has equally the aspect of 'I know and you don't', however much callous and self-alienated life requires that distinction as its corrective.

Doctrine of Antinomies

Yet the excessive zeal with which first philosophy offers its knowledge to the fools immediately testifies to its insecurity. The claim of the absolute with which it enters is the medium of its 37 own convulsion. The system, which reduces this claim to a formula in the name of inclusiveness and completeness, runs up against the impossibility of satisfying it. Idealism, which through reduction to the absolute unity of the 'I think' was the very first to be amenable to a systematics developing on all fronts, has, by the measure of its own radicalism, revealed how questionable is the residue it crystallized out.

Prima philosophia came to awareness of this in the doctrine of the antinomies in the *Critique of Pure Reason*. The search for the utterly first, the absolute cause, results in infinite regress. Infinity cannot be posited as given with a conclusion, even though this positing seems unavoidable to total spirit. The concept of the given, the last refuge of the irreducible in idealism, collides with the concept of spirit as complete reducibility, viz. with idealism itself. Antinomy explodes the system, whose only idea is the attained identity, which as anticipated identity, as finitude of the infinite, is not at one with itself. The recourse to subjective immanence occurred only to remove what was not already contained in a first. Otherwise philosophy of immanence forfeits its *raison d'être*. But its own course, the analysis of consciousness, brings to light that it does not contain some such absolutely first, independent of its material and from what 'befits' consciousness. The ontologically first is the ontologically non-first and thus its idea falters. Kant helped himself quite ingeniously and artificially out of the difficulty with the distinction between form and content. In the specification of contradiction and its necessity, which really forbids the arbitration which Kant himself sought, there lies – in comparison with later idealism, for its part – the less forgiving truth.

But as apologist of first philosophy, Kant did later advocate the primacy of form. The reciprocal dependence of form and matter, which he himself arrived at, could not touch the onset of system. Forms as givenness *sui generis* became for him the absolutely first. As the second version of the Transcendental Deduction[34] says, no 'further ground' may be named for those forms. That is the model for Husserl's later procedure of describing transcendental structures. Kant certainly seeks to unravel the secret and deduce the somewhat paradoxical givenness of the forms. Thus he arrives at pure identity, pure thought itself, the subject which, as 'pure' and cut off from all content, is made into a simple non-entity (*nicht-seienden*) and yet hypostatized. The Transcendental Deduction flows into reason as absolute being; the Transcendental Dialectic criticizes the absoluteness of both being and reason. So in a certain way the Deduction lags behind the doctrine of antinomies. In spite of this, the antinomies presuppose the Deduction and the proof of the subjective character of the category in order to ward off the 'naive' unreflective positing of the infinite. By the retreat to formalism, for which first Hegel and then the phenomenologists reproached Kant, he did honour to the non-identical. He did not deign to involve it in the identity of the subject without residue (*ohne Rest*). As a result, however, he narrowed the very idea of truth which no longer expected more than to classify the

---

[34] Immanuel Kant, *Kritik der reinen Vernunft*, ed. Raymund Schmidt (Meiner, Hamburg, 1956), B 146; cf. tr., Norman Kemp-Smith (St Martin's Press, New York, 1965), ibid.

heterogeneous by concepts of order. Husserl's restorative phenomenology is anxiously on its guard against that. That is its genuine pre-critical element which qualified it as a pacemaker for ontology, but it is also its legitimate objection to formalism.

Nothing distinguishes phenomenology and what came of it so emphatically from the otherwise closely related neo-Kantianism as the fact that Husserl every time, in writings which determined his later course, hardly allows the question of infinitesimality to be posed, or else neutralizes it to the possibility of continuous arbitrary variability and 'unrestricted (*entschränkten*) horizons'. The infinite was the paradoxical shape in which absolute and, in its sovereignty, open thought takes control of what is not exhausted in thought and blocks up its absoluteness. Ever since humanity really begins to be absorbed in closed systems of administration, the concept of infinity atrophies and the physical law of the finitude of space begins to suit it.

Nominalism

According to Kant, the antinomies appear wherever thought transcends the possibility of experience. But *prima philosophia*, the system, is endangered by experience. Thus the Kantian critique of reason has thought itself to death. In no way, however, does the problem of *prima philosophia* thereby coincide with the realism–nominalism debate. All philosophies of origins of modern times arose under the auspices of nominalism. Indeed Aristotle's *Metaphysics*, with the equivocity of its concept of οὐσία, already stands on the threshold. For it opens the question of whether every philosophy of the first may not comply with the nominalism it opposes in reflections where it tries to determine its substratum out of thought, the concept-construction procedure. The turn to the subject makes the concept the product of its thought. Insisting on the pure in-itself, *quod nulla re indiget ad existendum*,* transforms it into a for-another. Nominalism like realism stands under the primacy of the first. In both the game is one of *ante* or *post*, and all talk of *post* implies an *ante – in re* as the principle of the entity no less than in the universal.

* ['Which needs nothing to exist'. Trans.]

Nominalism, of course, once meant something else. The sophistry of Gorgias and the Cynicism of Antisthenes certainly will. As a theory of the foundation of science, it turns inevitably sophy of being. But ever since the fusion with science and the victory of the great schools, including those which arose from those untrustworthy groups, the impulse was deflected. Once it has sworn itself to the given and hence to subjective immanence as well as its counterpart, nominalism falls into the position of having to say B because it has said A, however much against its will. As a theory of the foundation of science, it turns inevitably to 'extreme empiricism'.[35] But, as Husserl well knew, extreme empiricism contradicts its own concept. The newer empiricism since Hume – not to speak of logical positivism – out-trumped absolutist metaphysics wherever possible in its concern for criteria of absolute certainty and thus for the fundamental. Conversely, the resignation before the absolute which is proclaimed by nominalistic and empiricist trends, was secretly not so foreign to absolutist metaphysics. For Husserl it was practically self-evident. The problem of the first itself is retrospective. 40 Thinking which like Plato's has its absolute in memory, can really no longer be expected.

The praise of the unchanging suggests that nothing should be otherwise than it has always been. A taboo is issued about the future. It is rationalized by the demand of all 'method' that the unknown be explained by the known. It is even at work in Plato who tacitly imputes a normative status to custom and general agreement in established language. With axioms like those of completeness and continuity, the thought of identity really always already presupposes total surveyability and acquaintance. The new is filtered out. It figures simply as 'material', contingent and as something of an intruder. What helps the subject out of its self-imprisonment is emphasized as negative. It is a danger which must be overpowered and immediately withdrawn into the preserve of the familiar. Thus empiricism agrees with its opponents and is linked to philosophy of origins.

[35] Cf. *LU* I, p. 84; and Findlay, p. 115.

Motivation and Tendency of Ontology

The turn to ontology, which Husserl hesitatingly began and speedily revoked, was conditioned by the downfall of the great systems, as it so abruptly and thus so imposingly terrified the Kantian critique of reason. Ontologies want to be first philosophy, but innocent of the compulsion and the impossibility of deducing itself and what is from a first principle. They want the advantages of a system without paying the penalty. They want to restore the obligation of order from spirit without grounding it in thought and the unity of the subject. Their twofold claim is rooted in arbitrariness, and thus the advance of ontology over the system is just as ambiguous as most late bourgeois progress. Resurrected ontology regresses. It casts off the compulsion for system, in order to abruptly appropriate that first for itself which became thoroughly questionable through its universal mediation. Its escape from immanence sacrifices rationality and critique in objective harmony with a society which descends into the darkness of immediate lordship.

But the subjective arbitrariness of the escape avenges itself. It fails. The tautological emptiness of the sacrosanct highest determinations is vainly concealed by contraband from psychology and anthropology, for its subjective descent is written all over it. What in the end fancies itself origin is simply antiquarian 41 and manifests, along with the *Jugendbewegung* in Germany, that allergy for the nineteenth century which does not so much surpass the present as it becomes uncontrollable and betrays freedom. Since the question of the immediately first is inappropriate to the current situation of spirit and must resolutely blind itself against mediation, it entreats an outmoded historical situation. What it timelessly disposes before the ontic is a changeling, a past which has been made unrecognizable.

Even Brentano's student, Husserl, whom many of his contemporaries felt to be a scholastic and in whose positive descriptive approach the trace of the critical was almost completely missing, inclined against his will to the archaic. After him critical reflection became fully and paradoxically silenced for the sake of the postulate of the binding as inherited from critique. The categories are dispensed from reflection as states-of-affairs which still just have to be recorded, or, in the language devised for that purpose, uttered (*zu sagende*). The abdication of the concept and the despairing need for something absent, and thus negative, is chosen as a positive *a priori*. The decree of positivity in itself through reason and against the ostensibly destructive drive of reason, is no doubt as old as urban bourgeois philosophy.

Yet the difference between the tradition of positivity and resurrected metaphysics has to do with the whole. Kant reckons to be sure about the reconstruction of truth out of the immanence of consciousness. And the 'How is it possible?' forms the determining figure of all his questions, since for him possibility itself poses no problems. Thus, like Hegel after him, he assumes the burden of carrying through that reconstruction on all fronts.

Husserl is in despair over this.[36] In the transcendental investigations which are his substitute for the system, that thought breaks off. He holds to singular determinations and the luckily newly attained concreteness is due not to more but rather less philosophy. Husserl's successors think the thought only to weaken it and yet canonize a binding and thus abstract dogma. If the critical completion of the themes which flow around phenomenology reveals its gaps, which it vainly plugs by switching from one concept to another, then in a certain sense phenomenology wills those very gaps in its ontological final phase. Its innermost irrationalistic intention profits from its involuntary irrationalities.

Hence phenomenology speaks the jargon of authenticity which meanwhile ruined the whole of cultivated German language and turned it into sacred gibberish. It struck a theological note devoid of theological content, or any other content except self-idolization. It feigns the incarnate presence of the first which is neither incarnate nor present. Its authority resembles that of the bureaucratic world which rests on nothing except the fact of bureaucracy itself. Socially, enthroning the completed abstract also enthrones sheer organization regardless of its social content, which is neglected for good reason.

In comparison with the doctrinal edifices of Aristotle and Thomas, which still hoped to accommodate all of creation, ontology today acts as if it found itself in a glass house with

[36] Cf. Herbert Marcuse, 'Begriff des Wesens', *Zeitschrift für Sozialforschung* 5 (1936), pp. 12 ff.

impenetrable but transparent walls, and spied the truth outside –
like an ungraspable fixed star, words whose sanctity one
approaches too closely if one but asks what they mean. All subject
matter, however, the life of concepts, is disdainfully relegated to
the individual sciences like history, psychology and sociology.
Yet these sciences' emancipation from philosophy also does not
lead to their blessedness. So philosophy should only be what
concerns itself with the utterly indifferent. Its value increases
with the indifference of its highest term which comprehends
everything and thus nothing. The new ontology returns peni-
tently to the beginning of Hegel's *Logic* and expires in the abstract
identity with which the whole game began.

Illusory Concretization and Formalism

Ever since Scheler's book on Kantian ethics, epistemological and
systematic formalism have been in disfavour. In its place, material
philosophizing was promised, though indeed immediately burdened with the exceedingly questionable concept of value drawn
from trade relations. Instruments needed no longer to be
sharpened, but rather, as Hegel wished, should be tried out
directly on matter. But the phenomenological movement which
began as epistemology, later started unflinchingly to withdraw 43
anew from all entities and even their highest concept, that of
existence (*Dasein*), which Husserl in fact originally wished to
eliminate.

Thus is ratified the necessarily formal character of πρώτη
φιλοσοφία itself, and not only its form of reflection in the
philosophy of immanence. Whoever wishes to name an absolutely first must eliminate whatever a direct first does not need.
Once, however, in the resistance to the accidental, the ontological
difference is asserted to be unmediated, solid and irremovable,
then the purifying process encroaches on the entity. It could, as
Husserl bluntly expresses it, when measured by the pure concept
of being, just as well not be. One ignores the contrary, that even
the idea of being may only be thinkable in relation to entities.
That would be fatal for resurrected ontology. In vain, though
necessarily, it projects the doom upon the structure of being in
itself. What has today become popular as the question of being

does not divulge apologetically cited originality so much as the need of philosophy of origins, through whose net the ontic slips, though it cannot do without one. Through hatred of mediation its concept of being must still ontologize the entity.

In the end, however, the question of being dissolves the ontico–ontological difference (*Differenz*) on the side of the sheer concept, while solemnly protesting to be beyond the difference.

Anti-idealism comes to itself in the sheer idea, just as Husserl's phenomenology already reverted to transcendental idealism. The necessarily false consciousness of this movement of thought is the prototype of ideology. The tendency of the doctrine is in that direction. If the entity merges indistinguishably with being most broadly extended, then the entity lets itself be absolutized when it chooses and historical opportunity presents itself. That is the schema of the ontological surpassing of formalism. In comparison, Husserl's old-fashioned loyalty to formalism has proved to be more justified. And finally ontology is repentant, but returns to formalism ashamed when it elaborates a ritual of the pure concept which denies that it is one.

The illusion of concretization was the *fascinosum* of scholastics. The spiritual should be intuitable and immediately certain. 44 Concepts are sensually tinted. The metaphorical, *art nouveau*, purely ornamental quality of such language, however, becomes obvious in Husserl himself in that the sensuousness claimed for thought has no consequences in the philosophical structure. Expressions from *Formal and Transcendental Logic* (which was, of course, published after *Being and Time*), such as 'authentification' (*Bewährung*),[37] 'rules throughout' (*durchherrscht*),[38] 'awakening' (*Weckung*),[39] possess a noticeably contrived selectivity and distance, slightly reminiscent of the Stefan George school. The ἐποχή changes into the esoteric. Husserl's epistemology furnished the auxiliary implements for an ideology, with which his scientific disposition wished to have nothing to do, but which, for its part, directly connected the pretension of the binding with what Husserl expounded in the posture of scientific reliability.

Thus critique of his specialized epistemology extends essentially beyond it. The aura of the concrete accrues to the concept,

[37] *Logik* [70]; cf. Cairns ⟨57⟩.
[38] Ibid. [134]; and ⟨114⟩.
[39] Ibid. [217]; and ⟨186⟩.

which presents itself to consciousness as unbesmirched by abstracting, through the theorems of the ideal unity of the species and ideation. Subjectively mediated determinations are credited to whatever completely lacks the subjective as qualities of its being in-itself. And so its authority is established. The counter-question as to the source of those determinations is blocked. But under the taboo against facticity, those concrete concepts are at the same time thoroughly flimsy. They feed themselves with ontic elements which are then simply labelled 'pure', pure consciousness or purely ontological. The illusion of the concrete rests on the reification of results, not unlike positive social science which records the products of social processes as ultimate facts to be accepted. Its metaphysical pathos, however, takes the illusory concrete directly from what is emphatically distant from the facts, viz. that spirituality which is pre-ordained to facticity in ontological idealism as in all German Idealism. No participant in idealism need dirty his hands with those mere entities from which characteristic concepts borrow their tone.

In this mode of procedure late $\pi\varrho\dot{\omega}\tau\eta\ \varphi\iota\lambda o\sigma o\varphi\acute{\iota}a$ energetically forgets the critique of the crude thesis that the logically superior is also the metaphysically superior. No less, however, does it forget the logical process itself. Such forgetfulness institutes the logical in-itself. As method (*Weise*), the ancient wisdom understands that in the end all the scars of its miscarriages should be presented as monuments. Everything strikes it as for the good. Because mediations were frightened into the dark, the determinations, which must be renounced in the formation of general concepts, can without notice, nevertheless, be added, by philosophical need, back to the result. One does not need to observe what was left aside in order to reach 'being in general'. Since, however, this being contains everything conceivable within itself, it lets itself be undisputedly filled with what is contained.

Being is transcribed in the most sensual metaphors with a partiality for such early historical achievements, because every criterion, which allowed removal of the metaphors from what was meant, disappeared from the concept. The harmless scientific maxims of Husserl's phenomenology to intuit (*erschauen*) the essence of concepts in descriptively faithful analyses of meaning – as if every individual concept had an unshakeable solid essence without reference to the others and their constellation – are already a stimulus to illusory concretization. In contrast, the obsolete concept of system still possesses its corrective truth as knowledge of the impossibility of the isolating praxis of spirit. This became the prerogative to magically attach those colours to the concept which it lost in the historical process of alienation. They are, however, a fleeting phantasmagoria as long as the concept which conjures up essentiality denies its own essence. Husserl commended his discussions as radical and since then fictively radical issues have shot up everywhere. They become their own answer and, moreover, rely completely on that old answer which is supposed to be their truth.

The concept was radically castrated with the help of theology. If the *Theses on Feuerbach* were meant to find the root of the evil, then the concept should now still borrow its force from the question which admits of no further inquiry – a forestalling of the answer which does not exist. No information is left to thought (which brackets out the multiplicity of facts in the determination of the first for the sake of their conditionality and mediacy) other than that which the new ontology secretes. This is the paradoxical news which Leibniz imparted to Lockean empiricism: *intellectus* 46 *ipse*. In this paradox, as in its abstract opposite, the doctrine of *tabula rasa*, is expressed the impossibility of the polarization of cognition and thus the impossibility of the very question of the first.

New and Old

With the concept of the first also collapses that of the absolutely new in which phenomenology participated without really coming up with any new themes and so phantasmagorically. The first and the absolutely new are complementary, and dialectical thought had to dispose of (*sich entäußern*) both of them. Whoever refuses obedience to the jurisdiction of philosophy of origins has, since the Preface to Hegel's *Phenomenology*, known the mediacy of the new as well as that of the old. It is qualified as already contained in the older form as the non-identity of its identity. Dialectics is the quest to see the new in the old instead of just the old in the new. As it mediates the new, so it also preserves the old as the mediated. If it were to proceed according to the schema of sheer flow and indiscriminate vitality (*Lebendigkeit*), then it would degrade itself to a replica of the amorphous structure of nature, which it should not sanction through mimicry, but surpass through cognition. Dialectic gives its own to the old as reified and consolidated, which dialectic can move only by releasing the force of its own weight. Dialectic reaches the insight that the closed process also includes the non-included. It thus reaches a boundary to knowledge itself. Dialectic itself would only be surpassed by transformed praxis. But before that, the new is just as much in its jurisdiction as the old. If the old wants the mastery of the autochthonous to date back to the divine, then the new idolizes the primacy of production, in which the principle of mastery is concealed, just as, on the market of spirit, the question of what novelty has been offered tends to become synonymous with that of origins.

The spitefulness of this question and thus the devaluation of the new in general is basic bourgeois. Out of the familiar nothing unfamiliar, nothing other should possibly arise. All the stones in the game are supposed to have been played. Thus speaks the self-contempt of the father, mutilated and condemned to unfreedom, a father who does not allow his son to become better and happier than the inherited disgrace. The wife in patriarchal society, on the other hand, unlike the son, does not completely participate. One moment of the debit structure forms the awareness that it could 47 not be breached. Seeing through the law of identity, however, means not exculpating oneself from the fact that what has escaped can breach the jurisdiction of origin.

All music was once in the service of shortening the *longueurs* of the high-born. But the Late Quartets are hardly background music. According to psychoanalysis, tenderness is training in reaction to barbaric sadism. But it has become a model for humanity. Even the decaying concepts of epistemology point beyond themselves. Right up to their highest formalisms and, before that, in their miscarriages, they are to be rescued as a bit of unconscious transcription of history. For they must be helped to procure self-consciousness against what they explicitly mean.

This salvation, mindfulness of the suffering that sedimented itself in concepts, waits for the moment of their ruin. It is the idea of philosophical critique. It has no other measure than the ruin of illusion. If the age of interpreting the world is over and the point now is to change it, then philosophy bids farewell, and in its farewell concepts leave off and yet persist (*innehalten*) and become images. Should philosophy as scientific semantics desire to translate speech into logic, then it is left to it as speculative philosophy to bring logic to speech. It is time not for first philosophy but last philosophy.

Critique of Logical Absolutism

If an angel were ever to tell us something about his
philosophy, I reckon we would hear many sentences like
'2+2=13'

Lichtenberg

Philosophy, Metaphysics and Science

Since Descartes' time a contradiction has come to the fore in the
relations between philosophy and the sciences, though it was
already implicit in Aristotle. Philosophy seeks to think the
unconditioned, to transcend positivity and the accepted existence
of sciences – arbitrarily dedicated to separate objects, and which
starkly isolate matter and method – and to contrast the scientific
domain with the unfettered truth. Yet philosophy takes science as
its model. Scientific labour overlaps the realm of inherited
metaphysics. As long as there has been cosmological speculation,
science has constantly robbed metaphysics of what it thought to
be its own. At the same time it outlined an ideal of doubt-free
certainty compared to which metaphysics appeared vain and
dogmatic, so long as it did not practise scientific discipline.

The possibility of metaphysics as a science is a transcription not
merely of the themes of the Kantian critique of reason as
epistemology. It also points up the impulse behind modern
philosophy as a whole. From the outset, however, that impulse
does not merely aim at some 'problem' to be solved in peaceful
progress, such as purifying philosophy from its pre-scientific
concepts through reflection on itself. The transformation of
philosophy into science, even into the first science which would
ground the individual sciences, or the highest science, the queen

of the sciences – which is the upshot of numerous apologies and excuses – is not fortunate maturation in which thought divests itself of its childish rudiments and subjective wishes and projections. Rather, it also undermines the concept of philosophy itself. As long as philosophy is no more than the cult of what 'is the case', in Wittgenstein's formula, it enters into competition with the sciences to which in delusion it assimilates itself – and loses. If it dissociates itself from the sciences, however, and in refreshed merriment thinks itself free of them, it becomes a powerless reserve, the shadow of shadowy Sunday religion. So not limited factual science, but rather objective compulsion bears the blame for philosophy falling into disrepute with the sciences.

Contradiction in Scientificization

One can read off the movement of philosophical thought itself what befalls it with the inalienable progress of its scientific control and self-control. By becoming truer, it renounces truth. Whoever freely reflects about objects confiscated from organized science, may often escape *taedium scientiae*. But he is not only rewarded for that with the ignominious praise of the stimulating and the intuitive, but must in addition put up with the proof, of either deficient knowledge of the subject matter or the staleness of what is instantly twisted into hypothesis and ground between the millstones of 'Where is the proof?' and 'Where is the novelty?'

But if, to escape from that danger, philosophy withdraws into itself, then it falls into a conceptual game which is either empty or non-binding and scholastic. Pathetic neologisms, which, as De Maistre says, the greatest writers fear, cannot conceal this.[1] Thoughts which grope to conceive it – though over conceiving itself lies the taboo of the unscientific – find everything already occupied. They are not only wholesomely cautioned against the amateurish, that complement of the expert. They are also paralyzed and rendered unable to acquiesce to such things as the manufacture of the spiritual link (whose absence Faust lamented) between all that has been ascertained. For the 'synthesis' which

---

[1] Cf. J. De Maistre, *Oeuvres* (Lyon, 1891), vol. IV, p. 151 ('Les soirées de Saint Petersbourg').

puts up with ever available scientific findings remains outside the spontaneous relation of thought to object. It also contributes to that organization which it presumes to countermand.

The conservative ideal of science, which once helped to free philosophy from the chains of theology, has itself meanwhile become a shackle which forbids thought from thinking. That is, however, as little due to simply faulty development as its fellow-traveller in that society where philosophy dwells. Thus it will not be arbitrarily corrected through insight and resolve. It submits the scientificization of thought to the division of labour. Either it proceeds according to the pre-established schemata, which economize on superfluous exertion, of the established separate disciplines, or it establishes itself as a supplementary separate discipline which holds its own on the market through its difference from other disciplines. When thought shuts itself off from the division of labour, it falls behind the development of forces and behaves 'archaically'. If as a science, however, it integrates itself into the sciences, then it renounces its proper impulse at the very point where it most needs it. It remains reified, a mere imitation modelled on societal categories and ultimately relations of production. This is so even when it credits itself with making scientific judgements about so-called issues of principle, such as the subject–object relation. Science reifies whenever it defines coagulated spiritual labour, knowledge unconscious of its societal mediations, as straightforward knowledge. Its demands and prohibtions express that completely.

Hence every thematic is laid out on the scientific map before-hand. Somewhat as mathematics customarily dismisses the question of what a number is as extra-mathematical, philosophy also is not supposed to deal with anything except the structure and conditions of the universally valid. But since the themes are already prepared and furnished ready-made from the societal workshop, scientific thought does not fit with what these themes want from themselves. It rather submits them to procedures demanded or inculcated by society.

The primacy of method has today already gone so far that only those research tasks can be undertaken which can be discharged by means of available devices. The primacy of method is the primacy of organization. The availability of knowledge through logical and classificatory ordering has become its own criterion.

51 What does not fit in appears on the periphery as 'data', that waits in its place; and if no place can be found, it is cast off. Like citizens of a tightly organized commonwealth, all laws of continuity must fit in with all the others. The 'unconnected' or non-integrable becomes mortal sin. Thoughts are drastically and fully brought under control by societal organization. For every scientific assertion is on principle tested by every approved scientist of the discipline, irrespective of his mental (*geistig*) constitution. And all spiritual activity should be repeatable afterwards by any other arbitrary individual. Understanding must practically present its staff ID, if it wishes to be tolerated. It is 'evidence' sought not for its intrinsic merit or content, but rather as a print-out of directions for future data.

Thus cognition does not linger over its object for the sake of elucidating it. It does not really refer to (*meinen*) its object at all, but rather degrades it to a mere function of the schema under which it is haughtily subsumed. The more objectively cognition poses and the more purified from all delusion and supplement from the observer, the more subjective it becomes in the totality of its procedure. The form of organization which is immanent to science and which philosophy absorbs gets in the way of the goal which is visible to philosophy.

If, however, the relation of philosophy to science is antagonistic in itself – i.e. if as science it enters into opposition with its own *raison d'être*, and yet whenever it gives a cold shoulder to science literally loses its reason – then its attempt to regard itself as science must lead to contradiction. The Hegelian principle of dialectic, understood through the tension between speculation and science, is the positive expression of such negativity. Hegel seeks to recast it as the organon of truth. What all philosophy works at – philosophy which expects to be 'raised to the status of a science' with the *Phenomenology of Spirit*, the conceptual movement which strives for lordship over contradictoriness by settling it – becomes equated with the essence of philosophy. One more step and the metaphysician of absolute spirit, for whom the world is always right, could be called the consistent positivist.

Concept of Intuition

52

Bergson sought to cut through the Gordian knot, and his intuitionism bears ready comparison to Husserl's essential insight. For he postulated an immediate-intuitive awareness of the living against conceptual-classificatory thought. His critique of scientism was unique in denouncing the triumph of the reified conventional copy over the authentic. With his dualism of two sorts of cognition and 'worlds', however, he turned philosophy into a reserve and thus paradoxically re-incorporated it right back into reified life, such as contributes to the sense of the entirety of late bourgeois irrationalism, which Bergson otherwise so thoroughly transcends in depth of experience and proximity to the phenomenon, just as impressionism towers over neo-Romantic ideologies.

In the mechanism of reification of thought, ordering conceptuality – which Bergson blames for all the mischief, though it is itself merely a derivative of mercantile society – just constitutes a moment.[2] On the other hand, living knowledge, whose salvation is Bergson's concern, certainly does not dispose in itself of a 'foreign' faculty of knowledge. Such an assumption, rather, reflects the split between method and matter which belongs to the realm Bergson detests. Bergson shares with bourgeois thought the belief in isolable and true method. He just assigns to it precisely those attributes which since Descartes have been denied it. He never realized that, whenever a well-defined method has been made independent of its changing objects, then rigidity has already been sanctioned which the magic glance of intuition is supposed to dissolve. Experience in the emphatic sense – the net of ungarbled cognition, such as may serve as a model for philosophy – differs from science not through a higher principle or apparatus, but rather through the use which it makes of its materials, especially the conceptual (which as such match those of science), and through its position towards objectivity. What Bergson calls intuition cannot be denied in such experience, but neither can it be hypostatized. The intuitions which intertwine with concepts and ordering forms achieve more legality with the

---

[2] Cf. Max Horkheimer, 'Zu Bergsons Metaphysik der Zeit', *Zeitschrift für Sozialforschung* 3 (1934), pp. 321 ff.

expansion and hardening of socialized and organized existence.
53 But those acts do not constitute an absolute source of knowledge,
cut off from discursive thought by an ontological abyss. They
certainly seem precipitate and occasionally involuntary (though
artists know that they can also be commanded). And they break
open the closed structure of deductive procedures. But this does
not mean that they have tumbled from heaven. Only the
positivists thought of them in that way, though Bergson's roots,
like Husserl's, are not far from positivism. Rather, they make
succeed what with better knowledge escapes the conversion in
which anti-intellectualism and science come to an understanding.

The suddenness of intuition competes in its resistance to social
control, which wants to scare thoughts out of their hiding place.
So-called inspirations are neither as irrational, nor as rhapsodical,
as both Bergson and scientism claim. Unconscious knowledge not
entirely subject to mechanisms of control explodes in inspiration
and bursts through the wall of conventionalized judgements
'fitting reality'. Since they do not participate in the manipulative
activity of ego-regulated cognition, but rather passively and
spontaneously recall what organizational thought calls sheer
scandal in things, they are in fact 'ego-alien'. But whatever is at
work in rational cognition also enters into inspirations –
sedimented and newly remembered – in order to turn for an
instant against all the devices over whose shadow thought by
itself cannot leap. Discontinuity in intuition does honour to
continuity falsified by organization. Only lightning bolts of
knowledge are saturated with memory and prescience. Official
and 'obligatory' knowledge, as Bergson indeed saw, fall as such
directly out of time and memory. The cognizer is overwhelmed at
the moment of intuition and delivered out of subsumption alone
and from the current present of past judgements, conclusions and
especially relations whose unification brings to light what in the
54 object is more than a placeholder in the systematic. In intuitions
ratio recollects what it forgot. In this sense, which he certainly
hardly intended, Freud was right when he attributed its own sort
of rationality to the unconscious.

Intuition is not a simple antithesis to logic. Intuition belongs to
logic, and reminds it of the moment of its untruth. As the blind
spots in the process of cognition – from which they still cannot
escape – intuitions prevent reason from reflecting upon itself as a

mere form of reflection of arbitrariness, in order to prepare an end for arbitrariness. In non-arbitrary memory, arbitrary thought seeks, however hopelessly, something to cure it from what it must nevertheless perpetrate. Bergson did not realize that. By passing intuitions off as the immediate voice of that life which nevertheless continues to live only as mediated, he diluted them to an abstract principle that quickly allies itself with the abstract world against which it had been devised. The construction of pure immediacy, the negation of everything rigid, leads him in the text on laughter to say:

> Every temperament is comic, as long as we understand by temperament what is finished about our personality, the set mechanism about us, which can function automatically.[3]

But he sees temperament as nothing more than 'obduracy against social life'.[4] That is, that resistance which is the truth of intuition. The absolutization of intuitive cognizing corresponds practically to a mode of procedure of absolute adaptation. Whoever neglects to 'remain attentive to what surrounds him' and elects to 'shut himself up in his temperament as in an ivory tower',[5] is rejected.

Whoever wishes to change petrified relations stamped out by mechanistic concepts needs just that. No concept of the living can be thought unless it includes a moment of the identically persisting. The abstract negation of mediation, the cult of pure contemporaneity, which opposes this, thereby falls right into conventions and conformism. While Bergson expunges the societal callouses from spirit, he surrenders it to social reality which causes them.

Husserl's Scientism

Husserl's attempt to break the spell of reification through philo- 55
sophical meditations and 'to come to grips' with 'the things themselves' in 'originary dator intuition', as phenomenologists

---

[3] Henri Bergson, *Le rire, essai sur la signification comique* (Alcan, Paris, 1913), pp. 151–2.
[4] Ibid. p. 137.
[5] Ibid. p. 138.

liked to say, remains, by its proper intention and in contrast to
Bergson, in harmony with science. He, of course, submits science
to the verdict of philosophy, but at the same time acknowledges it
as the ideal of philosophy. Thus he seems incomparably more
academic than Bergson. In spite of the expression, 'To the things
themselves!', his texts are still, in their most fruitful sections,
generally formal and full of terminological distinctions. He also
speaks of the 'stream' of consciousness, but his conception of
truth is traditional, i.e. static and timeless. He seeks to surpass
science in sobriety. His considerable capacity for verbal presentation stays hermetically non-artificial (*kunstfremd*). His thought is
non-radical and contemplative and burdened beforehand with
everything against which it remonstrates.

But since he does not deny his antagonistic relationship in itself
to science, but rather lets it work itself out, he avoids the fraud of
irrationalism that abstract negation has power over reification. He
ingeniously scorns the powerless fate of an approach which
ignores its opponent, instead of appropriating his power. The less
reconciled contradictions appear in his philosophy, the more
evident their necessity, which intuitionism blithely ignores. And
the closer their un-self-conscious development comes to that of
truth. Husserl accepts thinking in its reified shape, but he follows
it so incorruptibly that it eventually surpasses itself. His programme thinks philosophy as a 'rigorous science'[6] involving the
'suspension of all sciences . . . natural and moral, as sciences,
with all the knowledge they have accumulated . . .'[7]. And indeed
this includes not only, as he wishes, the specialized sciences
'which require the natural attitude',[8] but even 'pure logic as
mathesis universalis',[9] without which the very concept of a rigorous
science would be meaningless, though Husserl so qualifies
phenomenology. Thought and consciousness as 'spheres of being
of absolute origins'[10] are dealt with under the primacy of the
scientific ideal as a pure research subject, purified from all
prejudice and theoretical supplement.

[6] Edmund Husserl, 'Philosophie als strenge Wissenschaft', *Logos* I (1910–11), pp.
   316 ff; cf. tr. Quentin Lauer, 'Philosophy as Rigorous Science', *Phenomenology and the Crisis of Philosophy* (Harper and Row, New York, 1965), pp. 71–147.
[7] *Ideen* [108]; *Ideas*, p. 155.
[8] Ibid.
[9] Ibid. [111]; ibid. p. 158.
[10] Ibid. [107]; ibid. p. 154.

But consciousness thus congeals into what, by essence and possibility, should just arise out of it. Thought 'observed' by thought reduces to an objective existent and an element which passively registers such objectivity. The form of phenomenological description borrowed from the sciences, which is supposed to add nothing to thought, does change it in itself. Thought is driven out of thought. Despite the reduction of the natural world, that is the strict fact of the case with reification. Even the doctrine of 'logical absolutism' is prototypical of that. Husserl was not just the first to work intensively with it. He also developed it into the theory of the ideal state-of-affairs, resulting in the construction of essential insight (*Wesensschau*), the point at which the extremes of Husserl and Bergson meet. Irrationalism clings inalienably to European rationalism.

Dialectic in Spite of Itself

Nothing could be further from Husserl than the assessment of such interactions. The concept of science, on which his conception of philosophy rests, clings to the sense of the late nineteenth century for the triumph of solid research work over dialectical and speculative delusion. Any dialectic in his philosophy occurs in spite of itself, and can be extracted from it only with the force of its own consistency. Along with most of his contemporaries in Germany, Husserl took the appearance of sophistry in the dialectic at face value. Never does he speak of Hegel otherwise than scornfully, even though the name 'phenomenology' may have been chosen in recollection of the one of spirit. He speaks the language of scientific rancour against a reason which does not capitulate before common sense.

In the factical thought of normal persons the actual denial of a law of thought does not usually occur, but it can scarcely be said that it cannot thus occur, since great philosophers like Epicurus and Hegel have denied the law of non-contradiction. Perhaps genius and madness are in this respect allied, perhaps there are also lunatic rejectors of the laws of thought: these will certainly also have to count as men.[11]

[11] *LU* I, p. 141; cf. Findlay, p. 158.

Even when Husserl regarded his own task to be a 'critique of logical reason', he still protected himself against the suspicion that his concern was a 'merely frivolous inquiry of a dialectic that argues back and forth between sceptical negativism and relativism and logical absolutism'.[12] The *Cartesian Meditations* are similarly obdurate.

This idealism [that of Husserl's later transcendental philosophy] is not a product of sportive argumentations, a prize to be won in the dialectical contest with 'realism'.[13]

The inflexibility of such dogmatic positivity, which cannot imagine the 'contest' or conceptual movement otherwise than as shadow boxing, is all the more surprising – protesting resistance to the pull of his own thought – since the mature Husserl rejected the positivity of the sciences in an almost orthodox Hegelian fashion.

For such a grounding is now the incessant demand; everywhere it is what makes a scientific purpose specifically philosophic; everywhere it makes the difference between genuine science, which is nothing other than philosophy, and science in naive positivity (which can be accepted only as a stage preliminary to genuine science and not as genuine science itself).[14]

Before Husserl followed scientific usage and warned philosophy against concept constructions. Now he rejects as naive the idea of science that strutted forth in such a warning. Hence the phenomenologist must let himself reproach another philosopher who confronts no contradictions, namely Wilhelm Wundt, to the effect that

he himself in the second volume of his work falls to a logicism such as disappeared from history since the days of scholastic conceptual and verbal dialectic.[15]

---

[12] *Logik* [208]; Cairns ⟨178⟩.
[13] *CM*, p. 88; Cairns ⟨119–20⟩.
[14] *Logik* [278]; Cairns ⟨240⟩.
[15] Wilhelm Wundt, *Logik*, 5th ed. (Stuttgart, 1924), vol. 1, p. 7.

A Head-Start for Science

Yet Husserl's philosophy was motivated scientifically as a 'philo-sophical clarification'[16] of pure mathematics and logic which is supposed to rely upon the success of the sciences.

Whether a science is truly a science, or a method a method, depends on whether it accords with the aims that it strives for. Logic seeks to search into what pertains to genuine, valid science as such, what constitutes the idea of science, so as to be able to use the latter to measure the empirically given sciences as to their agreement with their idea, the degree to which they approach it, and where they offend against it. In this logic shows itself to be a normative science, and separates itself off from the comparative mode of treatment which tries to conceive of the sciences, according to their typical communities and peculiarities, as concrete cultural products of their era, and to explain them through the *58* relationships which obtain in their time.[17]

Sentences of this sort appear at the outset of far-reaching theoretical discussions as plausible and even indifferently self-evident. But they hide what remains to be proved. Husserl's concept of logic presupposes the success of the sciences as its supreme court. It also assigns its field to the system of the sciences. Scientificity is measured by the purposiveness of the means – the method – versus the 'goal' which is not even considered. This is quite similar to Max Weber's theory of purposive rationality. The stringency of its own foundational structure serves as a criterion for scientificity, and not a relation to things of whatever sort.

But then even logic is tacitly detached from thought. It is not supposed to be the form of thought so much as that of current science. Since research assumes the existence of science, the thread between logic and history is snapped, before the reasoning leading to it even gets off the ground. The analysis of the formal constituents of science is supposed to show what logic is. History, however, is concerned with the sciences only as 'concrete cultural products of a time', and not as such with the thought functions

---

[16] *LU* I, Vorwort, p. v; cf. Findlay, p. 41.
[17] Ibid. p. 26; ibid. p. 71.

which have sedimented in the sciences. How these functions have been formed in the operation between subjective and objective moments, and what the precipitate of their analysis may be, all remains outside the cautious line of demarcation of scientific 'regions'.

That is how the spiritual division of labour affects the immanent shapes of questions which arise as if they were pre-ordained before any subject matter. Husserl's logical absolutism mirrors in its own foundation the fetishization of the sciences, which mistake themselves and their hierarchy as an entity in itself. In fact, Husserl says in the passage of the 'Prolegomena to Pure Logic' which outlines the relationship between philosophy and mathematics (for Husserl throughout the equivalent of pure logic): 'The nature of the matter really demands a thoroughgoing division of labour here.'[18] Then the interdisciplinary quarrel is arbitrated in the sense of the hierarchical priority of the deductive sciences.

It is not the mathematician, but the philosopher, who oversteps his legal bounds when he attacks 'mathematicizing' theories of logic, and refuses to hand over his temporary foster-children to their natural parents.[19]

The only worry which bothers him is 'If the development of all true theories falls in the domain of mathematics, what is left over for philosophers?'[20] Even if the left-over were the formal characteristica of thought, positive science lays claim to precedence over its self-reflection. Science declares it is a 'domain' by right of possession. But the more abstract and isolated the scientific 'area', the greater the temptation and readiness to hypostatize it. The drive to disconnection as the possibility of science itself knows no bounds, for the bound-setting procedure of science is raised to a metaphysical principle.

Meanwhile we cannot suspend transcendents without limit. Transcendental purification cannot mean the suspension of all transcendents, for that might leave behind a pure consciousness, but no possibility of a science of pure consciousness.[21]

[18] Ibid. p. 252; ibid. p. 244.
[19] Ibid. p. 253; ibid.
[20] Ibid.
[21] Ideen [111]; cf. Ideas, p. 159.

The critical, idealistic reference of every sort of objecthood – even that of science – back to the immanence of consciousness must not touch the prerogative of science. The analysis, which precedes all science, of what is encountered in pure consciousness must treat even that as a scientific object.

This paradox is the key to all phenomenology. Scientific reification is entrusted to the foundation of objecthood and science. Husserl, the transcendental philosopher, who approves of the entire positivistic critique of post-Kantian Idealism, does not venture with Fichte to equate science to the absolute. But he *60* will concede none of its primacy. Thus the idealistic hunt for the transcendental must first be called off and the bracketing of the transcendent interrupted. The transcendental is replaced by an ideal of knowledge which, despite all 'reductions', is derived from the empirically available sciences. This is Husserl's deepest resemblance to Kantian resignation. The question becomes not whether but how science is possible, and any other is branded as groundless speculation. None of Husserl's intellectual operations, however radically they may behave, ever give credence to the thought of the vanity of the sciences such as was harboured by Agrippa von Nettelsheim in the early period of bourgeois humanism.

In the *Cartesian Meditations*, the ideal of philosophy and that of science – 'universal science' – remain the same. Philosophy is described faithfully to the schema of Cartesian rationalism as a hierarchy of scientific cognitions.[22] Though, in comparison with the unrefined Descartes, the project of doubt appears to be extended to the sciences, Husserl means no more than that the unreflective 'purported' sciences, including formal logic, should also justify themselves before a more rigorous concept of science, that of the seamless stratification of layers of evidence. Husserl does not worry about whether science is true, but rather whether the sciences are scientific enough. Turning established scientific methodology back to the legitimization of science itself in critique is as little an issue for Husserl as for any of his positivist opponents.

This explains why even for the later Husserl truth remains a reified advance, to be grasped 'descriptively'. Even the idealistic motifs of creation and origin petrify before the scientific glance

[22] Cf. *CM*, pp. 12–13 and 14; and Cairns ⟨52–3⟩.

into ascertainable states-of-affairs. His philosophy never gives credence to spontaneous participation in the process of creation, and thus also never to intervention into reality. Throughout the phenomenologist fancies himself as a 'researcher' who discovers and maps out 'areas'. He takes literally the Kantian metaphor of a
61 'land of truth' ('enchanting name').[23] The very term 'ontology' and later the attacks on scientific systematics could be motivated by Husserl's wish to raise the system of the sciences to an absolute.

The highest universals of each and every scientific subject realm are supposed, according to Husserl's conception, to match propositions of the highest formal type which cannot be further reduced. Their content is called ontology, and this is perhaps more in the spirit of Aristotle and Thomas, just as the newer ontologies held the floor in the beginning. Husserl's model at all stages is mathematics, in spite of the objection in *Ideas* that it not be confused with philosophy.[24] If in the 'Prolegomena' a value distinction is drawn within knowledge according to the standard of law-likeness,[25] then such mathematicism in form dominates all of Husserl's thought, up to the end, even where he was no longer content with the 'clarification of logic', but rather aimed at the critique of logical reason. Even though the Husserl of the phenomenological reductions may have 'bracketed out' the natural thing world, his own philosophizing had never qualified itself in any other way than by the form of sublimated apprehension of the reified, as it is sketched in the relation of consciousness to insight into mathematical 'states-of-affairs'.

'Realism' in Logic

That Husserl reverts to the beginnings of bourgeois philosophy, remains untroubled by Hegel's critique in the *Science of Logic*, and attributes primacy to mathematics, all occur because of mathematical 'purity'. The mathematician 'never asks about the

---

[23] Immanuel Kant, *Kritik der reinen Vernunft*, ed. Raymund Schmidt (Meiner, Hamburg, 1956); tr. Norman Kemp-Smith (St Martin's Press, New York, 1965), A 235/B 294.

[24] Cf. *Ideen* [133ff], esp. § 74 ([138ff]); and *Ideas*, pp. 185 ff, esp. § 74 (pp. 190 ff).

[25] Cf. *LU* I, p. 45; and Findlay, p. 86.

possible actuality of manifolds . . .'.[26] The analytic character of mathematics protects it from any intrusion by unforeseen experience. Thus unconditioned certainty and security matches its a priority.

Husserl divulges the price. 'This purity in restricting the theme to objective senses in their own essentialness – to "judgements" in the amplified sense – can also be exercised as it were unconsciously.'[27] The term 'unconsciously' indicates that the accomplishment of mathematical acts is independent not only from 'questions of possible actuality', but also from reflection on their own detachment. It is indeed possible that as a science, 62 mathematics requires such an unconsciousness of execution. Objectively, however, this ultimately undermines the very concept of truth. Blank manipulating is the bewitched form in which draining praxis, cut off from both theory and the quality of its objects, returns to theory. The question of any sort of meaning is replaced under the primacy of mathematics by a sort of faded, technical thought activity which perplexes whoever is concerned with meaning, while the mathematician smells sabotage to the machinery in any question of meaning and thus forbids it.

The mathematician's resolute unconsciousness testifies to the connection between division of labour and 'purity'. The mathematician is concerned with ideal objects like the paleontologist is with fossils. The blind acknowledgement of an externally posited thematic (as Husserl's manner of speaking throughout expects of philosophy also) releases the mathematician, according to Husserl, from the obligation to execute those acts which could reveal his 'subject area' (*Sachgebiet*) as a moment of the whole and the actual. Philosophy repeats what is substantially proven enough times and consecrates ignorance as the legal source for security. But the more hermetically the unconsciousness of the mathematician seals his propositions against any inkling of involvements, the more perfectly pure forms of thought, from which memory is expunged in abstraction, come to appear as the sole 'reality'. Its reification is the equivalent for the fact that it was broken loose from that objecthood without which the issue of 'form' would not even arise. Unconscious objecthood returns as the false consciousness of pure forms. It produces a

[26] *Logik* [145]; cf. Cairns ⟨124⟩.
[27] Ibid.

naive realism of logic. All of Husserl's realistic motifs emulate it and that realism motivates his attempt to break out of the epistemological theory of immanence.

The Logical In-Itself

Husserl's talk of a 'pure logic "dogmatically" treated'[28] expresses the fact that, in his transcendental philosophy phase, he also finally lost his patience with naive realism in logic. For this reason, he
63 wished in his old age to explain logical reason by means of pure consciousness.

He already ran into that problem, however, in his original formulation of logical absolutism. For among the ' "conditions of the possibility" of any theory whatever',[29] he includes the subjective.

The theory which validates knowledge is itself a piece of knowledge: its possibility depends on certain conditions, rooted, in purely conceptual fashion, in knowledge and its relation to the knowing subject. It is, e.g. part of the notion of knowledge, in the strict sense, that it is a judgement that does not merely claim to state truth but is also certain of this claim's justification, and actually possesses the justification in question. If the judging person were never in a position to have direct personal experience and apprehension of his judgement's self-justifying character, if all his judgements lacked that inner evidence which distinguishes them from blind prejudices, and yields him luminous certainties, it would be impossible to provide a rational account and a foundation for knowledge, or to discourse on theory and science.[30]

All this is already inferred in a transcendental philosophical manner from the consistency of reflection. It must not be allied to 'logical absolutism'. For the validity of logical propositions 'in themselves' is supported by – and restricted to – the demand for possible evidence in human consciousness. As a result all the epistemological worries, which logical absolutism had sought to ban, creep in once again. Husserl's rational impulse not only grappled with the dogmatic foundation of logic in psychology,

---

[28] *Ideen* [306]; cf. *Ideas*, p. 376.
[29] *LU* I, p. 110; cf. Findlay, p. 135.
[30] Ibid. pp. 110 ff; ibid.

but also logical dogmatism. It induced that turn which exposed him to the cheap reproach that he only eliminated psychologism to later smuggle it back in. The claim to a logical in-itself dissolves. The knowledge of the conditions of the possibility of logic itself is just divested of any movement of spontaneity and subordinated to the positivistic ideal of the sheer acceptance (*Hinnehmens*) of irreducible facts, i.e. 'givens'. That occurs through the concept of evidence. The central role of that concept in all of Husserl's thought is explained by the fact that evidence promises to cover the contradictory demands of foundation through recourse to the subjective and of observation of irreducible 'absolute' states-of-affairs.

A theory, therefore, violates the subjective conditions of its possibility as a theory, when, following our example, it in no way prefers an inwardly evident judgement to a blind one. It thereby destroys the very thing that distinguishes it from an arbitrary, unwarranted assertion.[31]

Hence the positivistic ideal of sense–certainty is already rudimentarily expanded and turned to its critical function. The demand for immediate givenness is transferred to the mental realm. The construction of categorial intuition comes close to making logical states-of-affairs in-themselves, absolute and yet in need of rational foundations. The later doctrine of such construction is nothing more than the incantation of evidence. But without such an auxiliary concept, in which the being-in-itself of the spiritual and its subjective justification converge, Husserl could not manage. If there are 'subjective conditions of the possibility of a theory', which arise in a structure of judgements, one cannot assert that logical theory is an in-itself. And yet Husserl must insist precisely on that from the outset. The same postulate of the 'independence from experience', that amounts to the 'realistic' construction of the logical in-itself and deals with logic and mathematics as if they were just there, demands both the ideality of logic and mathematics and their purity from the factual. Reification and idealization become correlates of this philosophy – and not at this point alone. If logical propositions were legitimized by the analysis of the 'how' of their 'appearance' – i.e. in consciousness, experiencing them – then the question of

[31] Ibid. p. 111; ibid. pp. 135 ff.

constitution would be broached and some existent would not be far behind. Logical propositions can only be 'experienced' at all as related to some sort of entity. Only thus is there motivation for their eventual execution. Otherwise their conception is empty – which is attributed to logical rigour, though the thought of logic does not gain insight into rigour.

Thus the naive realism of logic paradoxically merges with the assertion of the ideality of propositions in themselves over against entities. Thoughts must suspend themselves so that the privilege of self-sustaining absoluteness may be maintained for spirit alienated as logical automatism in which thought does not recognize itself. If science, however, is projected as a systematic, continuous immanent unity of 'propositions in themselves', such as permeates Husserl, then it slips into the character of fetish. 'Consider, for example, Husserl's phenomenological method where, in the final analysis, the whole realm of logic is transformed into a higher-order "facticity".'[32] But to expressly posit the narrow-mindedness of a method measured into 'domains'[33] and to see through such a method are by and large the same thing. By owning up to the reification of mathematics – and pure logic – Husserl reaches a second-level critique of positivism:

> Here we must note that the mathematician is not really the pure theoretician, but only the ingenious technician, the constructor, as it were, who, looking merely to formal interconnections, builds up his theory like a technical work of art. As the practical mechanic constructs machines without needing to have ultimate insight into the essence of nature and its laws, so the mathematician constructs theories of numbers, quantities, syllogisms, manifolds, without ultimate insight into the essence of theory in general, and that of the concepts and laws which are its conditions.[34]

Presupposition of Logical Abolutism

The fetishistic aspect of such a thought, which breaks off unconcerned with moving by itself to consistency, is nowhere

---

[32] Georg Lukács, *Werke*, vol. 2, *Geschichte und Klassenbewußtsein* (Luchterhand, Neuwied and Berlin, 1968), p. 295 (131); cf. *History and Class Consciousness* (MIT, Cambridge, 1971) p. 250.

[33] *LU* I, p. 252; cf. Findlay, p. 244.

[34] Ibid. p. 253; cf. ibid. pp. 244 ff.

clearer than in Husserl's discussion of F.A. Lange's *Logische Studien*.

Only sheer ignoring of the plain meaning-content of the logical law could permit us to ignore the further fact that this content is not at all relevant, directly or indirectly, to the actual elimination of contradiction in thought. This actual elimination plainly only concerns the judgement experienced by one and the same individual in one and the same time and act: it does not concern affirmation if divided among different individuals and in different times and acts. For the factual element here relevant such distinctions are essential, but they do not affect the logical law at all. For this says nothing concerning the conflict among contradictory judgements, among real, dated acts of this or that character; it only speaks of the law-based incompatibility of the timeless ideal unities we call contradictory propositions. The truth that the members of such a pair of propositions are not both true, contains no shadow of an empirical assertion about any consciousness and its acts of 66 judgement.[35]

Husserl criticizes the customary psychological grounding of logic to the effect that contradictory sentences cannot be unified in a single consciousness. Since the same judgement could be affirmed or denied by different individuals at different times, the argument does not suffice. But his reasoning is possible only because he isolates monadologically the consciousness of different individuals at different times. Collective unity in the execution of acts of consciousness, the social moment of the synthesis of thought, never enters his mind.

Since he does not concede that, but must acknowledge a validity of logical propositions reaching beyond the single individual, he finds himself forced to award an unmediated being in-itself to these propositions. If he were to conceive the subject of logical validity as social and in motion rather than as isolated and 'individual', then he would not need to drive an ontological cleft between thought and its own laws. If thought in fact belonged just to monads, then it would be a miracle that all monads would think according to the same laws, and theory would have no way out other than to appropriate this miracle through Platonic realism of logic. Yet thought is pre-arranged through language and signs for every single individual. The individual's intention

[35] Ibid. p. 97; cf. ibid. p. 125.

to think 'for himself' retains, in the utmost opposition to the universal, a moment of illusion. The part of his thoughts which belongs to the individual thinker is negligible both in form and in content. That is true of the doctrine of the transcendental subject, which has priority over the empirical.

But Husserl is blinded by individualism, and the only consciousness he knows belongs to monads. Thus, since he perceives that the validity of logical propositions is not exhausted in the abstraction from the monad, he has to hypostatize that validity. The emancipation of the pure law of thought from thinking reverts to that standpoint, whose critique has been the content of philosophy since Aristotle. By obstinately seeing that principle through, science itself is sentenced to the very mythology which it had sought to annul.

Essence and Development (Entfaltung)

The paradoxical origin of the reification of logic in the abstraction from all facticity, is evident when the early Husserl concerns himself with the motivation of his work as the 'philosophical clarification' of pure logic and mathematics.

The incomplete state of all sciences depends on this fact. We do not here mean the mere incompleteness with which the truths in a field have been charted, but the lack of inner clarity and rationality, which is a need independently of the expansion of science.[36]

Something in no way self-evident is again imputed self-evidence, viz. the dualism between the actual development of a science and its 'essence' which is supposed to characterize it formally – the idealistic dualism of form and content. The factual progress of knowledge in the sciences is supposed to have nothing to do with what they are in themselves. If the clarification of logic is undertaken strictly according to that postulate, however, then the theory commits a *petitio principii*. Objectivity and ideality in logic – its reified being in-itself – which is supposed to be proved by philosophical critique, is already presupposed by a method which attributes to logic a rationality and clarity

[36] Ibid. p. 10; ibid. p. 58.

independent of the state of its development and is thus satisfied with substantiating it descriptively.

Hence more is at issue than the 'self-referentiality' of logic which Husserl discussed later. It is certainly legitimate to apply logical propositions to logic. Otherwise no rational judgement could be made about it. But it is something else to question the essence of logic, which can only meaningfully be done if the answer is not prejudiced. Yet that occurs in Husserl's assumption of a fact-free formal *a priori* which is, as a result, indifferent to the 68 historical fact of scientific development. Arising only in a much advanced logic, whose constituents can be isolated, clarity and rationality are by their own essence laden with history. The fact that they first appear as results and are crystallized in the split between matter and method is not extrinsic to them, however obstinately they may resist that memory. Indifference to such a memory confers on the 'Prolegomena' a unique impotence, despite its great merit over psychologism which is in fact the mere correlate of reified logic. The argument constantly assumes implicit premises which it would like to exhibit as explicit results. The shadow of what Husserl has excluded falls necessarily over the protected zone of purity – and the fundamental operation of his philosophy is one of exclusion; it is defensive through and through.

Thus Husserl did not deny that 'practice and association' furnish essential and not simply accidental moments of every logical accomplishment. Thus, all the less can logic be cut off from thinking. Husserl sought to derive practice and association from the 'imprinted' law-likeness of logical form.[37] But he did not even raise the question, which was later so emphasized: how there can be pure logical cause of a psychic fact. Moreover, he is oddly undisturbed by the fact that those thought practices obviously belong to the factual performance of acts and not to pure form.

Calculators, Logic and Mechanics

Not only the presupposition of the argument for logical absolutism is controversial, however, but also the core of that argumentation itself. The passage in the first volume of the *Logical*

[37] Cf. ibid. pp. 21 ff; and ibid. pp. 67 ff.

Investigations, which contains the most compelling critique of psychologism, viz. the polemic against the belief that the laws of thought are 'supposed laws of nature which operate in isolation as causes of rational thought'[38] is also the victim of reification. Husserl argues[39] that it would be senseless to look upon logical laws as causal-psychological causes of the course of human thought. Calculators are constituted by 'natural laws' in such a way that numbers come up as mathematical propositions require. Yet no one would cite arithmetical instead of mechanical laws to explain the functioning of the machine. The same applies to man. He of course also has 'insight' into the correctness of what is thought through an 'other' law-governed thinking, perhaps another machine. His thought apparatus as such, however, functions no differently from that of the calculator.

In fact, Husserl showed strikingly by means of his example that the psychological cannot be derived from logical propositions and that the latter are not to be identified with laws of nature. Of course, without the ideal 'validity' of arithmetical propositions, the machine would have just as little chance of functioning as if it had not been organized according to the laws of mechanics. Even in the example, the split between spheres cannot succeed without a painful residue. But simile (which is not inconsequentially mechanical) cannot be applied to the living performance of insight at all. The impossibility of deducing factical thought performances from logical laws does not mean that there is a χωρισμός between the two. Hence, the comparison with machines is deceptive. The fact that in machines the mathematical correctness of the results and the causal-mechanical conditions of their functioning seem to have nothing to do with each other is due solely to a disregard for the construction of the machine. That construction demands some sort of connection between arithmetical propositions and the physical possibility of operating according to them. Without such a connection the machine would not produce correct answers, though that is the point of constructing it. The synthesis of the two is brought about not by the machine but certainly by the consciousness of the constructor. The machine becomes a 'thing' through the definitive establishment of the relation between logic and mechanics. But that

[38] Ibid. p. 64; ibid. p. 101.
[39] Cf. ibid. pp. 68 ff; and ibid. pp. 103 ff.

relation disappears in individual operations. The work of the constructor is hardened in the machine. The subject, which synchronized causal-mechanical procedure with states-of-affairs, abstracts itself from the machine like the God of the Deists from his creation.

The unmediated dualism of reality and mathematics came about historically through a forgetting, viz. the withdrawal of the subject. That happened not only with machines, but also to man *70* himself whenever his thought broke down into logical and psychological moments. The subject transmits to ontology his own cleavage into a disciplined mental functionary and an apparently isolated existent. Alienated from the subject, logical moments represent his encroaching. As thinker and actor, he is more than just himself. He becomes the bearer of social performance and also competes with the reality whose order precedes the divided being for-itself of his subjectivity. As psychological person, he does not feel alienated. But for his referral back to sheer self-identity, he must pay the price that the content of his consciousness is binding. Nor does he escape the fate from which the psychological person would like to be saved. Devoid of any relation to the universal, he shrivels up into a fact, succumbs to an external determination and yet also becomes a subjectless thing, a sort of solid unity of hardened subjectivity, like the law that governs him. The separate element lets as little come together from free and arbitrary thoughts in men as in machines. It is the social process which decides about separation and unification. Yet consciousness also remains the unity of separates. If self-alienation were radical, it would be death. Since it was caused by man, it also is an illusion.

This blinds the Husserl who is the unconscious but faithful historiographer of the self-alienation of thought. He projects self-alienation onto truth. Of course, he sees the limits of the machine analogy. But he hastily dismisses the objection.

The machine is no thought-machine, it understands neither itself nor the meaning of its performances. But our own thought-machine might very well function similarly, except that the real course of one kind of thought would always have to be recognized as correct by the insight brought forward in another.[40]

[40] Ibid. p. 68; ibid.

Yet even the hypothetical 'might' at a central point in the
argument must have puzzled the phenomenologist, who promised to abide purely by 'the things themselves'. But above all, the
subject of the argumentation does not subsist out of several
'thinkings' – the linguistic impossibility of a plural for 'thinking'
71 indicates a factual impossibility. Furthermore, the distinction
between reflective and directly performed acts would not establish an absolute dualism outside the unity of self-consciousness.
The very possibility of reflection presupposes the identity of the
reflecting spirit with the subject of the acts which it reflects upon.
But how could one assert a complete divergence between the
cognitive legitimization of logical propositions and the factical
performance of logical operations, if the two permeate each other
in one and the same consciousness? The unity of thinking which
becomes aware of the sense of its own operations when operating
logically, can be ignored only for a *thema probandum* which shifts a
distinction among scientific disciplines to the ground of being.
Without that unity one could not even imagine the consistency of
logic itself whose defence dragged Husserl into absolutism. The
fact that judgements can be made at all about objecthood
following logical laws would become a miracle if the thinking
which performs such judgements did not both obey and comprehend logic. Husserl's theory of a breach can itself be breached.

Reification of Logic

Husserl's discussion of the 'goals of thought economy' – the
concept of which he appropriated from the positivist critique of
knowledge of the end of the nineteenth century, particularly
Mach and Avenarius – needs to be pushed just a bit further to
reveal all. But he calls the mechanism of reification by name only
to capitulate before it.

It is, e.g., a most serious problem how mathematical disciplines are
possible disciplines not conducted in terms of relatively simple
thoughts, but in which veritable thought-towers, and thought combina-
tions intertwined in a thousand ways, are moved about with the most
sovereign freedom, and are spawned in ever increasing intricacy by our
researches. All this is due to art and method. They overcome the defects

of our mental constitution, and permit an indirect achievement by way of symbolic processes from which intuitability, as well as all genuine understanding and evidence are rejected, but which are rendered secure because a general proof of the performance potential of the method has been once and for all guaranteed.[41]

The contradiction could not be characterized better than as a rejection of intuitability, understanding and evidence. That mathematical work could only be performed through reification and by abandoning the actualization of whatever is meant, contradicts the fact that it presupposes the performance of what it taboos as contamination, taking that to be the legal basis for its own validity.

By describing, but not resolving the facts of the case, Husserl already sanctioned the fetishism which would put forward its illusory aspect sixty years later in fascination with the wonderful improvement of calculators and the corresponding concern with the science of cybernetics. He uses a good simile when he speaks of mathematical 'thought-towers', which are possible only because mathematical calculations are not performed in every operation by the mathematician, but rather take place between symbols. Accordingly the objectivity of mathematical procedure appears independent of subjective thought. Those 'towers' are artefacts which present themselves as if they are natural. Thus – to continue the image – an old bit of masonry is perceived as an element of the landscape, for its social origin and purpose has been forgotten. But the tower is not a crag, even though it was constructed from the stone which colours the landscape. In a move characteristic of his whole method, Husserl diagnoses the reification of logic in order to 'assume' it, and intentionally forgets again what logic had forgotten before.

The analogy is inevitable with vulgar economic thought which attributes value to goods in themselves and does not determine it through social relations. The mathematical method is 'artificial' only in that it does not provide thought with self-awareness. But such 'artificiality' directly transforms logic by magic into a second nature and lends it the aura of ideal being. For its sake Husserl retains mathematics within his philosophy as a sort of pre-philosophical model. He sees no scandal in the paradoxicality of

[41] Ibid. p. 198; ibid. p. 201.

'thought machinery'.[42] The sworn anti-positivist paradoxically encounters the logisticians also when he defines the products of the machinery which have been voided of living execution, viz. the universal arithmetical symbols for number concepts, as 'pure operational signs',

i.e. as signs whose meaning is wholly determined by external types of operation, each sign counting as a mere something-or-other to which this or that definite thing can be done on paper.[43]

Husserl's theory of language remains bound to the logicistic concept of the betting chip. For him words are simply 'sense signs' and thus interchangeable.[44] Logical absolutism sublates itself. Since Husserl dispenses concepts from their 'intelligibility' (*Einsichtigkeit*), they necessarily become 'external forms of operation', while their absolute validity for things becomes contingent. Rendering the formal self-evident and eternal and thus sparing it the confrontation with its own sense, also bisects the connection of what has been propounded as absolutely true with the idea of truth.

The Logical 'Object'

The first volume of the *Logical Investigations* propounds the thesis that logical propositions are valid for any and all possible judgements. Since they apply to any thinking at all of any object at all, they attain truth 'in itself'. Their validity has nothing to do with an object, simply because it concerns all objects. As in themselves, logical propositions are also supposed to be independent of acts which proceed logically or induce a logic reflected upon.

The talk of 'every object', however, is ambiguous. The fact that every single object may be ignored, since formal logic applies to all, does signify that in the highest universality of the category 'object in general', specific differences disappear altogether. What

---

[42] Ibid.; cf. also *LU* II, i, p. 403; and Findlay p. 202.
[43] Ibid. p. 196; ibid. p. 202.
[44] Cf. *LU* II, i, p. 73; and Findlay, p. 309.

does not disappear, however, is the relationship of the propositions of logic to an 'object in general'. They hold only 'for' objects.
Logic can apply only to propositions; only propositions can be
true or false. The law of non-contradiction, for example, could not
be expressed without reference to the concept of contradictorily
opposing propositions. But the concept of such propositions
necessarily involves some content, not only because of the
facticity of their proper execution, i.e. factual subjective judging,
but also because of the material elements which underlie even the
most abstract proposition, however mediated it may be, if it is
going to mean anything at all, i.e. be a proposition.   74

Thus the talk of logic as in-itself is strictly not permissible. Its
very possibility depends on existents, the propositions, with all
that this existence involves, just as conversely the propositions
depend on logic which they must satisfy in order to be true.
Formal logic is functional and not ideal being. But if the
'Whereupon in general' of phenomenologists is recognized as its
constitutive condition, then the conditions of the possibility of
such a 'Whereupon in general' would also be those of formal
logic. The 'Whereupon in general' and the propositions which are
subjected to logic, as syntheses, necessarily demand thinking,
even when what is compelling in synthesis conceals the moment
of spontaneity, and makes synthesis appear analogously to sense
perception as the sheer passive registering of something purely
objective. As a result, however, logical propositions also refer to a
subject matter which does not just arise in the thinking that acts
upon it.

By suppressing the subjective moment, thinking, as the condition of logic, Husserl also conjures away the objective, the
subject matter of thought which is inscrutable in thought. Its
place is taken by unilluminated thought which is thus extended
to objectivity directly. Without suspecting it, logical absolutism is from the beginning absolute idealism. Only the equivocality of the term 'object in general' permits Husserl to interpret
the propositions of formal logic as objects without an object
element.

In this way the mechanism of forgetting becomes that of
reification. The appeal to Hegel's *Logic*, for which abstract being
comes to nothing, just as in Husserl's 'object in general' all
objecthood can be eliminated, is useless. Hegel's 'Being, pure

being – without any further determination'[45] cannot be confused with the highest Husserlian substratum category, 'object in general'. Mainly Husserl feels no doubt about the law of identity. Concepts remain what they are. Husserl's 'nothingness', the elimination of facticity in the interpretation of logical states-of-affairs, demands absolute validity as an isolating judgement. Hence his terms have to relate to his own pet method, critical analysis of meaning.

Autosemantic and Synsemantic Expressions

Such an analysis is cleverly implemented in Oskar Kraus' Introduction to Brentano's *Psychology from an Empirical Standpoint*:

It is of utmost importance that we should be clear about the term 'object' (*Gegenstand, Objekt*). When it is used to mean the same as 'the case' (*Sache*), thing, or real entity (*Reales*), then it is an expression having a meaning of its own – it is autosemantic. In this case it refers simply to what we comprehend by the most universal concept that we can obtain by abstraction from perceptual data; and Brentano treats it as equivalent to the expressions 'entity' (*Wesen*), 'the case' (*Sache*) and real thing (*Reales*). But when 'object' is used in constructions such as 'to have something as an object', it has no meaning of its own, but rather a relative meaning, since this construction can be completely conveyed by the expression 'to have something in mind' – it is synsemantic. We can illustrate the ambiguity and occasional synsemantic meaning of the word 'object' by pointing out the equivalence of the two sentences 'I have something, i.e. a thing, a real entity as an object' and 'I have something, i.e. an object, as an object'. In the latter sentence, the first occurrence of 'object' stands for thing or real entity. It exemplifies the autosemantic use of the term, the second occurrence the synsemantic and means nothing in itself. Taken as a whole, the sentence is equivalent in meaning to 'I am thinking of a thing', 'A thing appears to me', 'A thing is a phenomenon of mine', 'A thing is objectual to me or

---

[45] G.W.F. Hegel, *Sämtliche Werke*, ed. Hermann Glockner, vol. 4, *Wissenschaft der Logik* 4th ed., Jubiläumsausgabe (Fromann, Stuttgart – Bad Cannstatt, 1964), p. 87; cf. *Hegel's Science of Logic*, tr. A.V. Miller (George Allen and Unwin, London, Humanities Press, New York, 1969), p. 82.

"given" or "phenomenal" or "immanent" ', 'I have something objectually'.[46]*

Kraus' demonstration of how a synsemantic concept may replace an autosemantic one characterizes meaning theoretically the result of reification, but, of course, does not develop it from its origin. Husserl's neglect, even in his theory of logic, of its 'object in general', i.e. its relation to objecthood which is implicit to the sense of logical propositions, and Kraus' turning logic itself into an object, while working out the error, are just two different aspects of the same thing. Since no thinking can break out of the subject–object polarity, nor ever even establish it and determine either distinct moment independently of the other, the object 76 which had been ejected in the hypostatization of pure logic returns within it. Logic becomes the object about which it had forgotten.

Logic necessarily misunderstands itself in its naiveté about its relation to objecthood. As pure form, logic takes credit for the stringency which is clearly gained in judgements about objects, and, as ontology, falsely appropriates it. But that affects not only the question of its 'foundations', but also its internal architecture. The much discussed inflexibility of Aristotelian logic, which only Russell and Whitehead rendered supple again, could have been produced by the reification of logic. For it shut itself off from its own object sense all the more completely the more it was improved as an individual science.

Logical Laws and Laws of Thought

The reification of logic as the self-alienation of thought is equivalent to and modelled on the reification of what thinking relates to, namely the unity of objects which are coagulated into the thought at work in them, and so to identity. Hence, neglecting their changing content, the sheer form of their unity can be established. Such an abstraction remains the obvious presupposition of all logic. It takes its cue from the form of

* ['I have something as an object' is an unavoidable Teutonism whose sense is explained in Kraus' text. It does not mean 'My purpose or point is . . .' Trans.]

[46] Franz Brentano, *Psychologie vom empirischen Standpunkt*, ed. Oskar Kraus (Felix Meiner, Hamburg, 1955), vol. 1, p. xix; cf. ed. Linda L. McAlister, tr. Anros C. Rancunello, D.B. Turrell and Linda L. McAlister, *Psychology from an Empirical Standpoint* (Humanities Press, New York, 1973).

commodities whose identity consists in the 'equivalence' of exchange values. By the same token, however, it also looks to a societal relation unperceptive about itself, false consciousness, the subject. Logical absolutism is two things. It is reflection in the subject of the reification which is performed by the subject, which itself ultimately becomes a thing. It is also the attempt to break the spell of universal subjectivization and intercept, by means of something straightforwardly irreducible, a subject which for all its power suspects itself of arbitrariness if not impotence. The most radical subjectivism becomes a fantasm of its own overcoming.

That is already Husserl's schema in the 'Prolegomena to Pure Logic'. His mode of procedure is already, as in the later epistemology, a 'crossing out' or 'bracketing out'. The reason is that residual concept of truth which, with the exception of Hegel and Nietzsche, is common to the whole of bourgeois philosophy. To this thought, truth appears as what 'remains left' after one deducts its production costs, the wages of the labour, as it were, in short what in the vulgar language of science enslaved to positivism is ultimately called 'subjective factors'. A consciousness in possession of the unalterable and inscrutable and thus of the surrogate for experience, which it breaks down into classificatory categories, is indifferent as to whether this does not lead to the amputation of what is substantial in knowledge, the fullness and movement of its object. The instrument which dissolves all absolutes proclaims itself the absolute. Just as Faust could only hold on to Helen's garments, ever-striving science consoles itself with the empty form of thought. Husserl calls himself a 'logical absolutist'[47] not without letting on to a slight unease in the appeasing formula, 'sit venia verbo'. He means the 'laws of pure logic, independent of the peculiarities of the human mind',[48] whose concept is also introduced with the hesitant parenthesis, 'if there are such things'.

Accordingly logical absolutism far surpasses the critique of the psychological interpretation of logic as the derivation of its validity from the dynamics of the 'life of the soul'. It far surpasses the excellent proof that logical laws are not merely a bit of intra-human soul. Husserl's theory is absolutist rather because it denies any dependence of logical laws on entities at all as the

[47] *LU* I, p. 139; cf. Findlay, p. 156.
[48] Ibid. p. 31; ibid. p. 75.

condition of its possible sense. His theory expresses no relation between consciousness and object. Rather, a sort of being *sui generis* is passed off on to it.

We for our part would say: Universal likeness of content, and constant functional laws of nature which regulate the production of such content do not constitute a genuine universal validity.[49]

For him such ideality agrees with absoluteness.

If all creatures of a genus are constitutionally compelled to judge alike, they are in empirical agreement, but, in the ideal sense demanded by a supra-empirical logic, there might as well have been disagreement as agreement. To define truth in terms of a community of nature is to abandon its concept. If truth were essentially related to thinking intelligences, their mental functions and modes of change, it would arise and perish with them, with the species at least, if not with the individual. With the genuine objectivity of truth, the objectivity of being, even the objectivity of subjective being or the being of the subject, would be gone. What if, e.g., no thinking creature were capable of postulating its own being as truly existing? Then they would both be and not be. Truth and being are 'categories' in the same sense, and plainly correlative: truth cannot be relativized, while the objectivity of being is maintained. The relativization of truth presupposes the objective being of the point to which things are relative: this is the contradiction in relativism.[50]

However conclusive that sounds, it nevertheless remains vulnerable to attack in detail. By cutting off the 'constraint' of like judgements from the judging subject and foisting it on ideal logic, the moment of compulsion in such a constraint, which follows from the things, is also neglected. This moment holds true only in the synthesis of judgement performed by the subject. Without constitutive mediation through thought, ostensible ideal laws could in no sense be applied to reality. Ideal being would not even have to do with real being as its 'form'. What Husserl takes as highest objectivity, 'logic elevated above everything empirical', would in such elevation be condemned to sheer subjectivity. Its relation to the real would obtain by chance.

   Even the plausible and perhaps convincing thesis in relation to

[49] Ibid. p. 131; ibid. p. 150.
[50] Ibid. pp. 131 ff; ibid. pp. 150 ff.

empiricism that the concept of truth would be abandoned, if it is determined by the 'community of nature', proves to be abstract negation and too crude. The thought of truth is exhausted neither in the subject, even the transcendental subject, nor in pure ideal lawfulness. Rather, it demands the relation of the subject to states-of-affairs. And this relation – and thus the objectivity of truth – likewise comprises thinking subjects, which, by fulfilling the synthesis, are brought to synthesis by things. Synthesis and constraint, meanwhile, cannot be isolated from each other. The objectivity of truth really demands the subject. Once cut off from the subject, it becomes the victim of sheer subjectivity. Husserl sees only the rigid alternative between the empirical, contingent subject – and the absolutely necessary ideal law purified of all facticity. This is not to say, however, that truth arises in neither of those. Rather it is a constellation of moments which cannot be reckoned a 'residuum' of either the subjective or of the objective side.

In seeking a *reductio ad absurdum* of 'subjectivistic' logic, Husserl insinuates that the same thinking creatures (*Wesen*) 'would both be and not be', if their disposition were to forbid them 'to posit their own being as truly existing (*seiend*)'. The absurdity is supposed to consist in the fact that such creatures, in spite of their defects, would indeed 'be'. But without the possibility of thinking, to which the concept of the subject is immanent, logical absolutism itself would be senseless. The apparently striking absurdity occurs only because Husserl in one instance assumes contingent psychophysical persons and in another logical laws. Persons certainly have no immediate power over such laws. Yet they are mediated by a concept of subjectivity which surpasses psychophysical individuals without simply eliminating them. Rather it preserves them as a moment of its own foundation.

Truth is as little identified by an ideality which is constituted only in virtue of a blindness to the factical implicates of ideality, as it is by the sheer facticity of subjective organization. Both the empiricist and the idealistic theory fall short of truth because they pin it down as an entity – Husserl calls it 'being'. Truth is, rather, a field of force. Certainly 'truth cannot be relativized while the objectivity of being is maintained'. But in place of such objectivity Husserl himself inserts its copy, pure form. For he cannot conceive of objectivity otherwise than as static and reified.

Aporia of Logical Absolutism

The idolization of logic as pure being demands an unconditioned split between genesis and validity. Otherwise the logical absolute would be compounded with entities and – accepting the standard of the χωρισμός – with the contingent and the relative. Husserl developed the split polemically against empiricism. According to him, psychologism, when dealing with logical theory, 'tends always to confuse the psychological origin of certain universal judgements in experience, on account of some supposed "naturalness", with a justification of the same judgements'.[51]   80

This elucidation of the terms does not really come to terms with the things themselves. It in no way follows from the fact that the generation and justification of judgements should not be 'confused', but rather that validity is something quite different from genesis, that the explication of the sense of validation features does not refer back to genetic moments as their necessary condition. Husserl, by the way, tacitly conceded this in his later transcendental philosophy, without expressly emending the thesis of logical absolutism. Insofar as the relation of logical validity to genesis is necessary, this relation itself belongs to logical sense which must be explained or 'awakened'. Husserl presented forcibly and with much authority the antinomies into which logical psychologism falls. But the unmediated opposing position of absolutism involves itself in no less harmful antinomies.

Two interpretations are possible of a logic whose validity is absolute and independent of all genesis and thus ultimately of all entities. Consciousness confronts logic and its 'ideal laws'. If consciousness wishes to substantiate the claim of logic as founded and not crudely assume it, then logical laws must be reasonable to thought. In that case, however, thinking must recognize them as its own laws, its proper essence. For thinking is the content of logical acts. Pure logic and pure thought could not be detached from each other. The radical dualism between logic and consciousness would be sublated, and the subject of thought would enter along into the foundation of logic. . . .

[51] Ibid. p. 86; ibid. p. 117.

Instead Husserl renounces, for the sake of the purity of the claim to absoluteness, the foundation of logic as a form which is immanent to thought and transparent to it as its own essence. In that case, however, logic would be given purely 'phenomenally' (to transfer an epistemological expression to the most formal states-of-affairs) to consciousness and not evident 'in itself'. Consciousness would know logic not as something that merely appears to consciousness to be accepted as heteronomous, but 81 rather as true only if logic itself were the knowledge of consciousness. If it were merely registered and accepted as a higher order 'phenomenon', the purity of the logical *a priori* may indeed be saved. Yet logic then also forfeits the character of unconditioned validity which is just as inviolable for logical absolutism as ideal purity. Its laws would then be valid only in the framework of its 'appearing'. They would remain dogmatic, unproven and contingent. Paradoxically they would become rules of experience and absolutism would turn into empiricism. If other logical laws were to 'appear' to consciousness, then it would have to submit to those just as it does to the laws of current logic. The phenomenologist would find himself precisely in that situation whose possibility Husserl himself denied to an angelic logic.[52] As Husserl refuses to concede to Erdmann, it may be 'that other beings might have quite different logical principles . . . .'.[53]

Both interpretations of the absolutistic claim lead just as much to aporia as the psychologistic counterposition. Logic is not being, but rather a process (*Prozeß*) which cannot be reduced purely to either a 'subjectivity' or an 'objectivity' pole. The consequence of the self-critique of logic is the dialectic.

Relating Genesis and Validity

Husserl, however, lays the greatest stress on the contrast between genesis and validity.

The question is not how experience, whether naive or scientific, is generated, but what must be its content if it is to have objective validity: we must ask on what ideal elements and laws such objective validity of

[52] Cf. ibid. pp. 145 ff; and ibid. pp. 161 ff.
[53] Ibid. p. 151; ibid. p. 165.

knowledge of the real is founded – more generally, on what any knowledge is founded – and how the performance involved in knowledge should be properly understood. We are, in other words, not interested in the origins and changes of our world-representation, but in the objective right which the world-representation of science claims against any other world-representation, which leads it to call its world the objectively true one.[54]

The thesis that what matters is not how experience is generated, but rather what content it would have to have to become objectively valid experience, ignores the fact that the content of experience is itself a 'generating' in which subjective and objective moments are chemically united, so to speak. Judgements must both express some thingly content and originate it through synthesis. Only if the immanent tension within judgement is 82 misunderstood, can the 'generation' of content be disregarded.

In fact, Husserl is not even concerned with content, in spite of his comments, but rather solely with the distilled form of the judgement. Thus, he eludes the very dynamic which is at play in the logical 'state-of-affairs' itself. The dualism of form and content is the schema of reification. Husserl explains that 'we', viz. future logicians, are interested not in becoming, but rather in the objective justice of the scientific representation of the world. Thus he arrogantly enthrones the 'interest', which is dictated by the scientific division of labour, as the criterion of the ontological dignity of ostensibly unchanging being as opposed to sheer becoming. The word 'interest', which points to an arbitrary turning to oneself, betrays, against Husserl's intention, the fact that such dignity arises not from the logical state-of-affairs in itself, but from the 'attitude' of a science, which anxiously fences itself off from the structure of science as a whole for the sake of its own putative dignity. The non-interest of the logician in the 'transformation of the representation of the world', credits only the opalescence of such a concept for the illusion of its evidence.

Logic is right not to worry about the transformation of the representation of the world as mere representation. It is wrong, however, to the extent that this representation is of the transformation of the world. The 'objective right which the world-representation of science claims as against any other', does not, as

---

[54] Ibid. pp. 205 ff; ibid. p. 207.

Husserl would like, have its God-given ground in the 'idea of science', but rather finds its measure and limit in the capacity of science to know its object. The division of labour both helps and hinders it from knowledge. Husserl's rigid objectivism of the logical proves to be a self-deceiving subjectivism also because the idea of science – the schema of order imposed on objects by human consciousness – is handled as if the need indicated in this schema were the order of the objects themselves. Every static ontology naively hypostatizes the subjective-categorial.

Genesis and Psychology

Husserl makes things easy on himself in his polemic against the
83 genetic interpretation of logic, because he confines himself to 'psychologism'. The genetic interpretation of logical laws must supposedly turn to the processes of consciousness in the psychological subject, the single human individual, as its ultimate substratum. That, of course, allows him to present the difference between psychological foundation in individual conscious acts and the objectivity of logical content.

But the implicit genesis of the logical is certainly not psychological motivation. It is a sort of social behaviour. According to Durkheim, logical propositions contain a deposit of social experiences such as the order of generation and property relations which claim priority over the being and consciousness of the individual. Both compelling and alienated from individual interest, these relations constantly confront the psychological subject as something valid and compelling in itself and yet as arbitrary also. This is also the case with Husserl's 'propositions in themselves' though much against his will. The power of logical absolutism over the psychological grounding of logic is borrowed from the objectivity of the social process which subjects individuals to compulsion while remaining opaque to them. Husserl's scientific reflection unreflectively takes the position of the individual within this social situation. He raises logic to an entity in itself just as pre-critical consciousness did to things. As a result, he correctly asserts that the laws of thought of the individual – psychologically speaking, of the ego, whose categories are indeed turned towards reality, and are formed in reciprocal action with reality, and are therefore 'objective' – do not receive their objectivity from the individual. The judgement that society is organized before the individual prevails in a distorted form.

The priority of the individual, the self-deception of traditional liberalism, is shattered by Husserl's post-liberal conception. But the ideology, nevertheless, maintains its power over him. The social process which he never understood was just the truth for him. Its objectivity was spiritualized into the ideal being of propositions in themselves.

Thinking and Psychologism

The response of the reference of logic back to thought and thus to 84 entities is too suggestive not to have occurred to Husserl.

It is irrelevant to object that talk of logical laws could never have arisen had we not lived experiences of representations and judgements, and abstracted the relevant, basic logical concepts from them, or that, wherever we understand and assert such laws, the existence of representations and judgements is implied, and can therefore be inferred. We need hardly observe that this does not follow from our law, but from the fact that we understand and assert such a law, and that a like consequence could be inferred from every assertion. One ought not, further, to confuse the psychological presuppositions or components of the assertion of a law, with the logical 'moments' of its content.[55]

What one 'need hardly observe' skates over the central difficulty. For the issue is not a mere subjective 'understanding and assertion' of a law, independent of the state-of-affairs and arbitrarily performable. Rather, the claim to the law's absolute-ness is equivalent to the claim to its correctness, and this latter cannot be gained otherwise than by current 'representations and judgements'. The 'law's' 'understanding and assertion' cannot be contrasted with it as an irrelevant mode of behaviour on the part of the observer where the law as 'law of thought' demands that it be thought to be legitimized, and where it can be stated only as a law for thinking – and 'understanding'.

The mistake of logical psychologism is to derive the validity of

[55] Ibid. p. 71; ibid. pp. 105–6.

logical propositions immediately from the psychic-factual, though this validity has become autonomous of factical psychic 'realization'. But the analysis of the sense of logical structure itself demands the reference to thought. No logic without propositions and no propositions without the synthetic function of thought. Husserl has drawn attention to the fact that the psychological presupposition of the assertion of a law may not be confused with its logical validity. But clearly logical laws are only 'meaningful' (sinnvoll) and can only be known, when they are inherently matched to the acts of thought which discharge them.

The sense of logic itself demands facticity. Otherwise, it could not be grounded rationally. Its ideality is not a pure in-itself, but rather must always also be for another, if it is to be anything at all. Husserl is correct when he contests the immediate identity of insight and state-of-affairs, genesis and validity, for developed scientific consciousness and the irrevocable position of alienation. He is wrong when he hypostatizes the difference.

The Law of Non-Contradiction

Husserl does not stop there. He expands his critique to the logical arch-principles of the law of non-contradiction and the law of identity. He sees Heyman and Sigwart as primarily responsible for the psychologistic misinterpretation of the law of non-contradiction, and he quotes from the latter's *Logik* the formulation that 'It is impossible consciously to affirm and deny the same proposition'. Husserl argues further against the grounding of the law of non-contradiction in the impossibility of psychological coexistence as it is presented in Mill's attack on Hamilton and in the *Logik* of Höfler and Meinong. The procedure is once again linguistic-critical, the good old Aristotelian analysis of equivocations.

The term 'thought', which in its wider sense covers all intellectual activities, is in the usage of certain logicians by preference applied to rational, 'logical' thought, to correct judgement. That in correct judgement, Yes and No exclude one another, is plain, but this is merely an equivalent to the logical law, and not at all a psychological proposition. It tells us that no judgement is correct in which the same state-of-affairs is at once affirmed and denied: it says nothing regarding a possible coexistence of contradictory acts of judgement, whether in one consciousness, or in several.[56]

Thus the coexistence of contradictory judgements would be impossible only to a thought whose 'correctness' (Korrektheit) already presupposes that it proceeds according to the law of non-contradiction. But then the law cannot be deduced from the impossibility of that coexistence. Yet the distinction between thought pure and simple and logical thought, which has such strikingly successful results for non-contradictory propositions, 86 does not present itself so unproblematically to reflection on the thought process. Logical principles crystallize not only around the logical pole, under compulsion from logical 'states-of-affairs'. Rather, such states-of-affairs in turn arise through the needs and tendencies of the thinking consciousnesses, which are reflected in the logical order. 'The universality of thoughts as developed by discursive logic, and lordship in the sphere of the concept, arises on the foundation of lordship in reality.'[57]
The historical development of that universality of thought is indeed that of its logical 'correctness'. Only contemplative arbitrariness could isolate the two. Correctness itself is just something which arises, a consequence of developing thought. If, however, thought and correct thought cannot be semantically distinguished in the way Husserl asserts, then the question of the possible coexistence of the contradictory judgements is not as indifferent for logic as he would like. His task is so easy because he shares with the psychologistic logicians the thesis of the impossibility of that coexistence and only argues against its having anything to do with the validity of the law of non-contradiction. If that thesis is no longer conceded him, i.e. if one inquires after the origin of thought, 'the primal history of logic', then the possibility of the coexistence of contradictories in factual judgements is no longer irrelevant. The psychological thesis of the impossibility of coexistence naively imitates the law that the same spatial location cannot simultaneously be occupied by two

[56] Ibid. p. 88; ibid. pp. 118–19.
[57] Max Horkheimer and Theodor W. Adorno, Dialektik der Aufklärung (Querido, Amsterdam, 1947), p. 25; cf. tr. John Cumming, Dialectic of Enlightenment (Herder and Herder, New York, 1972), p.14.

bits of matter. Such a 'point' in the life of consciousness is fictive, as the critique of the punctual interpretation of pure presence has long since shown. Thought of the contradictory seems to precede individuation.

Genetically logic presents itself as an attempt at integration and the solid ordering of the originally equivocal – as a decisive step in demythologization.[58] The law of non-contradiction is a sort of taboo which hangs over the diffuse. Its absolute authority which Husserl insists upon, directly originates in the imposition of the taboo and in the repression of powerful counter-tendencies. As a 'law of thought', its content is prohibition: Do not think diffusely. Do not let yourself be diverted by unarticulated nature, but rather hold tight to what you mean like a possession. By virtue of logic, the subject saves itself from falling into the amorphous, the inconstant, and the ambiguous. For it stamps itself on experience, it is the identity of the survivor as form. And the only assertions about nature it lets be valid are those which are captured by the identity of those forms.

Validity and rationality themselves are for such an interpretation of logic no longer irrational and not an inconceivable in-itself simply to be accepted. They are rather the demand, more powerful than all existence, that the subject not fall back into nature, revert to a beast, and leave behind that small advantage whereby humanity, self-perpetuating natural creatures, goes beyond, however powerlessly, nature and self-preservation. But logical validity is also objective by adopting the standard of nature in order to master it. Every logical synthesis is anticipated by its object, but its possibility remains abstract and is actualized only by the subject. They need each other.

The point is correctly made in logical absolutism that validity, the highest instrument for the mastery of nature, is not exhausted in such mastery. What is done and united in human logical synthesis, remains only humanity and not the empty form of its arbitrariness. Rather, in virtue of the shape of the object of synthesis, which would evaporate without synthesis, synthesis extends beyond sheer doing. Judging means ordering and more than mere ordering into one.

[58] Cf. ibid. passim.

The Law of Identity

In accord with the tradition, Husserl deals independently with the law of non-contradiction and the law of identity. With respect to the latter he especially seeks to separate the validity of logical propositions from their normative character.

The normative law is thought to presuppose absolute constancy among our concepts. The law would then only be valid on condition that we always used expressions with the same meaning, and where this condition was not fulfilled, it would not hold. This cannot be what [Sigwart] seriously believes. The empirical application of the law seriously presupposes that the concepts or propositions which function as the meanings of our expressions really are the same, since the law ideally extends to all possible pairs of propositions of opposed quality but identical subject matter. But this of course is no condition of the law's validity, as if this were merely hypothetical, but is the presupposition of the possible application of the law to previously given instances. Just as it is a supposition for applying a numerical law, that we have, in a *88* given case, numbers actually before us, and numbers of such a character as the law expressly refers to, so it is a presupposition for applying the logical law that propositions are before us; that they are propositions of identical subject matter is expressly stipulated.[59]

What Husserl calls 'presupposition', i.e. that expressions are related in identical reference, is nothing other than the content of the law itself. When it is not fulfilled, a law would in fact lose its validity, for it would present the sheer tautology of validity. The law of identity is not indeed a 'hypothesis' which would be verified or falsified depending on whether the referents of the expressions are seized or not. But without the confrontation of the expression with identical or non-identical 'matter', the law of identity could not be formulated at all. Husserl avoids the problem by attacking the normative interpretation of the law of identity as its devaluation to a hypothesis.

The question is not, however, whether the law would be relativized by its implicit reference to the propositions which fall under it, but rather whether it decays into senseless affirmation without such a reference.

[59] *LU* I pp. 99 ff; and Findlay p. 127.

Thus what I understand by the law of identity is not a 'principle' which would be acknowledged as true, but a demand to be fulfilled or left unfulfilled as we may wish. Unless it were fulfilled, however, . . . the opposition between truth and error in our assertions would lose its sense. The ostensible logical principle of identity which is customarily formulated in the allegedly self-evident proposition. 'A is a', does not at all express a self-evident truth, elevated above every doubt, unprovable and unexplainable, ultimate and mysterious. Rather, the truth of this proposition depends on the fulfilment of the principle of identity in the above sense, i.e. on the fulfilment of the demand to retain the referents of the signs. It follows from the fulfilment of such a demand. If this demand is not fulfilled with respect to the sign 'a', the proposition 'A is a' is no longer correct. For if we do not mean the same thing by the second 'a' in this proposition as by the first, then the first 'a' is not the second 'a'. That is, the proposition 'A is a' is no longer valid.[60]

The law of identity, therefore, is not a state-of-affairs, but rather a rule of how to think which, once detached from the acts for which it was advanced, hangs in the wind. Its meaning includes the relation to those acts.

Husserl obviously means that the identical use of terms belongs to the side of facticity and that the law of identity independently possesses an ideal validity 'in itself'. But this validity would have to be sought in its meaning, and it means nothing unless terms are used factually. Moreover, the 'presupposition for applying the logical law of contradiction, that propositions are before us', which Husserl does not contest so much as trivialize, would already suffice to debilitate logical absolutism, just as long as all its implications were followed up.

Contingency

Husserl will not follow it through because of a *horror intellectualis* of the arbitrary. Contingency is as unbearable to him as it was to the early days of the bourgeoisie, whose theoretical impulses ultimately flare up once again in Husserl, sublimated in every reflection. All bourgeois – all first – philosophy has struggled in vain with contingency. For every such philosophy seeks to reconcile a really self-antagonistic whole.

[60] Hans Cornelius, *Transzendentale Systematik* (Munich, 1916), pp. 159 ff.

Philosophical consciousness qualifies the antagonism as one of subject and object. Since it cannot sublate the antagonism in itself, it strives to remove it for itself, i.e. through reduction of being to consciousness. Reconciliation demands – equating everything with itself. And that is also the contradiction of reconciliation.

Contingency remains, however, the 'Menetekel'* of lordship. This is always covert, though lordship eventually openly confesses it: totalitarianism. It subsumes as chance whatever is not like it, the slightest non-homonymy. One has no power over what 90 occurs by chance. No matter where contingency arises, it gives the lie to the universal mastery of spirit, its identity with matter. It is the mutilated, abstract shape of the in-itself from which the subject has usurped everything commensurable. The more recklessly the subject insists upon identity and the more purely it strives to establish its mastery, the more threateningly looms the shadow of non-identity. The threat of contingency is simply advanced by the pure *a priori* which is its enemy and should allay it.

Pure spirit, that wishes to be identical with the entity must, for the sake of the illusion of identity, of indifference between subject and object, ever more completely withdraw into itself, let more and more go. Namely everything factical. 'It is now clear that, in this pregnant sense, any theory is logically absurd (*widersinnig*), which deduces logical principles from any matters of fact.'[61] *Prima philosophia* as a residual theory of truth which bases itself on what survives of the indubitably certain, is complemented by a contingency it cannot manage, but which it must exclude, so as not to endanger its claim to purity. As the claim to be *a priori* is interpreted more rigorously, less corresponds to it and more gets stuck in the realm of chance. Hence, the universal lordship of spirit always also includes its own resignation. Nevertheless, the unsolvability of the 'problem of contingency', the irreducibility of the entity to its conceptual determination, is also deceit. Contingency only extends to where reason shows solidarity with the claim to lordship, and will not endure what it has not captured.

The false point of departure of the philosophy of identity comes to light in the insolubility of contingency. The world cannot be

* [The writing on the wall from Daniel, chapter 5. Trans.]

[61] *LU* I, p. 123; cf. Findlay, pp. 144 ff.

thought as a product of consciousness. Contingency is frightening only in the structure of delusion. If thought were to escape from this structure, contingency would silence and extinguish it. Husserl, however, is compelled to the Sisyphean labour of overcoming contingency as soon as the unity of bourgeois society as a self-producing and reproducing system – as it was envisioned from the Hegelian heights – broke down. For Husserl, 'chance' plays no role in 'scientific connections of validation' which constitute the model of his entire philosophy, only 'reason and order, i.e. regulative laws'.[62]

Nowhere more disastrously than here does he apply the already advanced method of an individual science to the whole. He believes that he can turn scepticism upside down, since it denies the laws that 'essentially constitute the concept of theoretical unity',[63]* i.e. the 'definite sense'[64] of terms such as theory, truth, object and constitution. Logically, therefore, scepticism sublates itself in that its content is the contesting of laws, 'without which theory as such would have no "rational", i.e. definite sense'.[65] But it is not settled whether what is certainly not defined beforehand as a mathematical manifold is inwardly solid and satisfies the form of pure freedom from contradiction. Only in the mathematical ideal of connections of validity is the exemption from contingency imposed on philosophy which must conform to it. But really it should first find out whether it does not thereby regress to pre-critical rationalism. This reflection is no longer performed by Husserl. For him the ideas of the real diluted to pure forms are nowhere more the master. They nowhere enter into reality and nowhere reflect it into itself. Humanity itself as a result is, as a bit of reality, contingent to the idea and is expelled from the paradise of *prima philosophia*, the kingdom of its own reason. If contingency as scepticism has in the history of recent philosophy dragged ideas into its vortex, then Husserl now proceeds literally according to the dictum that if the facts do not obey ideas, all the worse for the facts. They are explained as

* [Quoted by Adorno as 'insight' (*Einsicht*) rather than 'unity' (*Einheit*). Trans.]

[62] Ibid. p. 18; ibid. p. 64.
[63] Ibid. p. 111; ibid. p. 136.
[64] Ibid. p. 112; ibid.
[65] Ibid.

unamenable to philosophy and ignored. An ironic twilight hangs over the concept of concretion of recent anthropological philosophies, for the theory which inaugurated the 'material' turn, far surpassed, in the formalism of its idea of truth, the Kantian version, the object of Scheler's war cry. Material essentialities, towards which description later tendentially but already in 92 Husserl turned, are inaccessible to the very entities to which they claim to return. Hence the ghostliness of all phenomenological concretion. Husserl reinterprets the need for the contingency of the factual in idealism as the virtue of purity in the idea. Ideas remain behind as the *caput mortuum* of life forsaken by spirit.

Abandoning the Empirical

The individual material sciences are frankly conceived from an empiricist standpoint. 'The realm of psychology is indeed part of the realm of biology.' The higher the demands to be *a priori* are raised, the more completely is the empirical conjured away, somewhat like the bourgeois arranges love according to the schema of sacred or profane. As a variation on the Kantian formula, the doctrine of logical absolutism in the Prolegomena could be called empirical relativism. It treats of the intersubjective world in the style of the sociology of knowledge.

Psychological laws determine the emergence, out of our first roughly agreeing mental collocations, of the representation of the single world common to everyone, and of an empirically blind belief in its existence. One should, however, note that this world is not the same for everyone, but only so 'on the whole'; it is the same only to an extent which affords a sufficient practical guarantee for our common representations and actions. It is not the same for the ordinary man and the scientific research worker: for the former it is a system merely approximate in its regularity, and shot through with countless accidents, whereas for the latter it is a nature ruled throughout by absolutely strict law.[66]

Such relativism is anything but enlightenment. Husserl's thought of 'absolutely strict law' takes things much too easily with the 'countless accidents', which do not in fact exist. For the

---

[66] Ibid. p. 205; ibid. p. 206.

researcher chance is the painful remainder which is deposited at the bottom of his concepts. For the 'ordinary man', whose name Husserl utters without hesitation, chance is what befalls him and against which he is defenceless. The researcher imagines that he prescribes laws to the world. The 'ordinary man' must obey such laws in practice. He can do nothing about it, and it all may correctly seem arbitrary to him. The fact, however, that the world is composed of things such as are surrendered to accidents of that sort, and of other things which, though they may not make the law, can comfort themselves with its existence, is no accident. It is itself the law of real society. No philosophy which discusses the 'representation of the world' can overlook it.

93

But the abandonment of the empirical does not grant Husserl undiminished insight into such connections. Rather, he repeats with a shrug of the shoulders the lixiviated prejudice that it is all a matter of point of view. He is not so punctilious with the knowledge of the factual, since that remains afflicted anyway with the mark of the arbitrary. Reality becomes merely the object of what one means. No binding criterion is supposed to cover it. This modesty is as false as its complement, the hubris of the absolute. Husserl overestimates the arbitrariness of the life of consciousness no less than its opposite number, the being in-itself of the laws of thought. Abstract reflection on the fact that anything factual 'could also be different', cheats about universal determinations, which are based on the fact that things are not different.

Phenomenological and Eidetic Motifs

The abandonment of the world as the content of such contingent facticity already implies the contradiction between the two governing motifs of Husserl's philosophy, the phenomenological and the eidetic. The exclusion of the worldly leads by the old and familiar Cartesian schema to the ego, the contents of whose consciousness, as immediately certain, are simply to be accepted. But the ego, which constitutes the unity of thought, itself belongs to the world which is supposed to be excluded for the sake of the purity of logical forms of thought. Husserl observes,

There would, therefore, be no world 'in itself', but only a world for us, or for any other chance species of being. This may suit some, but it becomes dubious once we point out that the ego and its conscious contents also pertain to the world. That I am, and that I am experiencing this or that, might be false if my specific constitution were such as to force me to deny these propositions. And there would be absolutely no 94 world, not merely no world for this or that one, if no actual species of judging beings in the world was so constituted as to have to recognize a world (and itself in that world).[67]

The absurdity, however, occurs only because one step in the chain of argumentation is isolated and assessed by an already advanced logical absolutism. Of course, logical principles would not be 'false' if the human race were to die out. They would, nevertheless, lose the concept of a thought for which they were valid; they would be neither true nor false. They would not come into question at all. Thought, however, requires a subject, and a factical substratum of whatever sort cannot be driven from the concept of the subject. The possibility which Husserl derides as a 'pretty game', i.e. that 'man evolves from the world and the world from man; God creates man and man God',[68] should appear as horrendous only to a rigid, polar, and, in the Hegelian sense, abstract thought. It offers an admittedly crude and naturalistic but in no way meaningless entry into dialectical thought, which does not make out man and world as warring brothers, one of which must at any price claim the right of first born over the other. Rather, it develops them as reciprocally self-producing moments of the whole which come out of each other.

Husserl's hatred of scepticism, like his hatred of the dialectic with which he confuses it, expresses a state of consciousness in which despair over the loss of the static conception of truth does not reflect upon whether a defect in the traditional concept of truth may not appear in the loss, but rather stigmatizes all theories which bear witness to that loss. For all relativism lives off the consistency of absolutism. If every individual and restricted bit of knowledge is burdened with the necessity of being straightforwardly valid independently of every further qualification, then all knowledge is effortlessly delivered over to its own

[67] Ibid. p. 121; ibid. p. 143.
[68] Ibid.

relativity. Pure subjectivity and pure objectivity are the highest of such isolated and therefore inconsistent qualifications. If knowledge should be exclusively reducible to the subject or the object, then isolability and reduction are raised to a law of truth. The entirely isolated is sheer identity which refers to nothing beyond itself. The complete reduction to subject or object embodies the

95 ideal of such identity. The untruth of relativism is just that it abides by the negative determination – which is correct in itself – of all individuals, instead of going further. In its faithfulness to mere appearance (*Schein*), it is just as absolutistic as absolutism. If knowledge is not unconditioned, then it should forthwith be untenable.

In a gestus that is not gratuitously suggestive of the two-phased thought of many psychotics, the judgement is two-valued according to the schema of all or nothing. Husserl has come to all too good an understanding with the opponents he chooses. Both are interminably right to call the other 'standpoint philosophers', by which term Husserl like Hegel rejects his opponents.[69] Husserl is right in that he demonstrates to his opponents that their criteria of truth break down truth itself. The opponents are correct in that they remind him that truth which forsakes those criteria is a chimera. But this robs his critique of its power, for that facticity can be other is a sheer possibility, while in the mode of procedure of thought which is constituted in one way and not another, is deposited the necessity of approximating an object and thus a moment of objectivity itself. The concept of objectivity, to which logical absolutism sacrifices the world, cannot renounce the concept from which objectivity draws its very model. This is the concept of an object: the world.

[69] *Logik* [123]; cf. Cairns ⟨105⟩.

2

Species and Intention

What only I mean (*meine*) is mine (*mein*). It belongs to me as this particular individual. If, however, language expresses only the universal, then I cannot say what only I mean.

Hegel, *Encyclopedia*

Propositions in Themselves and Essences

The renunciation of existence (*Dasein*) bestows much greater significance on Husserl's doctrine of logical absolutism than that of a mere style of interpreting formal logic. Logical axioms, elevated to propositions in themselves, offer the model of fact-free, pure essentialities whose foundation and description phenomenology as a whole chooses as its task and identifies with the concept of philosophy. Husserl's interpretation of the formal *a priori* dominated both his conception of all truth and that of his pupils, even the apostates among them. It even marks the thesis that being is organized before all entities.

The movement of the concept went beyond the Prolegomena, for empty forms of thought cannot be isolated from what are called problems of constitution in traditional epistemology. The validity of logical principles was, outside of dialectical doctrine, hardly controversial even before Husserl. The extraordinary effect of primarily his particular theorem can only be explained by the fact that it emphatically expressed the long since mature consciousness of a much troubled state-of-affairs. For the first time since the collapse of the great systems, the philosophical struggle against psychologism attests to the insufficiency of the individual as a legal ground for truth. It thus goes far beyond the neo-Kantian nuances given to the transcendental. But now anti-individualism does not proclaim the primacy of the whole over the particular, but just also acknowledges the ruin of the individual itself. Since every component of the legitimization of truth is taken away from the individual and its structure, logic, alienated from all reality, exposes the individual to its real nullity.

Far from culture-critical reasoning, Husserl conceives thoughts which blend the defeatism of the impotent individual with the sufferings of the monadological condition. Thus the Prolegomena functioned as an historical seismograph. It unifies the long-suppressed foreboding that individuation itself may be mere appearance and produced by the law implicit in it, with aversion to the very negative reality whose law in fact degrades the individual to mere appearance. Husserl's concept of essence scintillates with such ambiguity. Nothing is more timely than its timelessness. Phenomenological purity, idiosyncratically against all contact with the factical, still remains perishable like a flower ornament. 'Essence' was the cherished *Jugendstil* expression for the consumptive soul whose metaphysical lustre springs only from nothingness and the renunciation of existence. This soul's sisters are the Husserlian essentialities, phantasmagoric reflections of a subjectivity which hopes to obliterate itself within them as their 'sense'. The more subjective their ground, the more extravagant the pathos of their objectivity. The more manically they posit themselves as states-of-affairs, the more despairingly thought swears by a non-existent.

All of Husserl's philosophy is directed to resistance. It is the abstract negation of the subjectivism it sees through, though it remains imprisoned in the subjectivistic domain. It partakes of the feebleness it denounces. Phenomenology hovers in a region for which the favourite allegory in those years was the cloud daughters,* a no man's land between subject and object, the deceptive mirage of their reconciliation. Philosophically, the sphere in which pale disembodied young things in flower are called 'essences', is reflected by meaning (*Meinen*) as the subjective gesture towards an opposite, whose content is nevertheless exhausted in the subjective act.

Thus Husserl's ontology and doctrine of essence, the expansion

* [Possible reference to Strindberg's *Dream Play* where the daughter of Indra ascends and descends on a cloud. Trans.]

of the absolutistic motif to epistemology and metaphysics, is connected to his doctrine of intentions. He transfers to intentions the procedure which logical absolutism conjured up. What is thought becomes essence through the isolation of individual 'acts' and 'lived experiences' (*Erlebnisse*) over against an experience 98 (*Erfahrung*) which, as a whole, has by this time practically disappeared from the field of vision of his philosophy. The decaying individual is just the content of particular lived experiences which are touted as surrogates of concrete experience, but no longer have control over such experience itself. The peculiar lived experience which is lifted out of the monotony of reified life, the dispersed instant of decrepit, doomed fulfilment as the salvation of absent metaphysical sense – as Christian Morgenstern* scoffed at it ('Another lived experience full of honey') – is the historical model of Husserl's idea of the universal which is granted to singular intentions.

Lived Experience (Erlebnis) and 'Sense'

The Prolegomena makes no room for the concept of an essence derivable from the individual. It remains on the ground of traditional theory of abstraction.

Truths divide into individual and general truths. The former contain (whether explicitly or implicitly) assertions regarding the actual existence of individual singulars, whereas the latter are completely free from this and only permit us to infer (purely from concepts) the possible existence of what is individual. Individual truths are as such contingent.[1]

The individual and the factical are directly equated. It is not acknowledged that an individual can have an essence independently of its existence (*Existenz*).
It is only the doctrine of intentional acts which leads to that. For

---

* [Christian Morgenstern (1871–1914), German 'functionalist' poet, friend of Rudolf Steiner. Trans.]

[1] *LU* I, p. 231; cf. Findlay, p. 228.

the point of this doctrine from the beginning was the development of isolated 'lived experiences' corresponding to always
equally isolated 'unreal' sense implicates (*Sinnesimplikate*) which
are meant by the 'act'.

Here and now, at the very moment that we significantly utter a general
name, we mean (*meinen*) what is general, and our meaning differs from
our meaning when we mean what is individual. The difference must be
pinned down in the descriptive content of the isolated lived experience,
in the individually and actually performed general assertion.[2]

The fact, however, that meaning itself and thus the quality of the
act should vary, according to whether a universal or an individual
is meant, remains a bald assertion, provided that anything more
is supposed to be said than the tautology, that in both cases
intentional objects belong to distinct logical classes, and that acts
may also be divided according to the class of their object. It
99 remains, moreover, difficult to attribute distinct characteristica to
the individual acts which should form those classes. While
Husserl certainly does not attempt that either, he nevertheless
tacitly infers from the logical difference of objects that the
difference prescribed by the types of thing meant (*des Gemeinten*)
'must be pinned down . . . in the descriptive content of the
isolated lived experience'. Therefore, the constitution of the acts
as such is supposed to change.
    This apparently insignificant postulate, the subtle mistake of
dogmatically inferring absolute differences in the ways objects are
meant from the logical differences of objects of thought, has
enormous consequences. By seeking the difference in the descriptive content of the 'isolated lived experiences' and positing a
primordial split between meaning a particular and meaning a
universal, Husserl shifts this arbitrarily concocted split in the
character of meaning on to what is meant. As a result, universal
and particular are radically distinguished because different sorts
of act of meaning arise in each case. This distinction itself simply
mirrors that of the classes of what is meant and does not establish
it. Thus the distinctiveness of classes of what is meant still needs
to be derived. The 'descriptive content' of individual lived
experiences in any event adapts to the character of the 'finished

[2] *LU* II, i, p. 144; cf. ibid. p. 369.

products', the result of the completed distinction. But it does not establish any primary 'ideal unities' independent of multiplicities and abstraction.

Critique of Singular 'Senses'

Moreover, Husserl's actual procedure in his deduction contradicts the phenomenological programme. An analysis which seriously abides by what it supposedly encounters (*Vorfindlichkeiten*) in the life of consciousness, would not run into such singularities of lived experience and thus not into absolutely singular 'senses' either. Senses are in fact what the phenomenological Husserl criticized as theoretical constructions, rudiments of atomistic psychology of association. Just as no lived experience is 'singular' but rather interlaced with the totality of individual consciousness, and thus necessarily points beyond itself, so there are no such things as absolute senses or references (*Bedeutungen*). Any sense, of which thought becomes aware at all, possesses, by dint of thinking, an element of universality, and is 100 more than just itself. Even in the already much too simple case of remembering a person's name, this memory involves moments such as the relation of the name to its object, its identifying function, the quality of the name, inasmuch as it means this individual directly and not another, and innumerable vague or articulated other things. Describing the relationship between memory and what is remembered as absolutely individual and univocal would be logicist arbitrariness.

If one were to assume, however, that the construction of any individual act and any individual reference (*Bedeutung*) were necessary, indifferently as to whether they arise or not, in order to work out how consciousness becomes capable of articulated knowledge, then the traditional idealistic mode of procedure would be re-installed. But then it would be incomprehensible why one should adhere to the alleged 'pure references' in the construction, and not, rather, proceed in their analysis in the same way as the older epistemology where that sensation or ὕλη is necessarily attained, against which pure theory of meaning (*Bedeutung*) seeks to protect itself.

Husserl correctly criticizes Hume[3] to the effect that a 'conglomerate' of concrete images brings knowledge no further than the individual representation. But in the *Logical Investigations* he himself adheres to the Humean motif of the conglomerate, in that he transfers unity to the reference function (*Bedeutungsfunktion*) alone, i.e. to thought. He does not notice that the ostensible ultimate data are already not a conglomerate but rather – as Gestalt theory* has already proved *ad nauseam*– are structured and more than the sum of their parts. He also, however, ignores categorial connection or 'synthesis'.

Phenomenological conceptual realism is in no way the simple alternative to the nominalist tradition which adds together consciousness out of atomistic lived experiences. The two, rather, since Franz Brentano, are also complements. The two polar moments of the individual and unity congeal into absolute determinations as soon as they cease to be understood as reciprocally producing each other and thus also produced. Thinking, whose result is conjured into being, juxtaposes separated singularity and autonomized universality as elements having equal rights, independent of each other and ultimately valid. Both owe the illusion of their absoluteness to having been broken off and the emphasis on their positivity to something negative. And it is this very illusion, together with the abstractness to which separation condemns both, that permits the concept of an ideal being to be distilled from both of them and to be prepared through a selection of their qualities. The two may indeed be thereby found to be the same. Since for Husserl the materials of cognition are, in accord with idealist dogma, chaotic, he absolutizes the intentional object as something conjointly given and thus indubitable. It is determinate and to that extent an objective entity.

He does not agree with the customary epistemological distinc-

---

* When the *Logical Investigations* appeared, Gestalt theory was not yet fully developed. Yet Christian von Ehrenfels' treatise, 'Über Gestaltqualitäten' was certainly available (*Vierteljahreszeitschrift für wissenschaftliche Philosophie*, vol. 14, 1890), which already contains the elements of the critique of an atomistic interpretation of immediate givens. It is hardly likely that Brentano's student, Husserl, did not read it.

[3] Cf. ibid. p. 186; and ibid. p. 403.

tion between the act as immediately given and what is meant as mediately given. He is content to rigidly delimit the intentional object from both sides. From the side of sensation, since, as he correctly points out, one perceives not a complex of colours but rather 'the fir tree'.[4] From the side of the thing, since it is a matter of indifference whether the intentional object 'exists' in the time–space continuum. Thus the construction of perception, our meaning of something present to the senses, turns out to be a hybrid. The immediacy of the act is attributed to the act-sense. The symbolic content is invested with corporeality. The 'pure', fact-free intentional object remains an expedient. It does not produce what it should, i.e. an objectification of experiences, nor is the immediacy appropriate to it for whose sake Husserl claims that it is the canon of all cognition.

The two desiderata of the certainty of the given and the necessity of the spiritually transparent – which could not be made to overlap since Plato and Aristotle and whose mediation is the task of the entire history of idealism – were desperately identified with each other by Husserl who ultimately lost confidence in that mediation. He wished to force a draw in the divergence between sensibility and understanding and indeed that between subject 102 and object, as though in a momentary pause ignoring endurance and constitution. The hypostatized object is the primordial image (*Urbild*) of all later phenomenological essentialities as the indifference between ideality and objecthood.

Origin of Essential Insight (Wesensschau)

Husserl used the concept of essential insight itself long before the theory of categorial intuition. The second Logical Investigation of volume 2 is meant to show, according to the Preface in the Prolegomena,

that one can learn to see ideas in a type, represented e.g. by the idea 'red', and that one can become clear as to the essence of such 'seeing'.[5]

---

[4] Cf. ibid. pp. 197 ff; and ibid. pp. 411 ff.
[5] *LU* I, p. xv; cf. ibid. p. 49.

Husserl opposes the 'consciousness of meaning' (*Bedeutungs-bewußtsein*) of abstraction 'in that improper sense'

by which empiricist psychology and epistemology are dominated, a sense which altogether fails to seize what is specific, and whose inability to do so is even counted as a virtue.[6]

He was thus alerted that what is essential to a state-of-affairs and what befits a species, its 'specificity', cannot be attained through its sortal concept (*Artbegriff*), the unity of features of several states-of-affairs.

In this way he is in tune with the impulses of the other academic philosophers of his generation who otherwise diverge from him significantly, such as Dilthey, Simmel and Rickert, each of whom in his own way recalled what had already motivated Kant's *Critique of Judgment* and thereafter became a banality, i.e. that causal-mechanical and classificatory explanation does not go to the heart of the object and forgets what is most important about it. No scholar at the end of the nineteenth century, even those who were disinclined to any metaphysical speculation, could ignore this, as long as he studied 'individual things'. Even Husserl frequently found in a unique concrete thing – insistently contemplated and elucidated – deeper and more binding insight into far-reaching relations than would a procedure which tolerates in the individual only what can be subsumed under general concepts.

Not without irony, nor irrelevantly to philosophical history, at the same time as Husserl undertook to rescue the essence of comparative universality, his countryman and opposite number, Sigmund Freud, against the entire claim and tendency of whose 103 psychology Husserl's polemic against psychologism could have been directed, employed, in spite of a flawless scientific position and with the most enduring effect, the very procedure for determining the essence of the individual 'case' whose epistemological formula Husserl sought. But like Freud Husserl was also a child of his period. For he would think those essentialities which arise from the individual in no other way than as universal concepts of the type of the logic of the exact sciences. In fact, the

[6] *LU* II, i, p. 107; cf. ibid. p. 337.

energy of his project has its centre here. He rejected the split between natural and cultural sciences which was in favour at the beginning of his career, i.e. the split between divergent ways of cognizing the individual or historical on the one hand, and mathematical universals on the other. He stood for the idea of a single truth, and tried to force together the unspoiled concretion of individual experience and the binding force of the concept. He never rested content with the pluralism of truth according to the realms of knowledge.

That indeed accounts for the magnetic force of his starting point. But it also involves him in difficulties, which the Southwest German academic philosophers comfortably avoided. Since he is impressed by mathematics and thus does not venture to conceive the specific or 'essential', to which he is addicted, otherwise than as the class of scientific concept formation, he must turn to deducing the classificatory concept from singularity and so distinguishes those two types of abstraction.

'Ideational Abstraction'

Husserl calls improper what is otherwise known as abstraction, i.e. the construction of concepts by isolating and organizing a single feature from a multiplicity of objects. Against abstraction, he insists that essence, which constitutes a type, arises in a single act of meaning (*Bedeutens*).

When we mean red *in specie*, a red object appears before us, and in this sense we look towards the red object to which we are nevertheless not referring (*meinen*). The aspect of red is at the same time emphasized in this object, and to that extent we can again say that we are looking towards this aspect of red. But we do not mean this individually definite trait in the object as we do when, e.g., we make the phenomenological observation that the aspects of red in the separate portions of the apparent object's surface are themselves separate. While the red object 104 and its emphasized aspect of red appear before us, we rather mean the single identical red, and mean it in a novel and conscious manner, through which precisely the species, and not the individual, becomes the object.[7]

[7] Ibid. pp. 106 ff; ibid.

When we 'mean' (*meinen*) a particular, in this case 'a red object of intuition', its 'moment of redness' also comes forward, that feature which constitutes the species. It is this that we 'look towards' and thus secure for ourselves the ideal unity of the species, without the need for other examples, other 'red objects'.

The weakness of the argumentation lies in the use of the term 'identical'. For in that act we are indeed supposed to become conscious of 'the single identical red' and thus encounter the species itself instead of simply the individual. Yet one can speak meaningfully (*sinnvoll*) about identity only in relation to multiplicity. There is 'identical red' at all only for several objects which are red in common with each other. The expression need minimally apply to the continuity of perceived colours in a thing, i.e. to something purely phenomenal.

The two merge in Husserl. The fact that what is perceived in that act during perception is and remains one and the same, is substituted for the identity of the concept as the unity of features of distinct examples. The red perceived as self-identical is not, by dint of such an identity, already the species red. Unless, of course, Husserl assumes comparative operations – though unavowedly. 'Identical' may in the strict sense signify nothing other at the crucial point than what is meant in a specific act. This identity, the relation of an intention to a captured 'This here', is, however, interpreted as if it were already the identity of the universal concept. If that concept were to become an intentional object, then it would have to be given in advance, i.e. already constituted. The act as such, on the other hand, is indifferent to whether in it an individual or something conceptual is 'meant'.

Pure meaning (*Meinen*) pays no attention to the constitution and justification of what is meant. Otherwise it would already be 105 a judgement. The 'red' which is ideated out of the singular colour perception would only be a 'reduced' 'This here' decorated with the obligatory phenomenological brackets. Only language, which denotes both the singular red moment and the species red, entices one to the hypostasis of the latter. Husserl's 'ideational abstraction' – the counter-concept which he invents against the comparative and prevailing logical concept – postulates that the elementary forms of consciousness already reify their subject matter, without any heed to comparison. These forms fix the subject matter, as it were, under an optical lens, and so push absolute singularity into the 'identical' – an identical which is independent of the way in which it is identical.

At the suggestion of the alleged system of sciences, Husserl finds in one case pure truths of reason, *vérités de raison*, which have been diluted to ideal unities of validity, and in the other (his own) the equally 'pure' (i.e. cleansed of all naturalistic prejudices) immanence of consciousness. There is no relation between the two except that pure immanence of consciousness is supposed to be a peep-hole open to those ideal unities. That is the construction of meaning (*Meinens*). Since the point of origin of ideal objects, as simply meant, is not epistemologically evident, Husserl makes them independent of the acts of consciousness which compose them. The pure object of intention should be the ideal unity. The in-itself should appear in the act. Husserl will do justice to the desideratum, 'Learn to see ideas', by introducing a type of act

in which the objects apprehended in these manifold forms of thought are self-evidently 'given', with the acts, in other words, in which our conceptual intentions are fulfilled, achieve self-evidence and clarity. Thus we directly apprehend the specific unity 'redness' on the basis of a singular intuition of something red. We look to its moment of red, but we perform a peculiar act, whose intention is directed to the 'idea', the 'universal'. Abstraction in the sense of this act is wholly different from the mere attention to, or emphasis on, the moment of red; to indicate this difference we have repeatedly spoken of ideational or generalizing abstraction.[8]

Thus he succumbs to the very contamination of which he accuses Locke and Lockean doctrine.[9] He immediately interprets *106* the act which is directed to the 'abstract part moment' of content as the intuition of the species, as long as that moment is based on something hyletic. He profits to a degree from two mutually exclusive qualifications: First, the immediacy with which something red is perceived should guarantee the intuitive (*anschauliches*) character of the act; but secondly, so that the sense perceptible does not thus present itself as isolated, but rather as interwined with thought, that immediacy should also turn the

[8] Ibid. p. 223; ibid. p. 432.
[9] Cf. ibid. p. 217; and ibid. p. 427.

immediately intuited into something mental (*geistig*), i.e. a concept, which shines immediately on singularity, heedless of the character of the concept as the abstract unity of identical moments. The doctrine comes down to the fact that, if someone observes a red object and becomes conscious of this object as something red – though the relation between these two moments is unclear – then he has not only the specific sensation but also has in this sensation a concept of red in general.

Now, it is certainly not to be denied that, thanks to its categorial moments, the act surpasses pure sensation. That is, moreover, a tautology, since this difference simply terminologically defines the difference between sensation and act. If this distinction were consequently disavowed as a mere theoretical auxiliary construction, and if the existence of category-free data were denied, and along with Hegel immediacy were determined as always already mediated in itself, then the very concept of immediate knowledge would be eliminated, though Husserl's polemic against abstraction theory rests on this concept.

Husserl, however, unscrupulously adheres to the traditional difference between the hyletic and the categorial. Yet one can meaningfully speak of categorial activity only when the immediate is related to the past and the future, memory and expectation. As soon as consciousness does not abide by the pure concept-free 'This here', but rather forms any concept however primitive, then it brings into play knowledge of non-present moments which are not 'here', not intuitive and not absolutely singular, but distilled from some other. Always more belongs to the 'proper sense' of an act than its proper sense, the canon of Husserl's method. Every act transcends its periphery in that its meant content, in order to be meant, always demands the co-meaning of another. Thus no act analysis either is capable of restricting itself to the bounds of the singularity of the putative (*vermeinten*) object.

Hence the appeal to the act sense as something constant and reposing in itself – such as Husserl demands in accord with the schema of a naive realism which he elsewhere eliminates from epistemology – changes from an ultimate principle into something insufficient or at least merely propaedeutic. The assumption of such an act sense, however, which is solid in itself, unvarying and free of dynamics, is the model for Husserl's construction of essence. His essentialities are singularities which lack nothing other than to be factical (*Faktisch-Sein*), in that they are determined as purely mental, i.e. 'meant'. If one were to think away from a sensation of colour that it is in space and time, i.e. that it is real (*wirklich*), then this sensation would become the concept of a sensed colour. But in that case the simplest thing is misunderstood. The sheer idea of this one τόδε τί remains left over and its species is never attained.

Essentialities are in no sense to be distinguished from what is conceived as rigidly reified and also as (purely intentional) unreal act sense. They are not, e.g., 'ideal unities'. That is imputed to them from the outside. The emancipation of the ideal unity of the species from the performance of abstraction is illusory, analogously to the emancipation of the proposition in itself from thought. What can only be determined as a result, in this case the concept, is hypostatized for the sake of a guarantee, which does not devolve upon the concept, e.g., as something detached, but rather just in its relation to the totality of experience.

However true it may be that the species is not exhausted in the process of abstraction, since identical moments must be at hand for a concept to be formed at all from abstraction from the diverse, nevertheless these identical moments cannot be separated from the abstracting operation and discursive thought. And, just as in logical absolutism, Husserl again conjures away subjectivity – in this case, thinking as synthesis. For he breaks open particulars and forges those moments in them, which are functions of their structure, into singular characteristica. The mechanism of the Husserlian ontology is throughout one of isolation – as is the case 108 for all static doctrines of ideas since Plato. It is thus the very scientific-classificatory technique which Husserl's attempt to reproduce pure immediacy actually opposes. Goal and method cannot be united.

Abstraction and τόδε τί

What is called 'ideational abstraction' in Husserl's example, is, as he says, nothing radically different from distinguishing and focusing on a dependent content in a complex perception. It is, rather, just an interpretation of that mental performance which is contrived for the sake of the epistemological *thema probandum*.

When thus focused, the partial content is meant as something abstract in the literal understanding and distilled from the complex phenomenon. But, as part of a concrete intuition, it is also supposed to be intuited.

Thus fraudulent plausibility devolves on to the paradox of intuitive abstraction. Husserl merely suppresses the fact that even the focusing on the moment red (in psychological terminology, the directing of attention) is no longer identical with the pure datum. As soon as one turns one's view to 'red itself' (*'das' Rot*), then one categorizes and breaks up the unity of the act of perception, which applies to this colour, for example, together with other things observed here and now. The accentuated 'red moment' isolates the moment 'colour' from the present perception. If ever this were isolated as an autonomous unity, it would thereby fall into relations with other colours. Otherwise the colour moment could not be set off as autonomous at all, since in present perception it is simply blended into other things. It attains autonomy only by being brought together with a completely distinct dimension of experience, viz. past acquaintance with colour as such. It must be representative of 'colour' as is accorded to consciousness beyond sheer present experience.

Its concept is presupposed, however primitive and little actualized it may be; it does not come out of the *hic et nunc*. Believing that the subject could purely intuit 'red' out of the *hic et nunc* would be pure self-deception, even if the possibility of such singularities of lived experience were hypothetically assumed. 109 Red – 'redness' – is colour not a datum of sensation, and the consciousness of colour demands reflection. It is not satisfied with impressions.

Husserl confuses our meaning (*meinen*) red here and now with the knowledge of red which our meaning necessarily requires. He substitutes the singular meaning of universal objects for the constitution and grounded knowledge of universals. He equates our meaning of the abstract with sensible (*einsichtig*) judgements about the abstract, while the 'ideal' content which is apparently proper only to the individual act, refers back to manifolds and experience. That alone yields his static conception of essence. Though later in his unremitting analysis of foundational relations and especially of judgement he brings experience to bear, and implicitly justifies rectifying the universal, still the most pressing result is omitted, viz. the revision of the doctrine of essence which clings to that hypostatization. This doctrine retained to the end a key characteristic of Husserl's philosophy despite its striking inconsistency.*

That doctrine, however, is parasitic upon the fact that the singular acts, which support it, are in truth not singular at all but rather always already include the very manifolds which Husserl's Platonic realism rejects. This is the only way to get hold of the individual in the universal, for the individual itself is saturated with the universal. It is mediated in itself. Thus disintegrates Husserl's fundamental postulate to remain strictly with what is given originarily in 'pure lived experience'.[10] Immediacy is no longer the criterion of truth.

Hence phenomenology has not critically reflected; it resigns itself to a demand for positivism as scientifically self-evident. Husserl presupposes the possibility of a pure apprehension (*Hinnehmen*) of the state-of-affairs in thought. And yet the concept of the state-of-affairs belongs rather to the very realm of the

110

---

* Husserl, of course, already dropped the theory of the essence of the species – which occurs in the individual act and is to be immediately dissected out – in *Ideas*. For he there relates act analysis to the continuity of the stream of consciousness. He rediscovered for himself that such an absolutely singular act does not exist, especially in perception; every act is more than just itself and as a result the species cannot be based on the individual act.

As in the second Logical Investigation of volume 2, however, he persists in maintaining that phenomenology 'drops only individuation', while 'it raises the whole essential content in the fullness of its concretion into eidetic consciousness'. (*Ideen* [140]; cf. *Ideas*, p. 192). He thus never gives up the paradoxical concept of 'eidetic singularities' (ibid.). He goes on to say that this 'concrete' essential content belonging to singularity 'could particularize itself not only *hic et nunc* but in numberless instances' (ibid.). So the concept of every particular individual would be inferred simply by ignoring its spatio-temporal locus irrespective of other individuations. But, surely under the influence of William James, he still states considerations opposing that sort of absolute singularity as such. 'We can see at once that a conceptual and terminological fixation of this and every similar flowing *concretum* is not to be thought of, and that this applies to each of its immediate and no less flowing parts and abstract moments.' (ibid.) It follows that essence is no longer to be sought in individual intention as the second Logical Investigation had taught. This difficulty contributed greatly to the conception of categorial intuition as a cognitive process *sui generis*.

[10] Cf. *Ideen* [187]; and *Ideas*, p. 243.

factical which should be phenomenologically and eidetically 'reduced'. The transfer of 'unprejudiced research' to epistemological analysis forms a persistent pre-phenomenological residue. It can be accomplished only through those means whose justification is unfortunately considered by phenomenology as its principal task. That is, categorial intuition, a ὕστερον πρότερον of method.

Theoretical thought cannot at all, as Husserl would like, take a given purely as what it gives itself to be. For thinking it means determining it and making it more than mere givenness. The primal model of reification in Husserl does not lie only in the extension of the concept of objecthood to the phenomenal, but rather already in the dogmatic position of what apparently precedes all reification, the immediate .datum. Because he does not see through the immediate datum as mediated in itself, he considers the actually highly abstract τόδε τί as a sort of thing in itself, the ultimate solid substratum. But the τόδε τί, which Husserl 'posits (gesetzt) in the idea', is neither the species nor what is individuated, but rather something beneath, almost pre-logical, and actually the construction of a primal given free from all categorization. He merely strips it of the 'naturalistic' thesis of its facticity.

111 Eidetic singularity, as represented by the 'moment of redness' in Husserl's example, is thus not like concepts, i.e. more encompassing than the τόδε τί. It is, rather, still just the latter's shadow. The belief, however, is deceptive that the essence of something ideal is the quiddity (das Was) of individuation. For this quiddity in its strict selfhood could no longer be distinguished from the individual at all. Pure τόδε τί and essence, the individual and its concept, coincide. No determination of difference can be identified other than that the former is factical and the latter not.

Obviously this mere duplication of the individual through its eidetic reduction has nothing to do with what is called a concept. The pure τόδε τί and so the concept would remain empty and undetermined so long as they are not surpassed and the τόδε τί set in relation to something it is not. Singularity slips away from a thought that does not know multiplicity. Even positing a 'one' (Einen) as determined by its oneness implies a many (Mehr). This many, however, is transferred to the τόδε τί in itself by Husserl as something which simply precedes the determining cognition of the individual. The 'too little' in the pure τόδε τί, that indeter-

minacy which Hegel used to call 'abstract' in the specific sense, is
directly turned into that sort of many, viz. the substitute for what
is abstract in the customary sense, the universal concept. The
moment of truth in all of this – that pure immediacy is mediated
in itself as abstraction, that the absolutely particular is universal –
needs, in order to be redeemed, that the process of cognition
directly reveal this mediation of the immediate. But that is just
what Husserl's theory of individual essence is supposed to
dispense with. Since the τόδε τί is everything and nothing, one
can assert that it exemplarily comprises the universal concept
within it. And that assertion, as abstractly adduced as the τόδε τί
itself, need not be exposed to contradiction. Excess of facticity
becomes the vehicle for denying its own facticity. Hypostatized
fact (Faktum) and hypostatized essence murkily merge.

The ambiguity of the abstract τόδε τί, its lack of that determinacy which alone makes it an individual, raises the claim of the 112
superindividual, the universal, the essential – the surrogate of
that concretizing of the concept which still in Husserl slips
through the mesh of the classificatory net. In its quest for such
concretization, Husserl's philosophy wanders helplessly around
between its two abstract poles, that of the sheer 'here' and that of
the sheer 'in general'. It splits asunder in positivism and logic and
shatters in the violent attempt to unite the irreconcilable poles.
Husserl transposes his representation of the sheer 'here' or datum
to the content of higher categorial functions in such a way that at
every step he is encouraged by the predicates of a rigid being-in-
itself (Ansichsein) untouched by the subject–object dialectic.

If, however, the subject really could perceive a red object as
absolute singularity, like an island in the stream of consciousness
– which, in other respects, consciousness hardly 'runs into' –
though the conspicuousness of the moment of redness as 'red'
does not in some way include abstraction and knowledge of the
past, and if it could then 'posit in idea' the isolated moment of
colour, then what had been grasped in that way would be in no
sense the species, but rather indeed the subsumed (Darunter), the
pure 'This here', the Aristotelian πρώτη οὐσία which is distinguished from other sheer sense moments only by the fact that it
is placed between Husserl's brackets and therefore the thesis of
its bodily reality is suspended.

The pure 'This here' would not destroy its haeccitas, even in brackets, and would not raise itself to essence. The concrete moment of redness, isolated and not posited as reality, would thus still not have conceptual scope. If Husserl designates the ideal construction of an isolated hyletic moment as 'red', then he confuses the concept, to whose sense comparison and highlighting of the identical belongs, with the simple neutrality modification of a single solitary happenstance (*Einmalige*). The modification certainly drains existence in the specific sense from the happenstance, but that never meant that 'red in general' became universal. In strictly unique perception, there is no red, but only reflection on a sensation while ignoring its factual occurrence.

The Primacy of Meaning Analysis (Bedeutungsanalyse)

Prudently, however, Husserl's analysis does not descend to
113 sensation. He sticks with perception as consciousness of 'something', an objective thing, while sensation for him is actually introduced only with reference to perception as its hyletic core. Sensation changes from being the supporting substratum, as it has been for traditional epistemology, into something secondary, which is simply extracted from perception as its τέλος. It is drawn, as it were, from the matter of cognition for the confirmation of knowledge at the furthest edge of the intentional edifice.

He certainly takes account of the fact that the concept of sensation itself – as indeed that of perception, a level higher – presents an abstraction, and that individual sensations can hardly be isolated. This general proviso, which Husserl must indeed extract *in toto* from the concept (*Konzept*), must not delude one into believing that he attributes the central place of epistemology to 'consciousness of something' or intentionality. For breaking off analysis with the intentional act permits the construction of a mental entity (*Geistigen*) existing in itself to be presented as descriptively obvious. Uniting the doctrines of theory and of essence is the most convincing alibi for reification in Husserl's philosophy. 'Ideational abstraction', and thus originary cognitions in which pure singularity is supposed to be grasped in its essence, stand and fall with the fact that some object immediately arises from these cognitions, the ostensibly elementary performances of consciousness, as 'rays of vision' (*Blickstrahlen*), irrespective of their connection with the totality of experience.

As a result, absolute individuality, which does not match up to any plurality whatever, would still possess identity, namely the identity of its 'noema'. Hence acts become the organon of knowledge. Husserl can bestow upon the absolutely isolated the dignity of overreaching only because he forces it into original correlation with something already reified whose synthetic moments are invisible. Only by hypostatizing a situation whereby determinate classes of meanings (*Bedeutungen*) proceed 'directly and individually' not to the individual but to the universal, can he claim ideal universality for a conceptual realism whose excesses he occasionally deplores.[11] Husserl does indeed dispute the reality of the species, but he also attributes it 'objecthood'[12] with an inconsistency which recalls the Aristotelian ambiguity (*Doppelsinn*) concerning οὐσία. But he in no way exhibits the difference between the two expressions. Nevertheless, the expression 'objecthood' is quite clearly reminiscent of reification.

Since phenomenology concentrates on the 'direct and authentic intention' of 'names standing for species',[13] it strengthens the doctrine of the ideal unity of the species by meaning analyses.

The question as to whether it is possible or necessary to treat species as objects can plainly only be answered by going back to the meaning (*Bedeutung*) (the sense, our meaning (*Meinung*)) of the names standing for species, and to the meaning of the assertions claiming to hold for species. If these names and assertions can be interpreted as making the true objects of our intention individual, if the intention of the nominal and propositional thoughts which give them meaning can be thus understood, then we must yield to our opponents' doctrine. But if this is not so, if the meaning analysis of such expressions shows that their direct, true intention is plainly not directed upon individual objects, and if in particular their universal relation to a range of individual objects is plainly shown up as merely an indirect pointing to logical connections whose content (sense) will first be unfolded in new thoughts, or which will require new expressions – then our opponents' doctrine is evidently false.[14]

[11] Cf. *LU* II, i, p. 110; and Findlay, p. 340.
[12] Ibid.
[13] Ibid.
[14] Ibid.

Accordingly, the complaint is justified about a relapse into scholasticism, which was propagated in the early days of phenomenology and only stylishly forgotten under the primacy of existential ontology. Instead of epistemological critique, symbolically functioning expressions should be studied only in their relation to what is symbolized. The question as to 'whether it is possible or necessary' to take species as objects and thus as to whether Platonic realism is true or false, could be answered 'only' by referring to the sense of the names of the species. Semantic analysis immediately turns into judgement about things. What is meant is the answer to the controversy over realism and thus it literally usurps the thing-in-itself.

115   The already conceptually filtered world – which for Husserl is the world of science just as previously it had been that of theology – represents to itself the truth content of concepts. That is how Husserl is 'pre-critical'. The primacy of logic over epistemology, which still dominates in the structure of Husserl's thought even though he expressly rejects it, expresses the substitution of the conceptual net for the dialectic of concept and thing. Formal logic is the rule-governed operation with concepts alone, without regard to their material legitimacy. But this is also Husserl's procedure, wherever he discusses the possibility of logical states-of-affairs. By raising the meaning (*Bedeutung*) of concepts to the canon of their truth, he remains imprisoned within the immanence of the realm of their validity, even though it appears that he lays the foundation for this validity. This gives Husserl's phenomenology its peculiar hermetic character, a masturbatory quality, a powerful effort to lift India rubber weights. Something of this non-binding character clings to everything he produces and contributes to explaining the attraction which overcomes philosophers who want to pose radical questions unendangered by hazardous answers.

Whatever Husserl's historical importance, as particularly exemplified in his concept of essential insight, by the same token, he equalized the pattern of the world codified in science or alternatively language, viz. the system of concepts, with the in-itself. Whatever occurs cognitively in that second nature, gains the appearance of the immediate and intuitive. So nothing has really changed in such an autarchy of concepts except that the phenomenological method was used under other names to disclose

ostensible primordiality. The further its successors have distanced themselves from discursive thought, the more completely
do they presuppose a mechanism which has been dissected by
such thought. Resurrected speculation has everywhere just
strengthened the reification though it was supposed to be
eliminated. However impossible it may be to rip through the
conceptual net, it nevertheless makes all the difference whether
one becomes aware of one's own as such and reflects upon it
critically, or whether one, because of its imperviousness, takes it
for the 'phenomenon'.

This illusion also, of course, is a function of reality and
historical tendencies. The closer the form of socialization 116
approaches totalization and pre-forms every single person beginning with his language, and the less any individual consciousness
is capable of resisting it, the more already advanced forms assume
the character of fatality and of the entity in itself. Reified thought
is the copy of the reified world. By trusting its primordial
experiences, it lapses into delusion. There are no primordial
experiences.

The Function of the Noema

In the transition from logical absolutism to epistemology – from
the thesis of the being in itself of the highest formal principles to
that of the being in itself of universal concepts, the ideal unities of
objecthood – Husserl must give some account of how thought
may at all become conscious of objecthood and how in such a
consciousness real and ideal moments relate to one another. This
is not the least of the purposes of the doctrine of intentionality.

The polemic against psychologism in the 'Prolegomena to Pure
Logic' was already meaning analytical. Husserl argues throughout by inquiring after the 'sense' of logical propositions. Such a
'sense' then becomes the canon for the theory of authentic
consciousness. Cognition follows the structure of noesis and
noema – of acts of meaning and what is meant (*Vermeintes*) in
them. The idealist Husserl gives precedence to one of the
moments out of which, for Kantianism, the unity of self-
consciousness was composed: the moment of the symbolic
function, or, in the language of the critique of reason, the
reproduction of the imagination.

Husserl's positivistic *parti pris* for 'states-of-affairs' prevented him, till a much later phase, from forming a concept of the subject and, of course, of the unity of self-consciousness, which as spontaneity is outside of any description directed at the facts (*Tatbestände*).* The reified structure of Husserl's epistemology, thought's forgetting of itself, conforms to such a loss of the 117 subject. The symbolic function – the fact that certain facts of consciousness could 'mean' some other fact – commended itself to him, because, as isolated, no active subject seemed to be at work in it. Rather, meaning (*Meinen*) can be shifted to something static, viz. the expression, as its specific and even, as it were, thingly, definitely present quality. Intentionality serves so well as a foundation of the doctrine of essence, however, because the symbolized is voided of sheer existence in acts which always pass for pregnant 'consciousness', viz. consciousness of something.

Noema and εἶδος

Though the symbolized is encountered strictly within the framework of the analysis of consciousness, it should nevertheless be distinguished from the facticity of sensation; it should already possess that ideality whose justification is the point of Husserl's philosophy. In contrast to the Kantian continuum, no empirical reality is predicated of the meant (*Gemeinte*) as such.

But Husserl had to deal with the mediation of the concept of intentionality. For the position of the Prolegomena, viz. the 'naive realism of logic', not only refrained from engaging in epistemological reflection, but even actually excluded it by asserting an unconditioned antithesis between laws of logic and laws of thought. From an epistemological point of view, the programme of the Prolegomena to perform a demonstration of ideal being demands a revision of that demonstration. The analysis of consciousness must then track down a mental in-itelf. Thus

---

* These weaknesses have, of course, not escaped pre-Husserlian idealists. They were pointed out in particular in Heinrich Rickert's posthumous volume, *Unmittelbarkeit und Sinndeutung* (Tübingen,1939). Rickert criticizes with great acuity the alleged absolute certainty of beginning with the immediately given as the contents of the consciousness of every isolated and – on idealistic grounds – contingent subject.

Husserl's philosophy soon turns out to be a dialectic in spite of itself. In striving to lay epistemological foundations for logical absolutism, and to expand it, his philosophy dissolves elements of that doctrine.

Ideal states-of-affairs are sought out in thinking itself as unconditional (*unabdingbar*) moments of its structure. These are the noemata in *Ideas*, the unreal side of intentionality. They are supposed to be both objective and ideal and also unique to consciousness, accessible when the descriptive analysis of consciousness is limited to pure immanence. Thus they impart whatever the systematic demands. Noeses as factual thought acts or psychological facticities would be unsuitable for this. Sheer 'propositions in themselves', however, remain unconnected with *118* consciousness.

The knowledge of the essential two-sidedness of intentionality in the form of noesis and noema brings this consequence with it that a systematic phenomenology should not direct its effort one-sidedly towards a real (*reelle*) analysis of experiences, and more specifically of the intentional kind. But the temptation to do this is at first very great, because the historical and natural movement from psychology to phenomenology brings it about that as a matter of course we take the immanent study of pure experiences, the study of their own proper essence, to be a study of their components. On both sides in truth there open up vast domains of eidetic inquiry, and these are constantly related to each other, yet as it turns out keep separate for a long stretch. In great measure, what has been taken for noetic act-analysis has been obtained when observation was directed towards the 'meant as such', and it was really noematic structures which were there described.[15]

It is, however, the revenge of such bridge concepts that they always fall into conflict with what they aim at and reproduce the happily eliminated difficulties at higher levels. This is a bit of the distress of philosophy, the fatal configuration of all dialectic unenlightened about itself, which the dialectical method seeks to prevent by adapting to this configuration and practically proclaiming property rights over it.

[15] *Ideen* [265 ff]; cf. *Ideas*, p. 332.

Relation Between the Two Reductions

Noemata are supposed to be non-'real (*reelle*) components of lived experiences',[16]* and the question arises: 'what can be said on essential lines concerning this "of something" ',[17] namely the noema. 'Every intentional lived experience, thanks to its noetic moments, is indeed noetic; it is its essence to harbour in itself a "sense" of some sort or even many meanings.'[18] The concept of essence, by which noeses, which are supposed to 'have a sense' – an 'ideal state-of-affairs' – are characterized as universal, is burdened. The noesis–noema relation is with its help claimed to be ultimate and non-derivable, a 'law of essence'. It is so taken without regard for the functional structure in which traditional idealistic epistemology interpreted object and thought. In *Ideas* 119 the concept of essence of epistemology is systematically pre-arranged. All later phenomenological assertions try to be eidetic.

But it is difficult to separate the two reductions. Just as assertions about the noema make eidetic claims, so $ε'ίδη$ are, for their part, a class of noemata, species meant in intentional acts. Whatever occurs in the relation of noeses to noemata, of thinking to what is thought, is stood still. Spontaneity changes under the descriptive regard into a simple correlation. The 'intuitive' (*schauende*) method affects what is intuited. Indeed Husserl always talks about acts, but nothing remains of *actio* except a structure of reciprocally co-ordinated moments. Becoming is polarized in entities. Since it is the essence of noeses to have a 'sense', how that sense is constituted through thinking execution is ignored.

The sheer phenomenological definition of the concept of act confers substantiality on the ideal something, the noema. What is immanently meant in the act gets changed into the 'perceived', the 'remembered', the 'judged', and the 'pleasing' as such.[19] Given the mode of its emergence, this 'as such' is absolutely

* [Literally 'real components of intentional lived experiences'. Trans.]

[16] Cf. ibid.[181]; and ibid. p. 237.
[17] Ibid.
[18] Ibid.
[19] Cf. ibid. [182]; and ibid. p. 238.

identical to essence. Indeed, according to traditional usage, a great conceptual distance separates it from essence. The noema, or simply the concept, in Aristotle's terminology, could, in Husserl's language, be, e.g., a 'perceived tree as such', a singularity, while εἴδη are always universal concepts. But, according to the *Logical Investigations*, a singularity, such as the moment of redness intuited from a perception, suffices for consciousness of essence just as long as its facticity remains suspended. Concepts which have settled on various levels, the logical as well as the epistemological, converge. The pure individual essence, the τόδε τί whose facticity is expunged, converges with the noema, the 'complete' but purely meant state-of-affairs which is extracted from the 'natural attitude', the thing less its existence. Husserl simply does not demand from all noemata the exemplary, i.e. what reaches beyond singularity which is signified by the ideal unity which also arises in singularity.

Noema as Hybrid

The noema is a hybrid of 'ideal being' (that of all Husserlian philosophy) and the mediately given of older positivistic epistemology. Now this mongrelization, conditioned by systematic need, leads to contradictions. That can be demonstrated in the analysis of the noema of perception which Husserl performed. In such a perception – Husserl's example is the 'flowering apple tree' which he observes 'ambulando'[20] – the object has 'not forfeited the least shade of content from all the phases, qualities, characters with which it appeared in this perception, and "in" this pleasure proved "beautiful", "charming" and the like.' It is just that 'this thetic reality . . . simply does not exist by the measure of our judgement'.[21] 'And yet everything remains, so to speak, as of old.'[22]

Hence, the noema is totally identical to the perceived thing, with the simple mental reservation that nothing has been asserted

[20] Cf. ibid. [182 ff]; and ibid. pp. 238 ff.
[21] Ibid. [183]; and ibid. pp. 239–40.
[22] Ibid.

concerning its reality. Rather, the thing is considered only to the extent that it is meant in the isolated individual act, and thus without the possibility of verifying or falsifying the existential judgement through lived experience. Though the noema is not just supposed to bear the entire determination of the unreduced thing, yet, as always petrified and fixed, it is also more reified than things (which do change).

Once again, however, Husserl draws from this lack, this restriction to a point of non-experiential meaning, the positive side of the noema's invulnerable ideality. The noema, the content of sheer meaning (*Meinung*), is irrefutable. Thus Platonism is reversed and δόξα becomes essence. In defiance of all the totalizing protestations of anti-nominalists dating back to Husserl, the new ontology drags its mechanistic and atomistic origins along with it. That Husserl's construction is questionable, becomes blatantly evident in formulations such as the following: 'Like perception, every intentional lived experience – and this is indeed the fundamental mark of all intentionality – has its "intentional object" (*Objekt*), i.e. its sense, in an object (*Gegenstand*).'[23]

His use of terms is equivocal. The fact that an intentional lived experience has its intentional object is a sheer tautology. It says no more than that acts, in contrast to mere data, do indeed mean (*bedeuten*) something. Its 'object' (*Objekt*), however, and thus what is symbolized in every 'referring' act, is tacitly identified by Husserl with some sort of objecthood (*Gegenständlichen*) – wherever possible an entity in itself, whose existence (*Bestand*) in truth is certainly not exhausted in the individual act. Objectivity (*Objektivität*) as what is meant and objectivity as objecthood, which Husserl contaminates with the formula 'i.e.', are in no way the same. The formal meaning of the expression 'object' (*Gegenstand*) as the subject of possible predicates, is mixed up with the material reference of an identical core of experience for the texture of the act.

Thanks to this equivocation, Husserl succeeds in slipping into every individual act a result which is fulfilled not by the act but, idealistically speaking, by the synthetic unity of apperception. But the so 'constituted' object could no longer be given credit for the spacelessness and timelessness of essence.

---

[23] Ibid. [185]; and ibid. p. 241.

Essence and 'Factual States of Consciousness'

Anchoring the doctrine of essence in intentional acts does not simply strengthen the logical absolutism of 'propositions in themselves', it also contradicts the absolutistic conception. The terms 'abstract–universal' and 'idea' are still used as equivalents in the first Logical Investigation of volume 2. 'But since the concern of the pure logician is not with the concrete instance, but with its corresponding idea, its abstractly apprehended universal, he has, it would seem, no reason to leave the field of abstraction, nor to make concrete experiences the theme of his probing interest, instead of ideas.'[24] Husserl is directed to 'concrete lived experience' and thus to epistemology only by his opposition to the traditional doctrine of abstraction. Since the ideal unity is supposed to be independent of the multiplicity of what it deals with, it is located in cognitive consciousness and indeed in the singular act.

Along with Bergson and Gestalt theory, Husserl strives to restore metaphysics 'scientifically', that is with anti-metaphysical armature. This recalls, as opposed to classificatory thought, that the concept is not contingent and external to the thing and not established through arbitrary abstraction. Rather, in Hegelian language, the concept expresses the life of the thing itself. More is to be experienced from that life through immersion in the individuated than through recourse to everything else that the thing resembles in whatever respect. But Husserl thereby skipped *122* the moment of mediation, and at the Archimedean point of his philosophy ultimately, like Bergson, dogmatically contrasted to scientific procedure in concept formation a differently constituted procedure, rather than reflecting scientific procedure by itself. He could be led to this abstract negation of the scientific method – which first became completely obvious to his students – by the uncritical assumption of the positivistic principle, and the cult of the given and of immediacy.

Husserl's effort to save essence from contexts miscarries, for he does not penetrate individuation itself, does not disclose the atom as a field of force and thus does not articulate – by persevering

[24] *LU* II, i, p. 4; cf. Findlay, p. 250.

before the phenomenon – why the cognitive subject must always know more and have experienced more than just the phenomenon. Rather, he capitulates before the intention which has been sealed against its own dynamic. Thus concepts become the very thing they should have been protected from, an external thing, something always meant by individual acts of thought, which is in no sense pertinently motivated in these acts, but rather confronts them, as though finished, with the fallacious claim to 'primordial givenness'. εἴδη thus remain precisely the same as what is otherwise grounded through the mechanism of abstraction. And so they remain abstract universal concepts. Nothing about their traditional scientific structure changes; their genesis and hence their claims are just re-interpreted.

But the strategy is ostrich-like. By ignoring the continuity of consciousness and impaling individual intentional states-of-affairs instead, absolutistic logic would cast out the relativity which clings to abstract universal concepts, as long as it is a matter of choice which moment of a manifold is ever supposed to be stressed as identical, and to which logical context an individual should be adapted.

Antinomy of Subjectivism and Eidetics

But such a strategy does not diminish the distress. If Husserl cannot help legitimizing mental being-in-itself – 'essence' – through recourse to the facts (*Tatbestände*), then it is this very recourse which is the principal obstacle to that legitimization. 123 Plato's doctrine of Ideas could not flourish on Husserlian soil, that of epistemological, subjectively directed idealism. The thesis of an ontological transcendence of essentialities as opposed to the performance of abstraction would be self-consistent only if it were not derived from the factual states of consciousness alone. Yet as soon as the objectively true is determined as mediated in whatever way through the subject, it loses its static character and independence from those acts which mediate it.

Husserl's philosophy prevents this by tolerating no doubt about that static character. He desires a contradiction. He wishes to force εἴδη out of subjective cognitive functions as residing beyond subjective cognitive functions.

Husserl overcomes paradox, that congealed caricature of dialectic, by giving back to subjective mediation itself the appearance of the immediate and to thought the illusion of a straightforward awareness of states-of-affairs. This illusory appearance can most easily be maintained in intentional acts, which mean (*bedeuten*) something abstract without themselves abstracting. But a philosophical antimony is expressed in the paradox. Husserl must reduce to the subject, for otherwise, according to the traditional ground rules, the objectivity of universal concepts would remain dogmatic and scientifically injudicious. He must defend the eidetic in-itself, for otherwise the idea of truth could not be saved. Hence he must concern himself with imaginary cognitive productions.

The phantom disappears only for a thought that penetrates the concepts of subject and object themselves, for it leaves them unmolested. Examples are the constitutive, existence-establishing immanence of consciousness as well as the traditional truth theory of correspondence between judgement and thing. For the concept of the subject can so little be emancipated from existence or the 'object' as the object from subjective functions of thought. In empty confrontation, neither fulfils the purpose for which it was devised.

'Eidetic Variations'

The later Husserl who, as a transcendental philosopher, gave up trying to defend the crudely dualistic 'descriptive thesis' of the ideal unity of the species which comes to consciousness in isolated acts, inflected it into an extremely subtle theory, that of 'eidetic' variation. According to this theory, the individual is a preliminary 'example' for its εἶδος. The εἶδος is, of course, still 124 borne by the individual, but the same eidetic dignity does not devolve upon the individual as in earlier writings. The representation of the individual essence is controlled and the moment of universality in essence is confirmed. Essence should be more than the sheer space-less and time-less double for the individual. But it is not a multiplicity of individuals which is required for its constitution; rather, for any single individual, the consciousness of the essence which pervades it comes through the free activity of fantasy, or fiction.

That a something could stand in for the infinity of its possibilities, may be valid for mathematical manifolds, but is hardly so for anything material whose participation in a *totum* and its qualityless permutability is not defined beforehand. The outrageous exaggeration of the claim to a priority far beyond received idealism – the sharpening of the critical organs for whatever can be taken beyond arbitrariness, so to speak – brings about a regression into pre-critical rationalism.

This is not very different from the way the dynamics of late bourgeois society itself tends, for it abolishes 'experience', and aims at a system of almost pure concepts, a system of administration. In place of abstraction as a non-self-contained collecting, appears a calculus which relies on the individual element, as if the whole were already given to it beforehand. That is intimated in *Formal and Transcendental Logic* as a method of research into essences.

Everything that we have stated in our observations concerning constitution can, in the first place, be made a matter of insight on the basis of arbitrary examples of arbitrary sorts of already-given objects – that is: in a reflective interpretation of the intentionality in which we simply and straightforwardly 'have' a real or an ideal objecthood. We have made a significant advance when we recognize that what obviously holds good for factical single cases of reality or possibility still holds necessarily when we vary our examples quite as we please and then inquire retrospectively for the correlatively varying 'representations' – that is: 125 the constituting lived experiences – and for the 'subjective' manners of givenness, which change, sometimes continuously and sometimes discretely. Primarily we must inquire here for the manners of 'appearance' that are constitutive in the pregnant sense, the ones that are experiences of the exemplary objects or of their variants; and we must look for the manners in which the objects take shape as synthetic unities in the mode 'they themselves', in those experiences. . . . In this inquiry, the variation of the necessary initial example is the performance in which the 'eidos' should emerge and by means of which the evidence of the indissoluble eidetic correlation between constitution and constituted should also emerge. If it is to have these effects, it must be understood, not as an empirical variation, but as a variation carried on with the freedom of pure fantasy and with the consciousness of its purely optional character – the consciousness of the 'pure' Any Whatever (*Überhaupt*). Thus understood, the variation extends into an open horizon of endlessly manifold free possibilities of more and more variants.[25]

The 'universal essence'* should be the 'invariant' running through these variations. It is

the ontic essential form (*a priori* form), the eidos, corresponding to the example, in place of which any variant of the example could have served equally well.[26]

Husserl hopes to crystallize out of factical givens results, freed from facticity, by means of 'exemplary analysis'.[27]

In the first place, however, the 'significant advance' is really a dogmatic assertion that what 'obviously holds good for factical single cases of reality', also obtains 'when we vary our examples quite as we please'. As long as it is strictly just the example with which consciousness is acquainted, such an extrapolation would be inadmissible. One cannot see beforehand what would change in the ostensible states of the essence with variation, and indeed variation 'quite as we please'. The illusion of the indifference of the essence to variation can be protected only because in the refuge of the realm of fantasy, essence is spared the test of its invariance. Only experience can be enlightening as to whether such modifications touch upon essence or not. Sheer 'fantasy modification', which in no living way fulfils what it posits, does not provide a relevant criterion.

But is there more present to consciousness than just the isolated initiating representation of the 'example'? But then why insist upon such a representation? Furthermore, if the research into essences which Husserl professes needs to be initiated by an 'example' at all, then the tidy split between fact and ideality has already been revoked, for then the ideal needs something factical to even be representable. If essence cannot be attained without *126* fact, even an isolated fact, then that very relation between concept and experience, which Husserl had explained away, is

* ['allgemeinsame Wesen' ('universally common essence') in Husserl. Trans.]

[25] *Logik* [254 ff]; cf. Cairns ⟨218 ff⟩.
[26] Ibid.; and ibid. ⟨219⟩.
[27] Cf. ibid.

really implicitly revived. An essence form which must compare fictions with each another in order to gain its invariant, repeats, on allegedly higher levels, the theory of abstraction which Husserl had attacked.

In addition, the arbitrary fantasy variations, which Husserl does not want to see confused with empirical ones, although he gives no information as to the difference between them, are unavoidably alloyed with elements of experience. Even their deviations from experience cling to elements of experience. Their fictional character is itself simulated. The concept of example itself should have perplexed Husserl. For it arises from just that trivial abstraction theory which chooses one example and then another and prescinds what is essential out of its variety. The phenomenological doctrine of essence, by contrast, directly signified in its radical form the attempt to emancipate essence from 'examples'. Husserl rebelled against classificatory logic's dilution of the universal concept into a mere form of subsumed facts and its renunciation of the authentic, the 'essential'. This very procedure is the sphere of 'examples'. Since examples can be arbitrarily replaced, they deprive themselves of what was Husserl's concern. As soon as the concrete sinks to being a mere example of its concept, it reciprocally reduces the universal to a derivative from mere particulars, without claiming a substantiality in contrast to particulars.

At the decisive moment Husserl capitulates before traditional theory of abstraction, for his own initiation never escaped it. While he publicly sought essences in individuals, essence remained for him nothing other than the old universal concept of the prevailing logic.

Essence as Fiction

The theory of εἶδος as an invariant and facticity as a variation is more thoroughly worked out in the *Cartesian Meditations*.

By the method of transcendental reduction each of us, as Cartesian meditator, was led back to his transcendental ego – naturally with its 127 concrete-monadic content as this factual ego, the one and only absolute ego.[28]

[28] *CM*, p. 71; cf. Cairns ⟨103⟩.

The initial 'factical' empirical descriptions of the pure ego are nevertheless themselves supposed to assume to some degree the character of essential necessities.

But involuntarily we confined our description to such a universality that its results remain unaffected, regardless of what the situation may be with respect to the empirical factualities of the transcendental ego.[29]

Yet if the strict dualism of the 'parallelisms' between pure and ontic regions which Husserl preaches may be doubted, then only the 'involuntary' transition from the one to the other now effaces the entire difficulty. The profusion of concrete determinations, which so pleases Husserl and which alone permit of something like transcendental phenomenology, is derived from the content of experience and, no matter how much they are varied, they are directed to experience. Husserl does not want to renounce experience as drastic and dense, but he must save up to pay the toll. His assertions also thus remain caught in the web of experience and its determinacy. And indeed this is the filtered experience on whose concept his entire method is based, the concept of the philosophy of immanence of the personal consciousness of the meditator.

As long as the solipsistic point of departure is maintained and thus unquestionable, certainty is connected to the immediacy of the ego, no variation may surpass the circumference of this ego, provided the variation will not forsake that type of certainty for whose sake the entire *sum cogitans* was established. The framework of the immediate experience of the given meditator is prescribed to every modification of the empirical factualities of the transcendental ego'. Otherwise, it would fall, in accord with its own beginning, into the problem of conclusion from analogy, viz. relativity. One cannot both make use of that solipsistic beginning and overstep its bounds. Consistency of thought itself would have to negate that.

Instead Husserl spans the χωρισμός – which otherwise for his philosophy can never be deep enough – as if he were crossing a stream. The technique of fantasy variation claims nothing less than that it consciously attains that eidetic thing which should *128* unconsciously be attained by ego analysis.

[29] Ibid.; and ibid. ⟨104⟩.

Starting from this table-perception as an example, we vary the perceptual object, table, with a completely free choice, yet in such a manner that we keep perception fixed as perception of something, no matter what. Perhaps we begin by fictively changing the shape or the colour of the object quite arbitrarily, keeping identical only its perceptual appearing. In other words: Abstaining from acceptance of its being, we change the fact of this perception into a pure possibility one among other quite 'optional' pure possibilities – but possibilities that are possible perceptions. We, so to speak, shift the actual perception into the realm of non-actualities, the realm of the as-if, which supplies us with 'pure' possibilities, pure of everything that restricts to this fact or to any fact whatever. As regards the latter point, we keep the aforesaid possibilities, not as restricted even to the co-posited factical ego, but just as a completely free conceivability of fantasy. Accordingly from the very start we might have taken as our initial example a fantasizing ourselves into a perceiving, with no relation to the rest of our factical life. Perception, the universal type thus acquired, floats in the air, so to speak – in the atmosphere of absolutely pure imaginability.[30]

Between the sentence which Husserl introduces as ·a mere rephrasing of what preceded with the expression 'In other words', and what, in fact, preceded, there opens up, to use his terms, an 'abyss of sense'. For what the initially proffered variation yields is no 'pure' possibility. Rather, every new fact (*Faktum*) which takes its place through variation and can be subsumed under the universal concept 'object of perception', must nevertheless be potentially accessible to factical perception in order to remain subsumable in that way. One cannot 'variationally' (*variierend*) introduce the category of perception or of the something in general for all imaginable material contents of perception. Granted that Husserl's favourite example of the centaur is attained by varying within the concept 'animal' and ultimately by substituting for men, horses, dinosaurs, etc. So, as long as the identical concept 'object of perception' is held fast, its definition is realized, only if what is varied could for its part also in some way be brought to perception. If, however, that is not possible, as with centaurs, then the law prescribed to variations by the concept 'perceptual object' fails.

The pure fantasy object cannot be subsumed under it. That is not an object of perception. Fantasy in the Husserlian sense –

[30] Ibid. p. 72; and ibid.

which is, moreover, utterly foreign to the true sense – of simulation, is not, as he erroneously teaches, a 'free possibility'. 'Holding on to the concept' prescribes a rule which indeed does not invite a determinate facticity, but still necessarily contains the relation to the factical and not to something merely contrived. The formal correspondence between a fictional creature like the centaur and a real one does not detract from the fact that the centaur cannot be perceived, even though its representation were fitted out with ever so many perceptible features. For there are no centaurs, and the determination 'object of perception' is not indifferent to that fact.

While the route to facticity is obstructed for Husserlian variation as soon as he concerns himself with such figures, indeed while variations will have nothing to do with facticity, Husserl nevertheless draws the substantiality of his variations from facticity. Something is falsely mediated that Husserlian logic cannot mediate. The context of a concept demands the question of the existence of what is contained in the concept, and not just its meaning (*Meinen*). Even the later Husserl's doctrine of essences remains a prisoner in the hot house of intentionality. Corresponding to this is the reified and rigid view of fantasy as a mere discovery of objects distilled from the factical which should have no advantage over the factical except the fact that they are not. Husserl's qualification of essence settles for just that. He calls it fictional. What he calls 'the atmosphere of absolutely pure imaginability' in the *Cartesian Meditations*, in which the εἶδος 'floats', was the climate of his entire philosophy, the crystalline kingdom of a cognition which confuses the flight before fleeting existence and the negation of life with the citizenry of its infinity. Essences remain without essence, though the arbitrary thoughts of the subject dare, by their means, to fancy the desolate entity an ontology.

3

Epistemological Concepts in Dialectic

The road can be looked upon as the path of doubt, or more properly a highway of despair. For what happens there is not what is usually understood by doubting, a jostling against this or that supposed truth, the outcome of which is again a disappearance in due course of the doubt and a return to the former truth, so that at the end the matter is taken as it was before. On the contrary, that pathway is the conscious insight into the untruth of phenomenal knowledge.

Hegel*

Phenomenology as Epistemology

Husserl's self-criticism – which is by and large how we should take the 'Attempt at a Critique of Logical Reason' from his later period – gained control over impossibility by prying essentialities loose from the individual intention without making use of abstraction. The controversy over universals cannot be settled by a decree according to which the universal, as just the meant 'itself' converges with what exists, the given, the *res*. 'Intentionality is not something isolated; it can be observed only in the synthetic unity that connects every single pulse of psychic life teleologically, in the unity-relation to bits of objecthood – or rather in the double polarity, toward ego-pole and object-pole.'[1]

* [*Sämtliche Werke*, ed. Hermann Glockner, vol. 2, *Phänomenologie des Geistes*, 4th ed., Jubiläumsausgabe (Fromann, Stuttgart – Bod Canstatt, 1964), pp. 71 ff; cf. tr. J.B. Baillie, *The Phenomenology of Mind* (Harper and Row, New York and Evanston, 1967), pp. 135 ff. Trans.].

[1] *Logik* [269]; cf. Cairns ⟨232⟩.

This revision – which, by the way, is not explicitly opposed to the *Logical Investigations* – the admission of some sort of divergence between 'ego-pole and object-pole', between subject and object, does nevertheless reveal, in addition, that phenomenology is something that, in the name of 'research', viz. the description of the state-of-affairs, it passionately disowned till the very end: epistemology.[2] Phenomenology strains to bring the non-homony- *131* mous down to a common denominator, in this case the static higher concept of 'poles'. Its most effective thoughts were a vehicle designed for just that purpose. They were theoretical constructions. Only when we cease to be mesmerized by a radically new and original beginning, such as phenomenology and its successors aspire to realize, and only when we cease to deny phenomenology's epistemological inclination to ascertain how knowledge of objecthood is in general possible and how it may be identified in the structure of consciousness – only then will those categories, which phenomenology claims to have simply discovered, become clear.

These categories are revealed less in the output and states-of-affairs of the factual performance of cognition which the theory demands of them – they are dubious in all epistemologies – than in the function that such concepts fulfill for the sake of the consistency and unanimity of the theory itself, particularly of the mastery of its contradictions. The claim to novelty and theoretical impartiality, the battle cry 'To the things themselves!' arises directly out of an epistemological norm. That is the positivistic norm which restricts thought to the practically technical procedure of abbreviation and attributes the substance of cognition only to what is supposed to exist without the supplement of thought, and what certainly ends up as the flimsiest and most abstract of findings. By way of what was initially also a positivistic demand for pure immanence to consciousness, this positivistic criterion in Husserl got bound up with the subjective idealistic criterion, and from out of that crystallized the thesis of mental being-in-itself and of essentialities as a *sui generis* givenness.

Phenomenology let itself be defined as the paradoxical search for a theory-free theory. But then vengeance catches up. What is supposed to be in-itself is only for phenomenology. It has created

[2] Cf., e.g., ibid. [123]; and ibid. ⟨105⟩.

what it intuits (*erschaut*) in order to establish that it intuits. Like all theory, however, it becomes susceptible to critique in the difference between systematic function and the ostensibly encountered. Phenomenology falls everywhere into error because even those concepts introduced in the name of the description of the so-called states-of-affairs or encounterings (*Vorfindlichkeiten*) of pure consciousness do not at all describe cognitive processes or types of such processes. Rather, they just present those processes, so that something like a structural unity in the framework of the 'reduction' may be possible.

132

Like life philosophers and Gestalt theorists, Husserl has a feeling for this weakness on the part of concepts. But because of his scientific resistance to irrationalism, he cannot forego the classification of 'the contents of consciousness'. Thus he must provide cognitive classes with qualities which do not correspond to the products of cognition, and nevertheless violate the definitions of such cognitive classes, without which introducing them would have been unnecessary.

Positivism and Platonism

The tension – which is latent in all positivism, and still effective in its later variations – between the logical and the empirical element, both of which are required by the cognitive ideal formed by science, though it cannot unite them, is decided by Husserl in favour of the logical. Once again a sort of dialectic in spite of itself occurs. The injunction to follow the facts undermines the very concept of the factual, viz. the nominalistic priority of datum over concept. And yet the latter claims the positivistic solidity of the state-of-affairs.

Husserl, however, does not reflect on this reversal. He would like to bring his results into immediate correspondence with the traditional logic of non-contradiction whose justification induced that process completely. In non-dialectical systems, the dialectic in spite of itself becomes the source of errors and yet the medium of truth. For it drives all the epistemological categories, which it grasps, beyond itself, till the beginning itself is liquidated, i.e. the analysis of the form of cognition regardless of its concrete determinate content. The transformation of positivism into

Platonic realism will not succeed. For the positivistic demand for pure givenness may not be replaced by the sheer assumption of ideal states-of-affairs, nor may ideality, concept or logos be interpreted as givenness.

The characteristic categories of Husserl's philosophy – the same as those which entered into the apparatus of irrationalist ideology during the age of total rationalization – are devised throughout to *133* wipe away telltale dregs of earth within *prima philosophia*, the traces of the incompatible. The identity of extremes, of factically encountered things and pure validity, is tolerable to Husserl's philosophy of reflection only as itself immediate and not as again conceptually mediated concepts. Precisely because the concept of immediacy may not be emancipated from facticity and not be saved for ideality, its dogmatic use must take on the task of striking down critical consciousness. Hence the relation of the mutually irritating elements of Husserl's philosophy remains not an external one of incompatible world views which he sought to gather under a single rubric. The conflicts much rather obey an objective compulsion.

As a scientist and mathematician, Husserl does not see himself as simply facing some unformed manifold, but rather the unity of the entity in the concept as well. Since, however, he can neither create these unities out of the subject as 'spirit' (for that would be suspect to positivists as idealistic metaphysics), nor derive them from the unformed manifold of the factical itself, he must claim as in themselves the unified conceptual structures, which appear before his eyes in the developed sciences. Essentialities are settled beyond subjective spirit as well as merely existing, diffuse facticity. The Platonic turn is involuntary. He must present essentialities as an absolute and as ultimately given, because the positivistic norm of science prohibits a direct attack on the concept of givenness.

As early as the *Logical Investigations* Husserl accused the older positivism of not having been faithful enough to this norm and thus of having failed to recognize ideal givens.

They cannot bring themselves to take acts of thought for what they show themselves in pure phenomenological examination; they cannot let them count as wholly new 'act-characters', as new modes of consciousness opposed to direct intuition. They cannot see what is quite plain to anyone who approaches the matter unconfused by traditional prejudices, that these 'act-characters' are modes of meaning (*Meinen*), modes referring (*bedeuten*) to this or that significant content, behind which nothing whatever may be looked for that either differs or could differ from our meaning (*Meinen*) or significant reference (*Bedeuten*).[3]

And,

134 What 'meaning' (*Bedeutung*) is, is a matter as immediately given to us as is the nature of colour and sound. It cannot be further defined, it is ultimate in description.[4]

But everything meant is mediated by meaning. The fact that epistemology cannot refer behind the structures of consciousness as the 'symbolic function',[5] does not establish the referent of this function as an original phenomenon. Moreover, Husserl's broadening of the concept of givenness changes it qualitatively. Givenness loses what it was originally conceived for, a sense which Husserl maintains: the moment hinted at by the phrase, 'stubborn facts',* the opaque, what cannot be removed, what must simply be acknowledged, and which prescribes to thought its fixed boundaries. Husserl's interpretation of mediate givenness suffers from the fact that he further credits it with what vanishes with those modifications, viz. the immediacy of what is meant. This defect is responsible for any number of phenomenology's promises.

Husserl's Concept of Givenness

The concept of the datum is for Husserl and positivistic and empiricistic epistemology, as well as for Kant, primarily perceptible stuff, 'matter', ὕλη. 'Real' is directly defined in the third *Logical Investigation* of volume 2 as 'being a possible object of sense-perception'.[6] Hardly any concept of reality could be

---

* [In English in the text. Trans.]

[3] *LU* II, i, p. 182; cf. Findlay, pp. 399 ff.
[4] Ibid. p. 183; and ibid. p. 400.
[5] Cf. Hans Cornelius, *Transzendentale Systematik* (Munich, 1916), p. 90.
[6] Cf. *LU* II, i, p. 280; and Findlay, p. 479.

attained by means of traditional, subjectively oriented epistemology without recourse to something immediate, stuff-like and precategorial. At the same time, however, epistemological analysis of the immediate cannot explain away the fact that the immediate is also mediated.

That motivates dialectical logic, which raises such a contradiction to being a determination of the thing itself (*die Sache selbst*), and thus maintains as well as negates the concept of the immediate. This conclusion, however, is forbidden to Husserl by the absolutism of formal logic which he himself proclaims, viz. pure freedom from contradiction. As a compensation his theory models all mediated knowledge on immediacy. The dynamic development of contradiction is replaced by the static auxiliary construction of a self-sufficient cognitive production which is primarily supposed to give the mediated.

The paradox of beginning, however, is incompatible with Husserl's own criterion of freedom from contradiction. Givenness has been held up as a model for all cognition since the *Logical* 135 *Investigations*. The terminology of this vacillates between sense intuition and the contents of all lived experiences as the immediate facts of consciousness. Underlying this is the truth which has been notorious since Bergson's early writings, that the strict analysis of consciousness into 'facts' and their classification suffers from a moment of caprice that can be explained by the need for a construction imitating the world of things,[7] even though in the present life of consciousness not only individual acts but also their characteristics merge much more into each other.

But Husserl certainly does not criticize epistemological classes. Rather, he preserves them in order to confound them and let the imprecision of their distinction from the validity of the concept of givenness benefit the mediated. Indeed Bergson distinguished much more sharply between perception and memory. Speaking roughly and in terms of traditional concepts: since acts of thought as such may be immediate facts of consciousness just as much as impressions of sense-perception, then what for Husserl is in each case thought in acts of thought, is mediated by them, becomes for

[7] Cf., e.g., Henri Bergson, *Les données immédiates de la conscience* (PUF, Paris, 1948), pp. 92 ff.

its part, immediacy. Givenness at the moment is identified in the sixth *Logical Investigation* with consciousness.[8] Hence intentionality in the pregnant sense, which Husserl gave the term, would in the end be identical with givenness. Since the mediated, what is already thought through intention, should simply be assumed, the concept of immediate givenness becomes total. Perception becomes knowledge of something, this knowledge becomes the primary, irreducible factual state of consciousness and the perceived thing world becomes, so to speak, a radical first.

The equivocity is transmitted to the fundamental qualifications of *Ideas*, where the concept of original and originary givenness is directly co-ordinated with objecthood and thus lifts the stumbling block by terminological decree:

136 Every science has its own object-realm as a domain of research, and to all that it knows, i.e. in this connection to all its correct assertions, there correspond as original sources of the reasoned justification that support them certain intuitions in which objects of the region appear as self-given and in part at least as given in an originary sense. The dator intuition of the first 'natural' sphere of knowledge and of all its sciences is natural experience, and the originary dator experience is perception in the ordinary sense of the term. To have something real (*Reales*) originarily given, and to 'become aware' of it and 'perceive' it in simple intuition, are one and the same thing.[9]

This pre-critical relation of the sciences to the objects which they deal with is completely unabashedly presupposed in the course of *Ideas* for epistemological issues of constitution as it had been before for logic. Even in the 'phenomenological attitude' 'objects' are supposed to 'appear as self-given' without the much-evoked 'reduction' changing a thing about it. The critique of reason descends to mere suspension of judgement. Superiority to crude facticity does not hinder the acceptance of the thing world 'as it gives itself'. This is aided by the fact that analysis stands by perception as its last resort. For perception in the German sense of the word (*Wahrnehmung*), to which Husserl certainly subscribes, is always already a perception of something. The complete thing, whose constitution is otherwise the concern of

[8] Cf. *LU* II, ii, p. 162; and Findlay, p. 800.
[9] *Ideen* [7 ff]; cf. *Ideas*, p. 45.

epistemology, is allotted to Husserl from the beginning and its analysis ends by a bit of objecthood rising to consciousness as if it were just there waiting to be discovered. This is the way *Ideas* uses, in contrast to reflection, the terms 'pre-given (*vorgegebenes*) lived experiences' and 'datum of lived experience'[10] which establish the latter as an entity in itself.

'Foundation' (Fundierung)

The talk about reflection on lived experiences, which signify thoughts directed to a univocal contour, presupposes nothing less than the reification of the concept of givenness. It presupposes that the subject of reference 'has' a lived experience in itself upon which it may reflect. The simple but, for the method of the analysis of consciousness, stringent consequence is avoided, that all talk of the given demands such reflection, and that the concept of the given itself, therefore, is mediated through the concept of reflection.

Reification nestles in the primal characteristica of the given (on which the whole of phenomenology is based) as something already determined. It nestles in the belief that one may obtain mental states-of-affairs without the ornament of thought. Yet Husserl clings so tenaciously to the concept of givenness that he 137 would sooner sacrifice epistemological consistency than this concept and continues to speak of perception as a 'primal mode of self-giving'[11] and the like in *Formal and Transcendental Logic*. He will not forego the doctrine of the foundedness of all cognition. One intention is supposed to rest in another. But then the only secure ground would be something absolutely primary. Yet this doctrine is incompatible with the view of the cognitive process as a functional cohesion towards which Husserl, the transcendental logician, inclined. Functional cohesion of cognition can only mean that what is formed on the higher categorial level does not just depend on the lower. The converse dependence also obtains.

Husserl either did not see that or he did not concede it. Paradoxically enough, the conception of cautiously divided acts

[10] Cf. ibid. p. 148; and ibid. p. 200.
[11] *Logik* [166] and passim; cf. Cairns ⟨141⟩ and passim.

and meanings, stratified like stones, the legacy of the insatiable positivistic demand for evidence for every assertion, inaugurated all the static ontological doctrines, which attached to Husserl, all the restorative organization of being which he was supposed to imply. Alongside there developed a functional epistemology. Only because he did not settle the conflict, there awakened the illusion that phenomenology could to a certain degree reproduce Aristotelian metaphysics on the basis of scientificity and criticism. In the end, he had to seek to really unite the two. His contribution was to re-interpret the originally foundational, givenness itself, the refuge of the entity in pure being and in its proper possibility, as a refuge in the possibility of something that should not be presupposed.

Ontologization of the Factical

This ingenious construction, which seeks to release the given from the curse of being given, holds the system together, but brings it to no good. Givenness itself is in Husserl sublated in the possibility of being given – in a way not so unrelated to Kant's theorem of pure intuition; thus the factical is sublated in the ontologically pure determination of essence, 'being factical'. Yet factical existence by no means follows from the pure possibility of the factical. Neither does the existence of those 'facts of consciousness', through which existence itself was obtained.

Husserl's earlier doctrine that 'pure essential truths do not make the slightest assertion concerning facts; hence from them alone we are not able to infer even the pettiest truth concerning the fact-world',[12] is cast to the winds. It is perverted into the thesis of the essential lawfulness of existence by way of the existing entity. The difference disappears, in that doctrine, between the irrevocability (*Unabdingbarkeit*) of the factual as a universal determination – by all means, a 'law of essence' – and the assertion that existence itself is essential. And that is disowned by the ontological difference.

Thus the method cuts off the ultimate relation to experience which sustains its specific claim. And relapse into pre-critical rationalism is irresistible. This means that the concept of an

138

12 *Ideen* [13]; cf. *Ideas*, p. 51.

existence (*Dasein*) prescribed by laws of essence itself implies the ontological difference which is supposed to be set aside to the glory of the greater purity of phenomenology. Husserl ventures the erroneous construction in order to weaken and yet save given-ness at any price. The given is the most internal arena of reification in epistemology. With unchangeable rigidity and unmoved sheer existence, it may be conceived as immanent and subject-proper. Yet this subject-proper thing also remains entirely alien from the subject. The knowing ego which brackets the given as its 'fact of consciousness' must accept it blindly and recognize it as a simple other independent of its own work. Indeed the subject in its spontaneity must still orient itself to the given, in a way not so different from how the economic subject acts as the simple bearer of the functions of its property.

This antagonism is made evident in Husserl's identification of the 'thing itself' with what is given subjectively. In the shape of givenness, the promise of security offered by naive realism is transferred to the sphere of the ego. Here it means to possess the absolutely solid and unchanging within itself, which otherwise has always become problematic when one turned to the subject. And thus, in a way, it also becomes a thing.

The later Husserl (under Bergson's influence, in fact) made similar critical observations.

The data-sensualism that is generally prevalent in psychology and epistemology and, for the most part, biases even those who, verbally polemicize against it, or against what they mean by the term, consists in constructing the life of consciousness out of data as, so to speak, finished objects. It is actually a matter of indifference here, whether one thinks of these data as separate 'psychic atoms' swept together into more or less cohesive bundles according to unintelligible laws of fact, like those of mechanics, or talks about wholes and Gestalt-qualities and *139* regards the wholes as antecedent to the elements distinguishable within them; likewise whether, within this realm of objects already existing in advance, one distinguishes between data of the senses and mental processes as data of another sort.[13]

That is hardly less than a disclaimer of the fundamental claim of phenomenology: to describe what is given in 'the stream of

---

[13] *Logik* [291 ff]; cf. Cairns ⟨252⟩.

consciousness', viz. phenomena. The interpretation of the facts of consciousness as relations of ultimate elements is analogously disputed in the *Cartesian Meditations*. Such facts are not constituted as such *a priori*.[14] Husserl even comes to the view that the 'objectively oriented' sciences, which always deal with already constituted things, furnish the model for epistemological analysis of elements, and that the concept of data itself is most closely related to the dogmatic concept of the thing-in-itself, which recourse to data precisely opposes.

This view touches both the ontological aspect of phenomenology and the metaphysics of being, to which phenomenology was raised, and which goes to the greatest lengths in its claim to immediate knowledge. The illusion of conclusiveness and definitiveness, which moves from 'persisting' things in themselves to givenness as the substratum of cognition in the philosophy of immanence, and nurtures the ontological pathos of a heaven of ideas entranced by discursive thought, gives way to a dynamic determination of cognition.

We have already touched on the fact that self-giving is, like every other single intentional lived experience, a function in the universal nexus of consciousness. The effect produced by a single intentional process, in particular its effect as a self-giving, its effect as evidence, is therefore not shut off singly. The single evidence, by its own intentionality, can implicitly 'demand' further self-givings; it can 'refer one' to them for a supplementation of its objectifying effect.[15]

140   Thus in Husserl's transcendental revision the doctrine of originary 'dator' intuition is actually replaced by a function concept in the style of the Marburg School. But Husserl's reflection ceased to decide the conflict between such a critique and the dogma of 'primal givenness'. The later Husserl himself clings to it, for otherwise he would overthrow phenomenological procedure. The given, as the absolute possession of the subject, remains the fetish of the transcendental subject as well. Only what 'belongs' to the subject as a part-moment of the 'life' of its consciousness, and indeed as the foundational moment, no longer needs – or so Husserl's prejudice believes – to be thought

[14] Cf. *CM*, pp. 50 ff; and Cairns ⟨86⟩.
[15] *Logik* [168]; cf. Cairns ⟨142 ff⟩.

by thinking but simply to be assumed without trouble and without the danger of error. Theory appears risky. Hence the nostalgia for the theory-free. Phenomenology remains theory since it necessarily reflects on cognition and does not 'directly' judge, so to speak, empirically. It wants to be theory-free, for its ideal is to transform every assertion into givenness and thus avoid the possibility of false conclusions as well as that of critique.

The two are incompatible. If philosophy were ever to give itself over to that dialectic at all, which arises with reflection on givenness, then its epistemological foundation, including the method of 'reductions' which Husserl taught to the very end, would have to turn out to be a hoax. If it is supposed to belong to the essence of 'self-giving', as a possibility prescribed in this self, to demand (*verlangen*) other self-givings, then its fundamental character is destroyed. Cognition is cast into a process where, as Hegel was well aware, the concept of an absolutely first loses its meaning.[16] As soon as the given, as 'demanding' (*forderndes*), refers beyond itself, it is not only degraded to a mere part-moment of the encroaching cognitive process, it also shows its own process character in itself.

The descriptive state-of-affairs has, to use the later Husserl's expression, its 'genetic sense implicates'.[17] But that touches on the dichotomy between genesis and validity which has been assumed since the 'Prolegomena to Pure Logic'. Validity no longer shuts out its origin. Thus the generation of validity is no longer independent of its own truth content. Rather, genesis falls into that very 'demanding' truth content. It is not, as relativism 141 would have it, truth in history, but rather history in truth. 'Now is the time for decisive renunciation of the concept of "timeless truth". Yet truth is not, as Marxism claims, a temporal function of cognizing, but rather bound to a core of time which resides both in the cognized and the cognizer.'[18]

[16] Cf., e.g., Hegel, *Sämtliche Werke*, vol. 8, *System der Philosophie*, part 1, *Die Logik*, Einleitung, p. 63; and *Hegel's Logic, Being Part One of the Encyclopædia of the Philosophical Sciences*, tr. William Wallace (Clarendon, Oxford, 1975), p. 22.

[17] Cf. *Logik* [215]; and Cairns ⟨183 ff⟩.

[18] Walter Benjamin, 'Paris, die Hauptstadt des xix. Jahrhunderts (Passagenarbeit)', Manuskript, Konvolut N, B1.3; cf. Benjamin, *Schriften*, vol. 1, ed. Theodor W. Adorno (Suhrkamp, Frankfurt, 1955), pp. 406–22; and *Gesammelte Schriften, Inhaltsverzeichnis*, Band I–IV (Suhrkamp, Frankfurt, 1977), p. 7; and tr. Harry Zohn 'Paris – the Capital of the Nineteenth Century', in *Charles Baudelaire: A Lyric Poet in the Era of High Capitalism* (NLB, London, 1973).

On the threshold of such insights, Husserl's philosophy of reflection came exceedingly close to that self-movement of the thing and of the concept which he otherwise would have dismissed to speculative philosophy as undischargeable extravagance. Hegel also asked no more than that the state-of-affairs should 'demand' a movement of consciousness. If heed were ever paid to that, then the traditional Cartesian idea of truth as fitting the concept to the thing would be shaken. As soon as the thing is thought, it ceases to be something to which one can fit oneself. The realm of truth becomes reciprocal dependence, the mutual production of subject and object. And this could no longer be thought as a static correspondence or even 'intention'. If the early genuinely phenomenological Husserl convincingly polemicizes against the picture and sign theories of cognition,[19] then that polemic could also be turned against the sublimated idea that cognition is a picture of its object through resemblance or *adaequatio*. Only with the idea of a pictureless truth would philosophy retrieve the prohibition of images.

Thing as Model of the Given

The demand for receptivity (*Hinnehmens*) within the framework of intuition directly and immediately unifies the mediated, and also what confronts the act-performing subject, with the subject itself. According to *Ideas*, the noema, as what is meant by the subject itself, is supposed to be 'evidently given'.[20] Astonishment over 'wondrously becoming conscious' of an obvious given – which is, nevertheless, 'something opposed, in principle other, unreal and transcendent to consciousness',[21] as Husserl immediately declares by the thesis of the self-evidence of the intended – betrays the discrepancy between what is both proper and foreign to the subject. Not only Husserl's doctrine of the noema, but every doctrine of the absolutely given suffers from this. Sheer receptivity is equivocal. It is both a memorial to the barrier which

---

[19] Cf. *LU* II, i, esp. pp. 421 ff; and Findlay, esp. pp. 593 ff; and *Ideen*, passim, esp. [79] and [99]; and *Ideas*, passim, esp. pp. 123 and 145.

[20] Cf. *Ideen* [204]; and *Ideas*, p, 262.

[21] Ibid.

spirit rebounds from whenever something is not its equal, and a bit of resignation and ideology.

The question of absolute origin pushes aside that of the 'labour' of social production as the condition of cognition. With that question one already forgets, before every individual phenomenological analysis, that, in the method, the 'principle of all principles', 'every originary dator intuition is a source of authority for cognition, that whatever presents itself in "intuition" originarily (as it were in its bodily reality), is simply to be received as it gives itself, though only within the limits in which it gives itself'.* This norm, which is binding on Husserl's entire philosophy, is based precisely on the fact that whatever offers itself in an intuition, whether sheer sensation or structured or categorially formed appearance, could be observed passively by consciousness without the observed changing through the act of observation and regardless of the internal composition of what 'appears'. The naive realistic experience that the thing remains identical, even when the subject turns away from it, is transferred to the concept of givenness, which is beholden to critical reflection alone. This approaches the legacy of the pre-critical substratum without thereby illuminating what has been modified by the turn to the immanence of consciousness. What has changed is that givenness in the immanence of consciousness may no longer claim that 'objectivity' on which unreflected experience relies. That is the price which the subject must pay for Cartesian freedom from doubt concerning the facts of consciousness.

Still, it becomes necessary to transfer the character of indisputable objectivity to the subject's own givens so it may affix the determinations of the philosophy of immanence in general to any entity at all. The reification of givenness is as necessary as it is untenable.

Only by reducing consciousness to mistaking itself in one of its moments and not only holding this moment to be proper to consciousness but also positing it as confronting itself and simply existing, can something like objecthood be spun out of sheer 143 consciousness in general. The idealistic attempt to add together the critically decomposed thing out of the interplay of the material

---

* *Ideen* [43 ff]. Cf. also [187] and *Ideas*, pp. 83 and 243, where the given to be received is assigned to a 'how' of its givenness, on which the phenomenologist is supposed to depend.

of sense-perception and categorial form is guilty of a *petitio principii*. What is supposed to be constructed as a thing is already inserted unawares into the conception of that towards which the mechanisms of the categorial constitution of the object had, by the initial intention, to be set in motion. What is still called chaotic multiplicity in Kant's critique of reason, is interpreted by Husserl fully on the pattern of the already constituted so that the objectivity of subjective constitution may be more plausibly demonstrated. In his supposition of that 'as which' an object gives itself to the subject is mirrored the subject itself to itself. For this very *quidditas* is what alone, according to the ground rules of the analysis of consciousness, lets thought determine the unqualified at all.

One concedes by such a contradiction that the determination of the 'What' cannot be executed as true judgement unless something corresponds to it in the ultimate substratum. Thus a truth is inherent to the dogmatism which indeed does not reduce the given so radically as the programme will, but rather leaves its 'as which' alone as its 'in itself'. This is an expression of the impracticability of idealistic construction as soon as it reached complete consistency. What is not proper to the subject appears phantasmagorically as reflection in transcendental phenomenology, though it fancies itself breaking directly out of the phantasmagoria in the mirroring of 'what gives itself as such'.

This is true to Benjamin's definition of *Jugendstil* as the dream in which the dreamer dreams that he has awakened.[22] Hence the meaning of Husserl's doctrine of essence and the epistemological cry 'To the things themselves!' What is not exhausted in the analysis of consciousness is sucked into it and then presented in the dominion proper to such analysis as if it were being pure and simple. The subject raises itself by attributing absolute authority to its product. What acts as the overcoming of idealism just drives the power of order in domineering thought into irrationality, as if disdaining the reconciliation of subject and object. Thought gives up its critical right over what is thought.

144

---

[22] Cf. Benjamin, 'Paris, die Haupstadt des xix. Jahrhunderts', Konvolut K, B1.2.

Givenness Mediated in Itself

The immanent proof of the mediacy of the immediately given in itself leads that concept into a contradiction. Yet the fact that that concept, which should ground reified existence as a structure of the given, is itself a product of reification, explains the contradiction. The composition of the object out of the 'elements' of cognition and their unity assumes what is to be deduced. Terms like stuff, matter or Husserl's ὕλη of cognition, such as denote the given in all philosophy of immanence, recall, and not by chance, that character of the established or in-itself which is distilled from transcendent things. The given as something independent of the spontaneity of consciousness, can be characterized only by turns of speech out of the thing world.

This constraint is more than merely verbal. What the ego is supposed to have as its most secure and yet cut off from it comes closest to the possessible – to the rigid and available. The boundedness of the given, as assumed by elementary analysis, is that of things as property, ultimately indeed derived from title deeds. Corresponding to this is the fact that from its inception the philosophy of immanence did not take on the task of seriously reducing the world of things or contesting its existence. This philosophy sought, rather, to reconstruct it 'critically', i.e. through the evidence of self-certainty. Hence it is sworn previously to the thing as its *terminus ad quem*.

Philosophy of immanence must justify through reflection the pre-critical world of experience as one of things. The formal constituents, however, the principles of pure reason, are incapable of that. They remain inauthentic, and even in Kant a mere conceptual net thrown over the entity and at each instance requiring some material for experience. They do not provide that indisputable security, in which alone the scientific justification of the thing world is confirmed. Hence security, along with a second, fetishistic dogmatism, is transferred to that material which was made into something entirely undetermined and abstract by being cut off from categorial form. Its abstractness is the refuge in which whatever cannot be created out of pure subjectivity entrenches itself against the thing. The all high 145 subjective, what seems to be immediately given without any intermediary, is also the residuum of the thing as that most foreign to the subject and over which the subject has no power. Without the model of the thing which is supposed to exist independently of subjective caprice, the category-free being in-itself of the given as such would not be plausible. Just as the thing once was, the given is that 'to which thinking relates'. It is supposed to involve content, being both 'there' and immanent.

That it has content may be contingent to consciousness, but is incompatible with its immanence and its essence of being proper to consciousness, even though epistemology must insist upon the immanence of the given so as not to violate against its principle. The construction of the immanence of consciousness itself cannot do without a concept of the given in order to be capable of content-laden assertions, viz. 'synthetic judgements'. The entire schema of form and content since Kant can be maintained by predicating of content the very being-in-itself which had been attacked by the critique of reason.

Now it is just this being-in-itself which the given may not have. Consciousness which claims to have it, knows of it only what is mediated through consciousness. The post-Kantian Idealists understood that. And even the substitution of the given for the being-in-itself of the thing does not help epistemology out of its distress. That abstractness of the given as the reduced remainder of complete experience, which equates it to the impenetrable substratum, also robs it of what it should guarantee, once it had gone astray through the division of cognition into form and content: the dignity of the absolutely existing entity. The given as the result of abstraction becomes discernible through its abstractness as itself just something produced.

The hunt for the given as a phenomenological factual state is in vain. Even assuming sheer encounterability, analysis constantly finds itself confronting anew structures which transcend such givenness. Hence Husserl's tendency to overthrow the inherited hierarchy of the philosophy of immanence and to build on intentionality instead of simple sensation. Ever since the Prolegomena he could make nothing of the self-evidence of the 146 unintelligible, the facts. And thus he erred also concerning the elementary components of the consciousness of objects, the immediately given. For that reason, he later timidly attempted to think the 'stream of consciousness' as an unending 'continuum',[23] that could, nevertheless, not be composed out of elementary classes of 'representations'. But 'every individual lived experience' is supposed 'to end as it began and so bring its duration to an end',[24] in such a stream of consciousness.

The traditional epistemology of 'lived experiences' is not liquidated; rather its order is simply inverted. Instead of giving up the given, as well as the illusion of the solid and reified which prepares for it, he claims the attribute of the support or the first, for what the language of epistemology calls the produced or the higher. Indeed Hegel's *Phenomenology* also was acquainted with immediacy at ever higher levels of consciousness and mediation. But Husserl never reflected on the process which effects mediation. Blindness to production entices him to take the product as given. Even the spheres of the most extreme abstraction are unconsciously governed by the entire tendency of society which, since it no longer expects any good from its own dynamic, must hypostatize each of its existing reified forms as definitive, viz. as categories. Already with Husserl is evident, in the most inner cells of epistemology, that fetishization of the currently existing, which in the era of overproduction extends, with the simultaneous fettering of the forces of production, over the total social consciousness. In this sense also Husserl's essentialities are 'second nature'.

The Subject of Givenness

The concept of givenness, however, as an ontic residuum within idealism, does not simply have the thing world as a model for its structure. Rather, though it claims to establish the thing world, this concept already presupposes it in the strictest sense. Givenness demands, by its own concept, a subject to which it can refer. One cannot just speak of any given, rather only of that which is given to 'someone', or, as the language of epistemology would have it, to 'me'. Idealistic and positivistic philosophies of immanence differed primarily in that the former stressed the need to determine the subject to which something must be given, or else

---

[23] Cf. *Ideen* [163]; and *Ideas*, p.217.
[24] Ibid.

147 the expression 'givenness' would surpass even metaphysics in arbitrariness, though it is an anti-metaphysical concept.

Even the search for the subject of givenness, however, leads to an antinomy. It must obviously not be the spatio-temporal, empirical and already constituted subject. Otherwise the necessary condition for the concept of givenness would be precisely what, in the wake of the entire tradition since Hume and Kant, turns out to be a structure of the given. But certainly nothing can be given to a 'pure' transcendental subject. For that subject is a determination of thought, a product of abstraction, which is certainly not to be straightaway brought to a denominator with the immediate. It is not a concrete ego possessing concrete contents of consciousness. The transcendental subject itself is supposed to be cut off from the given by the ontological difference which should disappear in the construction of the subject. The sense-perceptible does not exist immediately for the supersensual (*Unsinnliches*); rather, it exists only by the concept which 'is' not sense-perception, but means (*meint*) and therefore sublates it.

That was why Kant asserted there is a stratum of constitutive subjectivity in the Transcendental Aesthetic, a pure form of sensibility,* free from all empirical admixture, but also from every supplement of thought on the part of the subject. The dichotomy of form and matter leads to intransigent difficulties in the conception of the 'pure intuition', which it casts into form without isolating any content from it as independent. The entire formal transcendental subject, the sheer aggregate** of the conditions of possible experience, is thus incapable of 'pure' intuitions also. No subject emancipated from everything empirical can ever be a form for the given; to no such subject can something be given (referring to 'it' as 'it' or 'him' is already problematic); none can receive such content in whatever manner.

Kant's precipitous remark about the heterogeneity of pure

---

* [*Sinnlichkeit*, usually rendered in English versions of Husserl as 'sense-perception' or, incorrectly, 'sensuousness'. Since the translation of Kant's usage as 'sensibility' is well established in English, however, that will be retained where Adorno's reference is clearly to Kant. Trans.]

** [*Inbegriff*, 'sum' in Kemp-Smith. Trans.]

concepts of the understanding and sensible intuitions* shows that
he is aware of that, uncorrupted by the enticement of consistency 148
in his own system. Cognition can never rid itself of its mimetic
moment without some remainder, the resemblance of the subject
to nature, which it wants to dominate and which arose out of
cognition itself. The resemblance or 'identity' between subject
and object which Kant confronted is the moment of truth of what
is expressed in a different form in picture and sign theories, viz.
duplication theory. The fact that cognition or truth is a picture of
its object, is the substitute and consolation for the irreparable
cutting off of like from like. As false illusion, the picture character
of cognition conceals the fact that subject and object no longer
resemble one another. And that means nothing else than that
they are alienated from one another. Lost mimesis is sublimated
only by renouncing every such illusion, in the idea of a pictureless truth, and not in the preservation of its rudiments.

That idea lives on in Husserl's yearning for 'the things
themselves'. It would be 'the refuge of all images from the power
of the name, imageless'.[25] Epistemology, however, which wants

---

* Cf. Immanuel Kant, *Critique of Pure Reason*, tr. Norman Kemp-Smith
(St. Martin's Press, New York, 1965) A 143/B 182. Kant's remark has a long
pre-history in ancient philosophy. Theophrastus asserts in *De Sensu* that
Parmenides had already taught that what is perceived and what perceives
resemble each other, while Heraclitus pleaded that only the unlike and
contrasted can recognize the like. Plato followed the Eleatic tradition. Aristotle
turned Plato's own μέθεξις back into a doctrine of resemblance, viz. the
Pythagorean doctrine that things exist only in imitation of numbers (*Metaphysics*, α, 987 b). Among the proofs of the immortality of the soul in the *Phaedo*
the argument is not missing that, corresponding to a likeness between the
body and the world of appearances, is a likeness between the soul and the
world of Ideas. (p. 79). It is not far from that to the conclusion that the
resemblance between subject and object is the condition for the possibility of
knowledge.
  If rationality is altogether the demythologization of mimetic modes of
procedure (cf. Max Horkheimer and Theodor W.Adorno, *Dialektik der Aufklärung* (Querido, Amsterdam, 1947), pp. 38 ff, and John Cumming, tr., *Dialectic of
Enlightenment* (Herder and Herder, New York, 1972), p. 25), then it can be no
surprise that the mimetic motif survives in reflection on cognition. This is
perhaps not simply an archaic holdover, but is rather due to the fact that
cognition itself cannot be conceived without the supplement of mimesis,
however that may be sublimated. Without mimesis, the break between subject
and object would be absolute and cognition impossible.

[25] Benjamin, *Schriften*, vol. II (*Kurze Schatten (Suhrkamp, Frankfurt, 1955)*).

to establish the unity of what has been estranged from the subject, is allotted fixed concepts, such as form and content, as its elements. Hence it must seek a *tertium comparationis* to make
149 such a federation possible. The given of sense-perception, the ὕλη, which, according to Husserl himself, furnishes the content to all cognition, if only through 'fulfilment', requires something like itself if it is to exist at all. The sense-perceptible would not devolve on what should be free from all sense-perception. A subject, however abstractive and removed from the spatio-temporal continuum, could have no intuitions.

The anathema against 'naturalism' does not save epistemology from having recourse, in its analysis of the given, to the apparatus of sense-perception, the sense.organs. According to the ground rules of epistemology, however, such organs are a bit of the thing world. And thus epistemology gets caught in the ὕστερον πρότερον. The insistent demand to exclude the sense organs, as well as the individual person who bears them, from constitutional analysis, is just a bit of apologetic strategy.

Phenomenologically speaking, it belongs to the sense of seeing to be 'with one's eyes', and would not just be casual reflection and theoretical explanation.* Seeing simply could not be con-
150 ceived without eyes nor hearing without ears. The μετάβασις εἰς

---

* Husserl came surprisingly close to that in the 'Reduction of Transcendental Experience to the Sphere of Ownness' (*Cartesian Meditations and Paris Lectures*, § 44). 'Among the bodies belonging to this "nature" and included in my peculiar ownness, I then find my animate organism as uniquely singled out – namely as the only one of them that is not just a body but precisely an animate organism: the sole object within my abstract world-stratum to which, in accordance with experience, I ascribe fields of sensation (belonging to it, however, in different manners – a field of tactile sensations, a field of warmth and coldness, and so forth), the only object "in" which I "rule and govern" immediately, governing particularly in each of its "organs". Touching kinesthetically, I perceive "with" my hands; seeing kinesthetically, I perceive also "with" my eyes; and so forth; moreover I can perceive thus at any time. Meanwhile the kinesthesias pertaining to the organs flow in the mode "I am doing", and are subject to my "I can"; furthermore, by calling these kinesthesias into play, I can push, thrust, and so forth, and can thereby "act" somatically – immediately and then mediately.' (p. 99; Cairns ⟨128⟩).
The fact that fields of sensation are attributed to the body should be of immeasurable significance for the starting point of phenomenology, if the inferences were drawn from the description. 'Attribution' is here a vague expression for the inextricable unity of organ and perceptible ὕλη. The

ἄλλο γένος,* of deriving the given, the primary matter of cognition, as a consequence of the sense organs, viz. of what they themselves are meant to constitute, is no corrigible error of thought. Its unavoidability leads the starting point of philosophy of immanence to its own falsehood. Sense perceptible phenomena are commensurable only with the 'senses' and cannot be exhibited, do not 'exist' independently.

The deictic method, which in contrast to the method of definition seeks to seize the sense perceptually given, must expressly or not appeal to the sense organs in order to 'show' in some way what may be sensed and what is sense-perception. The 'I' which givenness necessarily requires is the subject as something sense perceptually determined, one that can see and hear, and just that is denied to a transcendental or pure subject. The static contrast of *constituens* and *constitutum* is insufficient. Had epistemology worked out that the *constitutum* needed the *constituens*, then analysis, on the other hand, must relate the facts of consciousness – which are supposed to hold as constitutive according to the content, indeed the possibility of epistemology – to what, traditional epistemology claims is just constituted. Otherwise epistemology would advance (*vorgibt*) its brand of ideality with the naiveté that naive realism advances reality. The presentiment of that survives in Husserl's insistence on noesis and noema. It remains impotent since he submits to the taboos of epistemology, which his deepest impulses would like to bring down.

Paradoxia of Pure Intuition

Kant's Transcendental Aesthetic comes to terms with the *quid pro quo* of *constitutens* and *constitutum* by de-sensifying

---

admission of such a unity, however, yields up nothing less than the fact that sensation, in Husserl's doctrine the immediate, irreducible factual state of the transcendental ego, cannot be isolated from the sense organs at all. It would be phenomenally fused with something that cannot be expressed as a fact of consciousness. The *constituens* would be as dependent on the *constitutum* as vice versa. At this point, Husserl's analysis must cease, unless it wants to rupture the entire ἐποχή by a finding gained within it.

* ['category mistake'. Trans.]

sense-perception. His pure intuition ceases to have anything to do with intuition. The reference of the given to something always already constituted descends in Kantian terminology to expressions such as the constantly recurring one that objects are given to 'us'.[26]

The contradiction between this and the doctrine of the object as mere appearance has been an obstacle since Maimon. For philosophers have not become aware of the implicit admission of 151 the bounds of a priority on that *constitutum* whose constitution should realize a priorism. But at the heart of Kant's attempt at reconciliation there abides a paradoxicality, which epitomizes the irresolvable contradiction. The contradiction is linguistically indicated by the nomenclature 'pure intuition' for space and time. Intuition as immediate sense-certainty, as givenness in the figure of the subject, names a type of experience, which precisely as such cannot be 'pure' and independent of experience. Pure intuition is a square circle, experience without experience. It would be of little help to interpret pure intuition as a loose turn of phrase for the forms of intuition purified of all specific content. The fact, rather, that Kant vacillates in the Transcendental Aesthetic between the expressions 'form of intuition' and 'pure intuition', attests to the inconsistency of the situation. Despairingly he wishes to reduce immediacy and a priority to a common denominator in a single blow, while the concept of form, as referred to some content, itself already presents a mediation, something categorial so to speak. Pure intuition as immediate and not conceptual would indeed itself be sense perceptual, viz. 'experience'. Pure sensibility, siphoned off from any relation to content, would no longer be intuition, but rather 'thought'. A form of sensibility which merits the predicate 'immediate' without, however, also being 'given', is absurd.

The forms of sensibility are so emphatically contrasted by Kant with the categories – among which Aristotle had indiscriminately included them, as Kant reminds us – only because otherwise ostensibly present and immediate givenness would be endangered in these forms. Kant would have had to concede that the 'material', with which categorial labour was supposed to deal, would itself already be pre-formed. 'Space' and 'time' as the Transcendental Aesthetic lays them out, are, in spite of all

[26] Cf. Kant, *Kritik der reinen Vernunft*, A 106.

assurances to the contrary, concepts, or in Kant's expression representations of a representation. They are not intuitive, but rather the highest universals under which the 'given' may be grasped. The fact, however, that a given independent of these concepts is not indeed possible, turns givenness itself into something mediated. So much is true in the Kantanian critique of speculative Idealism which fused the opposition of form and content. No matter can be isolated from form. Nevertheless, form is only as the mediation of matter. 152

Such a contradiction expresses a comprehension of non-identity and the impossibility of capturing in subjective concepts without surplus what is not of the subject. It expresses ultimately the breakdown of epistemology itself. The entire conception of the Schematism is objectively motivated by the fact that Kant eventually became aware of the categorial essence of what he calls sensibility. By letting what he held in the beginning to be the raw material of cognition be pre-formed by an 'art concealed in the depths of the human soul',[27] he can declare the similarity between categorial form and sensible content without which the two 'breeds' of cognition would simply not go together.

The doctrine of the Schematism tacitly retracts the Transcendental Aesthetic. For if in fact the Transcendental Aesthetic did function as the architecture of the system prescribes, then the transition to the Transcendental Logic would be a miracle. If, however, pure sensibility remained consistent to the programme of the Aesthetic and were dispossessed of its material, then it would also be reduced to something merely thought, a bit of the Transcendental Logic. We could not understand how thought supervenes at all. Kant himself, who contests the conceptual nature of space and time,[28] still does not get over the fact that space and time cannot be represented without spatial and temporal things. To that extent they are not intuitive, not 'sensible'. This aporia forces the contradictory assertions that space and time are, on the one hand, 'intuitions'[29] and, on the other, 'forms'.

[27] Ibid. A 141/B 180.
[28] Cf., e.g., ibid. A 56/B 81 and A62/B 87.
[29] Cf., e.g., ibid. A 56/B 81.

Matter as Fulfilment

In Husserl as in all philosophical jargon, the concept of givenness is equivocal. It contains both the moments of the life of consciousness in sense-perception and those having a symbolic function, or in Husserl's terminology, 'acts'. This equivocality arises in the
153 need to contrast the given to naturalistic concepts as well as to speculative caprice. It also makes apparent that the *ens concretissimum* of epistemology, the components of impressions or 'sensations' are themselves already abstractions. They never occur pure and independent of categorial moments, and can only be forcefully extracted from the complexes of consciousness at the cost of the state-of-affairs, givenness as such.

The analysis of consciousness cannot handle completely the dialectic of the concept of givenness. That dialectic reverberates in Husserlian formulations like the one that the stream of consciousness is constituted in the 'duality and unity of sensile (*sensuelle*) ὕλη and intentional μορφή'.[30] Now priority goes to the latter. 'Intentionality, apart from its puzzling forms and stages, resembled also a universal medium which in the last resort includes within itself all experiences, even those that are not characterized as intentional.'[31] The relation thus inverts the entire nominalistic tradition, and that type of dissection of consciousness whose ruling idea is that representations are something like faint copies of sensations. In that way Husserl accommodated epistemology to Platonic realism about logic and its assertion of the independence of universal concepts from abstraction.

For Husserl the material moment is, even in the process of cognition of content, not really the substratum of cognition but rather the sheer function of the spiritual moment, an accident. Equally, however, his positivistic composition of consciousness out of strata or classes of lived experience prevents him from thinking the mediation of immediacy which is implied in his own thesis of the priority of intentionality. Instead he just inverts the static hierarchy of traditional epistemological classes, without impugning the classes themselves. What the tradition took to be first, viz. sensation, Kant's 'material', becomes last for him, a

[30] *Ideen* [172]; cf. *Ideas*, p. 227.
[31] Ibid. [171]; and ibid. p. 226.

τέλος cited by the progress of knowledge, the ultimate 'fulfilment' of intentions.[32] The genuinely immediate material moment in complex perception appears to Husserl (for whom, of course, perception is an immediate knowledge of its object) as just subsequently supervenient.

The demand for the 'verification' (*Verifizierung*) of an act of perception – which as such succumbs to error – by the corrobora- 154 tion of expectations inherent to perception, leads to confusing the test of knowledge with its motivation. After the primacy of intentionality tendentially removed the concept of sensation, the fulfilment of the intention was supposed to join the lost matter back on. What is absurd about that is that perception indeed, as consciousness of something, is included among intentional acts, but thereby requires a new moment, viz. that of fulfilment, which on Husserl's theory, however, can be realized by nothing other than perception itself.

Husserl assigns a key role to this paradoxical concept of fulfilment. He defines evidence as fulfilment, and it functions for him as the criterion of truth.

The concept of corroboration (*Bestätigung*) relates exclusively to positing acts in relation to their positing fulfilment, and ultimately to their fulfilment through percepts. To this last pre-eminent case we now give closer consideration. It is a case in which the ideal of adequation yields us evidence (*Evidenz*). We speak somewhat loosely of evidence whenever a positing intention (specifically an assertion) is corroborated in a corresponding, fully accommodated percept, even if this be no more than a well-fitting synthesis of coherent single percepts.*

Thus perception as 'positing intention' should literally be fulfilled, corroborated and made evident through perception, which equivocally modulates into its second, hyletic meaning, while Husserl anxiously avoids the concept of sensation. Phenomenological doctrine earns a decisive advantage from the trivialization of the hyletic moment as mere 'corroboration' of

---

* Husserl, *Logical Investigations*, II, ii, p. 121; cf. Findlay, p. 765. Perception itself, however, was already expressly defined as fulfilment (cf. ibid. p. 116; and Findlay, p. 761).

[32] Cf. ibid. [300] and passim; and ibid. pp. 368 ff, esp. in the chapter 'Phenomenology of Reason'.

perception for its intensive endeavour to let vanish the heterogeneous moment wherein eidetic a priorism has its limits. Since it
is an essential law of meaning (*Meinen*) to demand fulfilment,
then fulfilment is also displaced to the realm of essence.

155   Facticity, the 'impure', whatever is opaque to reason in
producing the most obstinate resistance, i.e. with the foundation
of the reality of objecthood, is sublimated into something prog-
nosticated by reason, and thus ultimately a mere determination of
reason. If the sheer 'fulfilment' of the ὕλη of cognition were ever
to come out of itself, then the ὕλη would present itself faintly
reduplicated as a component of the categorial apparatus, a
mechanism for the progressive adjustment of consciousness to a
something which through this very treatment was analysed out.
The theory of fulfilment proves itself to be completely viciously
circular in that fulfilment is expected of the 'object' which
perception gives or presents as something present.[33] If, however,
the present thing of perception were, according to Husserl's
theory, not just ὕλη but rather something itself already
'categorized', viz. meant through intention, then the fulfilment of
perception as intention would be completed by the sense of this
intention and not by sensation. Phenomenological consciousness,
in seeking the *quid* to which it is related, always runs back into
itself.

When Husserl seeks to bring a halt to the infinity of reciprocally
grounding intentions, he gets caught up in the hall of mirrors of
intentions. His Sisyphean task of determining matter through
intention just becomes a further pretext for denying the ontological difference. Husserl's epistemology allies an analysis of consciousness oriented towards the 'things' – in this case the
progress of inconclusive meaning (*Meinen*) towards evidence –
with the absolutization of mind. The non-identical, with whose
treatment cognition begins according to older idealism and
positivism, is banished to the furthest bounds of cognition like
savages in the self-satisfied civilization of imperialism. Also
banished, however, is the critical motif, the decision about
existence, from epistemology. The fact that the conception of
fulfilment is demanded by the essential structure of consciousness as well, and thus mentally, is meant to compensate

---

[33] Cf. *LU* II, ii, p. 116; and Findlay, p. 761.

epistemology. It extracts itself from what it adds on to this structure as factical and non-mental, what, in Kantian terminology, is attached to the sheer concept. It thus extracts itself, *156* however, from the genuine question of right for knowledge.

Philosophy substitutes for its claim to discover the rightness and wrongness of judgements of content, a sketch of apophantic forms in which 'fulfilment' as well finds its modest place. The primacy of intentionality destroys, through endless protests of concrete plenitude, the relation of philosophy to the real, and permits a risk-free but non-binding phenomenology of all and everything, not so unlike the relativism which the Prolegomena was supposed to bring to ruin.

Sensation and Perception

The primacy of intentionality obscures the difference between it and the non-intentional. Indeed both moments do interpenetrate in truth. In the second volume of the *Logical Investigations*, Husserl will do justice to that through the concept of animation of complexes of sensations.

Sensations plainly only become represented objects in psychological reflection: in naive, intuitive representation they may be components of the lived experience of representation, parts of its descriptive content, but are not at all its objects. The perceptual representation arises in so far as an experienced complex of sensations gets informed by a certain act-character, one of conceiving or meaning. To the extent that this happens, the perceived object appears, while the sensational complexes are as little perceived as is the act in which the perceived object is as such constituted.[34]

If, on the other hand, the corresponding issue is the 'content of sensation', then phenomenological flexibility establishes, along with conservation of the traditional concepts, a highly consequential confusion. The concept of sensation becomes nugatory as soon as sensation is supposed to have a content, i.e. in some sense 'mean' something, and yet it is defined as $\ddot{v}\lambda\eta$, as absolute content. Husserl's concept of intentionality is total, but the

---

[34] *LU* II, i, p. 75; cf. ibid. pp. 309 ff.

difference of sensation and intentionality is not criticized by him as such and that weighs most heavily on his conception of the moment of matter. There results a *quid pro quo* between sensation and perception thanks to which immediate certainty secured by sense-impressions is bound up with the objecthood assumed in Husserl's conception of intentionality.

While Husserl classifies sensation along with 'functional problems' and makes it dependent on intention as 'fulfilment', i.e. turns it into perception and the 'giving' of objecthood, perception, on the other hand, gets turned into sensation in the name of simple sense-presence. Just to avoid the faculty psychology of the eighteenth century, the 'mythology of activities', he obeys the no less mythical command to stare fixedly at 'states-of-affairs' whenever their concept is· inadequate. Such staring magically transforms all becoming into being. Perception, which Husserl himself regards as an act, is transformed into the practically passive having of the object as a completed vis à vis towards consciousness. 'All thought of activity must be rigidly excluded',[35] even when (as in all thinking) spontaneity, an action of the subject itself, belongs to the phenomenological 'state-of-affairs'.

For the sake of the purification of the phenomenologically 'observed' from activity, perception is reduced to the passivity of absolute immediacy, translated back, so to speak, into sensation, though more cognitive performance is demanded of it than of sensation. But if intention means something 'itself',[36] as Husserl would have it, this self nevertheless does not thereby become something immediate like sensation. That would be the confusion of symbol and symbolized. Husserl's theory of perception, however, becomes guilty of that. It asserts that the 'itself' which is meant in perception is an absolute ultimate and immediate, though the expression 'itself' in the first instance just denotes logical identity. Thus it asserts that an act applying to an 'itself', for example, does not express as its meaning syntheses which establish this self.

Nothing should thereby be pre-judged as to whether this 'itself' would be a primary fact of consciousness or merely constituted (*stiften*). Husserl says,

[35] Ibid. p. 379; and ibid. p. 563.
[36] Cf., e.g., ibid. p. 20; and ibid. p. 264.

Perception, so far as it claims to give us the object 'itself', really claims thereby to be no mere intention, but an act, which may indeed be capable of offering fulfilment to other acts, but which itself requires no further fulfilment.[37]

That would be the negation of its act character; it would be *158* literally immediate knowledge. Hence the elementary case of perception of things could apprise of the fact that, in order to be cognition, this perception needs 'fulfilment' just as much as do other 'higher' acts. If one perceived a building in German cities after the Second World War from a strict frontal perspective, then one quite often had to go around to the side in order to know whether one really saw a building or simply the intact wall of a demolished structure. Husserl did not consider such a possibility. Perception of things, the consciousness of something mediated, remains in *Ideas* 'originary' and thus unmediated.

Conversely, starting from any lived experience which has already the character of such a modification, and remains then always so characterized in itself, we are led back to certain original lived experiences, to 'impressions' which exhibit experiences that in the phenomenological sense are absolutely originary. Thus perceptions of things are originary experiences in relation to all memories, fantasy presentifications and so forth. They are originary in the sense in which concrete lived experiences can be at all. For closer inspection reveals in their concreteness only one, but that always a continually flowing absolutely originary phase, that of the living 'now'.[38]

The connective 'thus . . . are', classifies perceptions of things under 'impressions' and thus effaces the distinction between sensation and perception. The consequences of such an apparently insignificant turn can hardly be over-stressed. For the fantasm of immediate knowledge of the mediated, which such a turn called up, remained the condition for the possibility, however inexpressible, of every subsequent revival of a metaphysics of being which takes itself to be dispensed from critique. Critique means nothing other than the confrontation of judgement with the mediations inherent to judgement.

[37] *LU* II, ii, p. 56; and ibid. p. 712.
[38] *Ideen* [149 ff]; cf. *Ideas*, pp. 202 ff.

Antinomy of the Doctrine of Perception

In Kantian terminology, perception is 'empirical consciousness, that is, a consciousness in which there is also sensation'.[39] Corresponding to this is Husserl's definition from the first Logical Investigation of volume 2. '. . . the essential mark of perception lies in the intuitive persuasion that a thing or event is itself before us for our grasping.'[40] Like Kant, Husserl contrasts perception and sensation, though in a certain way the latter is supposed to be 159 'contained' in the former. This leads to an even greater blindness to the opposition between perception as an intentional act – and thus immediate knowledge – and the immediacy of sensation. According to the sixth Logical Investigation, 'the cognitive act in lived experience is based on the act of perception,'[41] and later 'Perception as presentation so interprets the presenting content, that with and in this content the object appears as given itself'.[42]

But what can 'self-givenness' mean when the self-given and thus the immediate is given only 'with and in' something else, i.e. is given as mediated? Hence Husserl's doctrine of perception leads to a flagrant antinomy. In spite of the object's pure 'self-presentation' and thus immediate givenness, it is supposed to be distinct from the 'act', meant and mediated by it. And that would be possible only if the object were posited in itself before all critical analysis. As 'intentionality' and thus the priority of pure fact-free thought over all matter and everything existing increases, so does the alienation of the subjectively intended object from what intends or thinks.

In the sixth Logical Investigation, phenomenology turns its own delusion into a programme. In the analysis of perception Husserl wants to 'deliberately ignore categorial forms'.[43] Perception, however, which, according to historical usage, is always related to objecthood, can be understood (once naive realism has been rejected) only as a performance of thought, or as Kant would put it, as 'apprehension in intuition' or categorization. If categorial forms are subtracted, all that is left is sheer ὕλη.

[39] Kant, *Kritik der reinen Vernunft*, A 166/B 207.
[40] *LU* II, i, p. 34; cf. Findlay, p. 278.
[41] *LU* II, ii, p. 25; cf. ibid. p. 689.
[42] Ibid. p. 83; and ibid. p. 734.
[43] Ibid. p. 15; not in Findlay.

Naive realism would save the character of immediacy and pre-categoriality for perception, but it would also rupture immanence to consciousness on whose analysis the claim to certainty on the part of epistemology is grounded. The insistence on the categorial role in perception for epistemology certainly would remain immanent and 'critical'. But it would sacrifice immediacy and thus the claim of perception to originally and absolutely ground transcendent being in pure immanence.

Husserl, however, wants to have the one and not forego the other. Hence he does not theoretically resolve the antimony and so all the more falls victim to it. Since he chases after the phantom *160* of a simple first, though the analysis of 'pure consciousness' never leads to it, he must follow its proper concept and turn the first into a second and the second into a first. The structure of his epistemology, however, consists in unremitting effort to correct those contradictions through the introduction of auxiliary concepts, which are created from the misery of logic, and yet must always come forward as descriptions of states-of-affairs. This prescribes to phenomenology the fundamental law according to which it must constantly rediscover objects, regions and concepts, perhaps according to the model of mathematics, so that it may next describe and analyse them in the *gestus* of the disinterested observer or deeply moved discoverer.

Sensation and Materialism

Husserl falls into the difficulties of perception theory because, like Kant's successors, he wished to divest himself of ὕλη as an element heterogeneous to consciousness. Thus among the impulses of his philosophy the idealistic one gains the upper hand. But the thesis of the interlacing of perception with sensation also makes clear the knowledge that even sensation does not generate that absolute first which Husserl's epistemology seeks. Indeed sensation, the lowest level of the traditional hierarchy of mind, as of the Husserlian phenomenologically pure consciousness, marks a threshold. The material element simply cannot be rooted out of it. Bordering on physical pain and organic desire, it is a bit of nature which cannot be reduced to subjectivity.

But sensation does not become pure immediacy through the somatic moment. The insistence on the mediacy of each and every immediate is the direct model of dialectical thought as such, and also of materialistic thought insofar as it determines the social pre-formedness of contingent individual experience. But dialectic, therefore, has no materialistic foundation in sheer sensation, for sensation, despite its somatic essence, is completely diluted of full reality through the reduction to subjective immanence. If it were true that material reality extends into so-called 'conciousness' only as sensation and 'sense-certainty', then all the more would objectivity be turned into a categorial performance of the subject, a 'supplement', at the cost of the concept of a social reality prescribed to the isolated subject and comprehending it.

161

Understanding the subjective mediacy of sensation, on the other hand, leads to the reciprocal impossibility of thinking the mediated ego as pure; it can only be thought as spatio-temporal and thus once again as a moment of objectivity. The mediation of sensation in the subject is anything but purely ontological. The subject, without which there could be no question of sensation, is itself already *mondain* just to be capable of sensation. Its proper concept transcends the sphere of pure immanence in which the abstract concept of sensation remains imprisoned. The dialectic, on the other hand, cannot be resolved in the object either. Subjectivity pervades the object as a determination of difference and the question of the share of the two is not to be settled generally and invariably.

Only the critique of abstract sensation as well as the abstract 'ego cogito' and being in general makes room for a movement of the concept which is as little prejudiced by the thesis of the identity of subject and object as by that of their rigid dualism. But it does not follow that one would automatically break out of idealism as the simple conclusion of critique. Neither can the immediate moment of sensation be isolated from mediation, nor as in the post-Kantian Idealists, can mediation be isolated from the moment of immediacy. Sensation is not to be sublimated (*verflüchtigen*) in 'spirit'. That would be spiritualism and ideology. It should rather be checked by the constraint that if mediation and immediacy are split off from one another, one moment or the other would be absolutized.

Epistemology as Elementary Analysis

The two equally problematic concepts of perception and sensation generally obtain only within an 'analysis of elements', hence only if consciousness is analysed into its components, and the classificatory divisions (as a distinction between the 'faculties' of sensibility and understanding) are naively allotted to analysed consciousness in itself. If ever this habit of thought is criticized, then the binding qualifications of the two concepts can no longer be defended. No sheer sensation can be detached from perception in the real life of consciousness. The two can be distinguished 162 only by dint of a theory which posits sensation as a placeholder for the thing-in-itself.

On the other hand, however, individual perceptions are also not the source of justification for cognition. The foundational role which epistemology unjustly attributes to sensation cannot be arbitrarily transferred to the next higher level of consciousness. Perception as consciousness of each object, as rudimentary judgement, is for its part exposed to disillusion and not incontrovertibly there. Sensation occurs as little without perception as perception does without sensation (provided it is not entirely nugatory). If one were to turn seriously to experience and not to its surrogate in the philosophy of immanence, then one would encounter a 'perception as such' as little as a sensation as such. The fact that someone 'perceives this house' and nothing else occurs only in epistemological colloquia. The triviality of such examples says something about the inadequacy of epistemology to cognition. Of course, the concept of perception is just an expedient, devised simply to reconcile the demand for the originary with the fact that consciousness is not composed out of the partial moments into which epistemology must analyse it, in order to reproduce plausibly the world out of the closed structure of immanence. Epistemology could do that only if it were to have everything out of which the world is formed together in consciousness like a basket.

No philosophy of immanence can do without the Cartesian completeness axiom from the *Discourse on Method*.[44] Hence

---

[44] Réné Descartes, *Oeuvres philosophiques de Descartes*, ed. Ferdinand Alquié (Garnier, Paris, 1963), vol. 1 (1618–37), p. 587; cf. Elizabeth S. Haldane and

everything in the forms of consciousness must be provided for, ultimately even what is not itself form. Yet only the countable is complete, the sum of individual parts. Only thought which ceases to identify cognition with its subject could get by as the canon of cognition without the completeness of subjective forms of consciousness and would no longer need to add together experience out of the parts of the process of cognition. Until then all talk of entirety is twaddle.

'Gestalt'

Phenomenology's exigency that the epistemological classification of the facts of consciousness not be descriptively corroborated in 163 the 'experience of consciousness', moved authors like Scheler to transpose Gestalt theory from the psychology of perception into philosophy.[45] And Gestalt theoreticians themselves, notably Köhler, have supported him in this. The universal priority of the whole over its parts is supposed to settle the antinomies of classificatory analysis of consciousness.

Yet, whatever the psychological profits of Gestalt theory may be, from an epistemological point of view, the concept of Gestalt also has aporias. Abstraction, which effects the division into sensations* and reflections* is, together with the false consciousness it brings along with it, dictated by the reduction to subjective immanence. If social alienation through spirit is ever ratified by the theoretical split between subject and object, and if the cognitive subject must despairingly exert itself to set right a cosmos 'out of joint', as Hamlet says, then its 'material' is no whole, but rather just the ruins which the split left behind. With

---

* [In English in the text. Trans.]

G.R.T. Ross, tr., *The Philosopical Works of Descartes*, vol. 1, 'Discourse on the Method of Rightly Conducting the Reason and Seeking for Truth in the Sciences' (Cambridge University Press, Cambridge, 1968), p. 92.

[45] Cf., e.g., Max Scheler, 'Die deutsche Philosophie der Gegenwart', in *Deutsches Leben der Gegenwart* (Berlin, 1922), pp. 191 ff; *Vom Ewigen im Menschen*, 4th ed. (1954), p. 250; *Wesen und Formen der Sympathie*, 5th ed. (Frankfurt, 1948), pp. 29 and 284; *Wissensformen der Gesellschaft* (Leipzig, 1926), passim, esp. pp. 375 ff; and tr. Peter Heath, *The Nature of Sympathy* (Yale, New Haven, 1954); and tr. Bernard Noble, *On the Eternal in Man* (SCM Press, London, 1960).

Gestalt we suddenly recall that phenomenalism deceives – that the world is not created by the subject out of the chaotic. The task, meanwhile, of gluing the world together out of the 'facts of consciousness', under which Gestalts are then subsumed, itself already involves the principle of division. That is, all labour of the spirit deals with elements. That is the truth of the statements of the later Husserl to the effect that, if ever 'the life of consciousness is built up out of data, viz. so-called finished objects', then it does not matter whether these data are thought as 'psychic atoms' or 'acts'.

Philosophy expects nothing else from the succour of the concept of Gestalt than to free the already previously abstracted givenness from its isolation and concretize it. But if Gestalt theory correctly objects to Hume and the psychology of association that 'there are' no such things as unstructured, more or less chaotic 'impressions'* isolated from one another at all, then epistemology must not stop there. For data of the sort that epistemology cites Gestalt theory as appropriately describing simply do not exist. Living experience (*lebendige Erfahrung*) is just as little acquainted with the perception of a red 'Gestalt' 164 as it is with the ominous red percept. Both are the product of the laboratory.

Gestalt theory has been correctly reproached with wanting immediately to uncover metaphysical sense in the datum of the structure of positivistic research. It presents itself as a science without paying the price of demystification. Hence it serves to lay an ideological smokescreen for divided reality, which it claims to know as undivided and 'healthy', instead of naming the conditions of the division. Within epistemology, however, the concept of Gestalt becomes a source for errors. It makes epistemology neglect, in the name of the dominance of the whole over the parts, any insight into the reciprocal effects between the two moments and their mutual dependence. Epistemology must immediately equate the given as something elementary with the whole and hence makes as little room for mediation as does phenomenology. The very concept of the elementary is already based on division. This is the moment of untruth in Gestalt theory.

* [In English in the text. Trans.]

Thus Husserl's own stance towards it vaccilates. Atomic representations from the composition of consciousness[46] accompany Gestalt theoretical representations, such as the doctrine of 'background intuitions',[47] or that of the relative dependence of all lived experiences.[48] Husserl, the theoretician of reason, remonstrates against the irrationalistic implications of Gestalt theory, which he felt may compromise the reception of his own doctrine, though the insistence of the analyst of consciousness remained unsatisfied with the inherited classes of lived experiences of mosaic psychology.

Intentionality and Constitution

The necessary contradiction between a positivistic concept of givenness and an idealistic concept driven to the extreme of a 'pure' being, free of all empirical admixture, reaches its height in the doctrine of noesis and noema and its antinomies. Since the correlation of act and act sense is turned into the canon of the analysis of consciousness, the concept of intentionality, which is logically and meaning theoretically conceived, finds its application to traditional questions of constitution. The noetic–noematic structure, as the *a priori* of the structure of consciousness as such, is supposed to explain what had earlier been the business of transcendental synthesis and the original activity of mind.

The model of the doctrine is to be found in logical absolutism, according to which thought – as something which just grasps – confronts a state-of-affairs existing in itself with logical principles by passive 'meaning', so to speak. In order to qualify as a science also, phenomenology in all of its strata takes as a basis positive science and scientific method as valid, and yet tries to ground this foundation. It escapes the trap by avoiding any express decision about idealistic or non-idealistic beginnings and refers both 'things' and 'acts' to each other as equally justified moments. Phenomenology leaves off at their correlation and the description

---

[46] Cf. *Ideen* [149 ff and 245]; and *Ideas*, pp. 201 ff and 307; and Theodor W. Adorno, 'Die Transzendenz des Dinglichen und Noematischen in Husserls Phänomenologie' (Dissertation, Frankfurt, 1924), p. 31; in *Gesammelte Schriften* (Suhrkamp, Frankfurt, 1971). vol. 1.

[47] *Ideen* [62]; cf. *Ideas*, p. 106.

[48] Cf. ibid. [167]; and ibid. p. 221.

of their static coordination. It conceals the idealism of this procedure. Just like the species with respect to the process of abstraction, however, so is the noema a reification of the noesis, which mistakes itself as an in-itself.

The 'one-rayedness' (*Einstrahligkeit*) in which, according to the *Logical Investigations*, the act becomes aware of the species,[49] corresponds to the 'ray of vision' (*Blickstrahl*) with which, in *Ideas*, the *constitutum* or Kantian continuum is introduced as the counterpart of intention.

The noema is a hybrid of subjective immanence and transcendent objectivity. That is indicated most blatantly in the theory of judgement in *Ideas* in which the critical function belonging to every consciousness of reality, viz. existential judgement, becomes expressly 'a manner of givenness', an act-correlate which is to be assumed as such.

The whole that is formed out of [judged objects], the entire judged 'what', and in addition taken exactly with the characterization, and in the manner of givenness in which we are 'conscious' of it in lived experience, constitutes the full noematic correlate, the 'sense' (in its widest sense) of the lived experience of judgement. To put it more pregnantly, it is the 'sense in the how of its manner of givenness', insofar as this is traceable in it as a feature.[50]

Like abstraction in the doctrine of the ideal unity of the species, the performance of existential judgements and the motivating 166 process of object consciousness is in this case desiccated and emasculated into a mere result. The lack of interest on the part of the extremely objective Prolegomena in epistemology makes that evident in Husserl. He does not really deal in that text with the possibility of cognition so much as with what presents itself as a feature in the already executed.

This is, by the way, a displacement of the question such as already cast its shadow in Kant who, in the programme of the critique of reason, sought to investigate the How of the possibility of synthetic judgements *a priori* instead of that possibility itself. The neutralization of Kantian critical pretensions into the mere observation of what one may notice in acts of cognition, con-

[49] Cf. above, chapter 2, passim.
[50] *Ideen* [194 ff]; cf. *Ideas*, pp. 251 ff.

tributes essentially to the fact that Husserl's philosophy, which called itself transcendental, could ultimately without too much trouble be summoned to the denunciation of reason.

Enter Noesis and Noema

Though the term is not introduced, the concept of the noema, as things turn out, as a meant object is already touched upon before the question of its justification in the chapter on the idea of pure logic in the Prolegomena.[51] The fifth Logical Investigation of volume 2 then professes the entire doctrine of noesis and noema.

The sense-moment of colour, e.g., which in outer perception forms a real constituent of my concrete seeing (in the phenomenological sense of a visual seeing or appearing), is as much a 'lived experience' or 'conscious content' as is the character of perceiving, or as the full perceptual appearing of the coloured object. As opposed to this, however, this object, though perceived, is not itself a lived experience or conscious, and the same applies to the colouring perceived in it. If the object is non-existent, if the percept is open to criticism as delusive, hallucinatory, illusory etc., then the visually perceived colour, that of the object, does not exist either. Such differences of normal and abnormal, or veridical and delusive perception, do not affect the internal, purely descriptive (or phenomenological) character of perception.[52]

The expression 'noema' for the as such 'unreal' (*nicht reelles*) correlate itself, however, is first used in *Ideas*. In that text noesis and noema are supposed to be 'essentially related to each other' and yet 'in principle and of necessity not really and essentially one and united'.[53] The difference between relatedness and unity remains initially vague. Whatever is mutually related, is thereby united, and it would be nonsense to both assert that relatedness is a type of primordial structure and to deny that it is an internal dependence or functional articulation. The terminology caprice betrays how things in fact stand. The 'ray of vision of the ego', which is a functional element in the Kantian sense (i.e. the 'unity

[51] Cf. *LU* I, pp. 228 ff; and Findlay, pp. 226 ff.
[52] *LU* II, i, p. 348; cf. ibid. p. 537.
[53] *Ideen* [73]; cf. *Ideas*, p. 117.

of action' (*Handlung*))[54] and thus a becoming, is presented as a state-of-affairs – as being – so that it may be described and conceived as absolute givenness. That occurs in the thesis of 'correspondence'.

Corresponding at all points to the manifold data of the real noetic content, there is a variety of data displayable in really pure intuition, and in a correlative 'noematic content', or briefly 'noema' – terms which we shall henceforth be continually using.[55]

The fact that all 'acts' are the sort of lived experiences with which something is meant and thus really nothing other than the simple establishment of the term 'noesis', suborns Husserl into 'parallelizing' that something, the meant, with the meaning. Precisely because noesis and noema are unconditionally related to each other, their reference is ignored. The something is hypostatized and ultimately, like essence, constructed as something unreal and yet objectual.

The Forgotten Synthesis

The phenomenologist desperately forgets synthesis and fixates with manic obsession on the world of self-made things, a world reduced to infinity and thus phantasmagorical. Even when he encounters himself in those things, he does not recognize himself. The proscription of the other is strongest at the very point where Husserl speaks of an 'other in principle' – using a turn of phrase which surprisingly anticipates dialectical theology – as if he had escaped the structure of immanence.

The 'absolutely other', which should arise within the phenomenological ἐποχή, is, under the heel of the ἐποχή, nothing other than the reified performance of the subject radically alienated from its own origin. Thinking the other is, for the sake of its omnipotence, taboo in authentic phenomenology. All the meth- 168 odological foreplay of phenomenology ends up in the acquisition of an ostensibly 'pure' subjective region, but the subject itself is

[54] Kant, *Kritik der reinen Vernunft*, A 105.
[55] *Ideen* [181 ff]; cf. *Ideas*, p. 238.

not named. Rather that region appears, as the name suggests, to be relatively thingly and objective.

The phenomenological reduction to subjectivity believes to begin with that it can at all events manage without a concept of the subject. The representation of the subject and its activity may only pass muster in a rudimentary way, e.g. in the phrase 'ray of vision of the pure ego'. And even here the term 'ray' initially translates something functional, an activity into something fixed and linear. But though Husserl at a later point in *Ideas* – whose conclusion begins to prepare for the return to transcendental philosophy – deals with 'syntheses',[56] the concept of subjective 'spontaneity and activity',[57] which he cultivates there is completely different from original synthesis. 'Freedom' is attributed to such spontaneity as an arbitrary disposition of already constituted noemata.[58] Such freedom is the spectre of the production which Husserl forgot. The 'fiat' which he raises to a privilege of thought, comes about in a very un-Kantian manner in the already constituted opposition between the pre-given intentional object and sheer thought manipulation.

Critique of Correlation Theory

The *nervus probandi* of Husserl's theory of the ostensibly original state-of-affairs of 'correlation' is the fact that the 'phenomenological structure' of noeses is independent of whether the objects meant in noeses, viz. the noemata, exist or not. From a phenomenological standpoint, that is as long as it is not a question of the meant, hallucinations and perceptions are, as noeses, equivalent. The spatio-temporal reality of their correlates has no bearing on noeses. Even though it makes no difference for the character of our meaning acts whether they apply to the real or the unreal, the acts themselves still remain temporally determined 'psychic phenomena' and, by Husserl's own account, real events.

His expression 'lived experiences' (*Erlebnisse*), which so little harmonizes with the tone of eidetic phenomenology, is yet no

[56] Cf. ibid. [253 ff]; and ibid. pp. 315 ff.
[57] Ibid. [253]; and ibid. p. 315.
[58] Ibid.

accident. *Only* where 'lived experiences' exist as components of an intra-temporally constituted 'stream of consciousness', can 169 one ask after their phenomenological residuum at all. Over and above that, however, the assertion of the identity of the noetic stock (*Bestand*) in hallucination and perception is itself questionable, if ever more is meant than the tautology that both are noeses. According to Husserl, 'such differences . . . do not affect . . . the phenomenological character of perception'.[59]

What is common to perception and hallucination, however, is extremely abstract and isolated. Only if the singular act is observed irrespective of any relation between judgement and experience, does its character have nothing to do with what it means. But since, according to Husserl himself, 'objectifying' acts are intertwined with each other and with their correlates, their independence cannot be defended.

Only in the pathetic case of precisely hallucination can they be observed, and that thereby disqualifies itself as cognition. The fact that the hallucinatory act is sealed against its own constitution colours it as a 'phenomenological state'. It claims from the subject the acknowledgement of an absoluteness which is otherwise not peculiar to the cognitive act. It is characterized by a moment, inordinately familiar to psychiatry, of compulsiveness and non-addressibility. And insofar as it is interspersed in a not completely psychotic continuum, it is also ego-alien and inauthentic. The hallucination is lived as irresistible and yet illusory. The individual who despairingly struggles for its 'restitution', seeks in vain to reconcile the antagonistic moments of that 'act'. It is certainly never harmonious and univocal. Only an analysis which, in spite of all good intentions of descriptive faithfulness, is indifferent to the qualities of the types of consciousness, will be satisfied with the bald assertion of the fact that there is subjective perception in both cases irrespective of the reality of the object. If acts contact the reality or unreality of the object by their own phenomenological stock, however, then the claim of the independence in principle of noeses from their correlates crumbles. Ultimately, the phenomenological difference between perceptual and hallucinatory acts refers back to the existence (*Bestand*) or non-existence of what Husserl calls the 170

---

[59] *LU* II, i, p. 348; cf. Findlay, p. 537.

'hyletic core' of perception, i.e. to something non-mental. And this material component can also not be 'bracketed out' by Husserl as a constitutive mode of consciousness from the phenomenological continuum.

Pure Identity and Noematic Core

Since noeses are, so to speak, comprehended horizontally under the name 'act', i.e. simply through the feature of intentionality which is common to them all and highly abstract, and not, as in Kant, vertically derived from their function in the unity of consciousness, so Husserl shifts their unity to the sheer form of the something to which all acts are directed. The classificatory operation utimately secures for what is meant the value of an in-itself. The peculiarity of all noeses, viz. that they mean something, pays the price of passing off this something, which is given uniquely in noeses, as final and *a priori*. Absolute 'ontological' objectivity is supposed to be justified by the essence of that subjectivity which, nevertheless, re-posits the object in identity with itself by means of such a justification and revokes the absoluteness of the object.

Hence the noema is at once an in-itself and something completely mental. The assertion of such a being-in-itself remains the schema of all later ontology, though it does not exist, or, in Husserl's terminology, is not 'real' (*reell*). The representation of the logically absolute, which originated in the formal realm, is transferred to the realm of content, to transcendental logic in the Kantian sense.

Husserl now constructs things in themselves following the pattern of propositions in themselves, though they are not supposed to be things, and the polemic against psychologism runs parallel in both realms.[60] In either case he is interested in saving the objectivity of truth from the relativism which threatens all enlightenment with the regress to the subject. In either case – conforming to the tradition since Kant – the possibility of such a salvation is expected from the immersion in subjectivity itself. But the positivistic development since Kant has denigrated just that

[60] Cf. *Ideen* [265 ff]; and *Ideas*, pp. 331 ff.

immersion as 'speculative' and insisted on quasi-natural scientific research which fits the facts. That is why Husserl must for his part hypostatize the immanent object (which in Kant was the result of the interplay of the transcendental apparatus with sense content) as something encountered and halt the process of transcendental synthesis in descriptive contemplation without which the concept of an 'immanent' and in a definite sense 'ideal' object could not *171* be attained.

On the other hand, the progress of critical contemplation also radicalizes the idea of a priority. It becomes much more allergic than Kant to any trace of the factical. Thus the self-critical movement of critical philosophy extorts its own relapse into the pre-critical, viz. the assumption of dogmatic transcendence just as the transcendence of thought over experience. Both tendencies converge in the noema. In epistemology as in logic Husserl fetishizes his own forgotten thinking in the most literal understanding, i.e. in what is thought. He worships it as pure being. The noematic 'core', however, the genuine in-itself of Husserlian epistemology, is just the abstract identity of the something, that says no more and has no more content than the Kantian 'I think', out of which the noema is supposed to have 'realistically' escaped, though in truth the two just collapse together. Whatever 'qualities' are attributed to the noema, they would be, by the idealistic presupposition of the Husserlian reductions, a sheer projection of the suppressed effects of synthesis on the isolated 'as such' which is interpolated as static.

That is to be understood, e.g., in the 'Delimitation of the Essence, "Noematic Sense" 'in *Ideas*.

On the other hand, for the description of this intended bit of objecthood as such all such expressions as 'perceptively', 'recollectively', 'clearly and intuitionally', 'intellectually', 'given', are excluded – they belong to another dimension of descriptions, not to the objecthood we are aware of, but to the way in which we are aware of it. On the other hand, in the case of an appearing thing as object, it would fall again within the limits of the description in question to say: 'in front' its colour, shape, and so forth are of such and such a well-defined kind, 'behind' it has 'a' colour, but one that is 'not more closely defined', and generally in this and that respect it remains 'undetermined' whether it is thus or so.[61]

[61] Ibid. [269 ff]; and ibid. p. 335.

Under the taboo against all subjective expressions, objective ones are derived once again from an always already assumed 172 'naturalistic' thing, such as the reductions, however, simply exclude. Experiences, which were the first to determine the noema at all, are trivialized into accidents, which play into the content as its sheer 'quality' and, so to speak, recur contingently while, as in scholasticism, the quiddity of the object, the sheer form of predication, is granted autonomy. Husserl conceived qualities as external to the object and detachable from it so that he could raise the object out of the arbitrariness of experience. Thus the object itself becomes something completely empty and undetermined.

Hence the attempt to get hold of a sort of being proper to consciousness and yet transcendent in the noema fails. The Husserlian object is composed as a concoction out of qualities, logical determinations and an abstract-nugatory substratum. Perhaps we should seek the innermost epistemological drive to reification, and also the moment of unity of subjectivism and reifying thought, in the principle of abstract identity itself. As soon as predicates attach to something completely undetermined, and as soon as experience is cut off beforehand from what it refers to, then an unfitting in-itself is conceded to the referent (*dem Worauf*). Purified of every predication, it would be that nothingness into which for Hegel abstract being is converted, while this complete indeterminacy also secures the being-in-itself of the abstract point of reference from all critique. And yet as little can be made of that in-itself as of the Kantian thing-in-itself as the cause of all appearances.

To the extent that the pure moment of identity, as Husserl construes the noematic core, is nothing other than the result of abstraction from all predicates, and ultimately the pure form of thought, the construction of the noema obeys the mechanism which furnishes all being-in-itself in Husserl. The result of abstraction is broken off this construction; thought will know nothing about itself. The core of objecthood resides precisely in the predicates which Husserl separated from it in harmless imitation of linguistic usage and syntactic prejudices – not next to or under predicates as pure 'being'.

The πρῶτον ψεῦδος of the material metaphysics and existential ontologies which attach to Husserl is already posited in his formal-epistemological theorems. Being cannot be peeled off 173 objectivity in the widest sense as its innermost by the destruction of what objectivity allegedly just overlaps. What is extolled as origin is an extract and the first is a mildewed last. Objectivity falls to the share of only a complete concrete experience with all of its entanglements. The question of absolutely primary being, the predicate-free and noematic core, leads to nothing other than sheer thought functions. That thwarts Husserl's attempt to break out as well as those which were undertaken after him. They all either terminologically forbid idealism or write it off pathetically as the original sin of the Western spirit, for the name admonishes them of their own imprisonmment.

The Primacy of Objectifying Acts

The absolutization of the noematic core over its ostensibly mere predicates (which still contain what made it into an object) ultimately grounds Husserl's doctrine of the primacy of intentionality, the primacy of the 'objectifying act'. Since Husserl hypostatizes the something, the act that means the 'something' becomes for him the foundation of all cognition. In a thought whose structure fundamentally adapts itself to the primacy of reified objecthood as pre-given (*Vorgegebenen*), a primacy of object consciousness must also hold sway in such a way that every other consciousness is founded in object consciousness.

Thus results the peculiar subordination of all human consciousness which does not arise in cognition, under intentions which should be their fundamental support. Feeling and even practical behaviour are supposed to presuppose object consciousness in principle, as if object consciousness had not laboriously and unstably wrenched itself away from psychological types of reaction and blind action. The anti-psychologist Husserl panders to rationalistic psychology.

Every act, as also every act-correlate, harbours explicitly or implicitly a 'logical' factor . . . . It results from all this that all acts generally – even the acts of feeling and will – are 'objectifying' (*objektivierende*) acts, original factors in the 'constituting' of objects, the necessary sources of different regions of being and of the ontologies that belong therewith. For

example: valuing consciousness constitutes over and against the mere
thing world the typically new 'axiological' objecthood, an entity of a new
region, so far at any rate as actual doxic theses in virtue of the intrinsic
nature of the valuing consciousness generally are indicated in advance
as ideal possibilities which give prominence to sorts of objecthood with a
new type of content – values – as 'meant' or 'thought' (*vermeinte*) in the
valuing consciousness. In acts of feeling they are affectively meant; they
174 came, through actualizing the doxic content of these acts, to forms of
being meant (*Gemeintsein*) that are first doxic and then expressly
logical.[62]

That certainly holds as much truth as the fact that the split
sanctioned by the Kantian system between praxis, feeling and
cognition is in fact a simple division of labour, socially produced
'false consciousness'. No feeling is substantial which is not
inhabited by cognition and no praxis which is not justified by
theory. If *Husserl* separates the spheres and declares that the
rational is the foundation of them all, then he may point to the
current situation, the completed establishment of rationality. His
theorem may demand what certainly phenomenology as *philosophia perennis* would ultimately like to demand, suitability to the
historical instant. But then that theorem by its own sense forfeits
justification. Whatever in the psyche is not itself initially directed
at some objecthood – such as Husserl's glorified example of
perception – is also not subordinate to the primacy of the thing
which was established only in millennia of enlightenment.

Feelings and modes of behaviour do not essentially require
thing consciousness and are not a mere variant on it. Husserl's
epistemology falls into the dilemma, whenever it deals with
'intentions' whose accent does not lie on the dependence on
supposed objects. Levelling praxis down to a mere special case of
intentionality is the crassest consequence of his beginning by
reification. But if the relation of cognition to praxis were ever cut
off by the scientific postulate of cognitive purity, then 'pure'
thought itself, alienated from all doing, would also congeal into
something static, as it were, a thing.

[62] Ibid. [244]; and ibid. pp. 306–7.

Thing as Clue (Leitfaden)

The priority and special status of objectifying acts affirmed by Husserl till his revisionistic late phase, lets the constituted thing be used as a 'clue'[63] in constitutional analysis, and 'transcendental 175 structure' be read off thing consciousness. Methodologically, therefore, epistemology presupposes what, by its proper *raison d'être* it should have deduced. Indeed the noema is supposed to be neither a real component of the continuum of consciousness nor an 'unreduced' naively realistic object.

But since the correlation of noesis and noema, with the merely formal assertion of its phenomenological reducedness, reiterates precisely the 'naive' relation between thought and thing and attributes priority to the thing as the 'moment of unity', constitutive epistemology submits to reified thought. The noema becomes the camouflage (*Deckbild*) covering the only area of operations for the critique of reason. It is the placeholder for the concrete thing in pure phenomenology, and indeed represents both the old thing-in-itself and the object in the Kantian sense. The promise of a new beginning in phenomenology, together with its historical effect, clings to the illusion that the analysis of consciousness in the style of criticism is supposed to deliver what is simply beyond consciousness and escapes the structure of immanence of consciousness. Whereas the noema as what is just meant (*Vermeintes*) in acts, remains bound to the structure of immanence and is supposed to appear in ἐποχή without the risk of a naturalistic positing, it permits the straightforward interpretation of the meant (*des Gemeinten*) as being to let our meaning and the meant correspond to one another reciprocally in static ontological polarity.

Yet whenever all the characteristica of that as-such, the 'qualities' of the pure theory of objects, in which subjectivity, nevertheless, resides, are exclusively shifted to the as-such, and the consciousness of the subject, as sheer knowledge of already constituted objecthood, is contrasted to objecthood without recollection of the unity and mediation of the two, the 'complete' noema is turned into a thing as second nature. Thinking the

---

[63] Cf. ibid. [313 ff]; and ibid. pp. 383 ff.

thing, in which thinking forgets itself, becomes givenness of the thing.

But the most elementary reflection gives that the lie. All meaning is subject to error; the entire claim of self-givenness is to exclude error. Self-givenness is strictly possible only where the act and its object collapse into each other. But otherwise the object given in the act – in Husserl's own terminology as in the Hegelian which he ignores – is 'mediated'. It is 'thought' and bears within itself, even when it is thought as objective, categorial moments which cannot remove any of the operations of its 'self'. The expression 'self-givenness' is a *contradictio in adjecto*, and this is the point of Husserl's thesis.

Antinomy of the Noema

But whereas the noema – at least in the writings of Husserl's middle period which actually characterize phenomenology and are most consequential – is not considered to be constituted, but is just impaled on the isolated intention, which 'encounters' it, Husserl nevertheless does emphatically distinguish it from the thing. A most paradoxical situation arises. The reifying tendency of pure phenomenology which correlates whatever is meant and thus already completed with our meaning, directly brings about the difference from the complete thing of experience, even the Kantian thing. The meant unit, i.e. every noema and not only the universal concept, 'ideal unity of the species', evades not only corroborating or contrary experience, but also all determination in space and time as such. The 'abstractness' of the noema in the Hegelian sense, its isolating coordination with the isolated act, is entered ontologically on the credit side and ontically on the debit side.

Since what is meant here and now, which is envisioned only by the present act, does not change, this instantaneity takes on the predicate of infinity and transcends to essence. Hence the same χωρισμός opens up between the noematic object and the complete thing of experience which phenomenology otherwise so struggles to cover over. This schema of the infinitization of the referent (*Bedeuteten*), by ignoring the question of the existence of the object, whose bounds are drawn by the circumference of the ἐποχή, dominates the entire post-Husserlian development of the school. Even existential ontology is a *lucus a non lucendo*.* By circumspectly economizing with meanings alone and the appearance of their timelessness, it eliminates the question of the existence of the referent.

According to Husserl, the 'thing in nature' (i.e. what was the immanent, categorially constituted object for all of Kantianism) is fundamentally distinct from what is reduced, viz. the noema.[64] 177

The tree plain and simple, the thing in nature, is anything but this perceived tree as such [the noema], which as perceptual meaning belongs to the perception and that inseparably. The tree plain and simple can burn away, resolve itself into its chemical elements, and so forth. But the sense – the sense of this perception, something that belongs necessarily to its essence – cannot burn away; it has no chemical elements, no forces, no real properties.[65]

For such properties would, of course, devolve not upon individual intentions but rather only on their relation to the continuity of experience.

Husserl's argumentation is motivated by the difficulties of a duplicity in the consciousness of things. The idealistic notion of immanent things would have to reckon with two realities 'whereas only one of these is encounterable and possible'.

I perceive the thing, the object of nature, the tree there in the garden; that and nothing else is the real object of the perceiving 'intention'. A second immanent tree, or even an 'inner image' of the real tree that stands out there before me, is nowise given, and to suppose such a thing by way of assumption leads only to absurdity.[66]

But it certainly does not follow from the fact that the thing of transcendental idealism is immanently constituted that the tree is itself an 'inner picture' or otherwise a lived experience, i.e. that the thing is a real component of the structure of consciousness. Kant already conceived it as a law[67] and since Mach it has been

* ['A sacred grove because it has no light.' Trans.]

[64] Cf. Adorno, Dissertation, pp. 43 ff.
[65] *Ideen* [184]; cf. *Ideas*, p. 240.
[66] Ibid. [186]; and ibid. p. 243.
[67] Cf. Kant, *Kritik der reinen Vernunft*, B 163 ff.

expressly taken as a functional equation of the given, never itself as part of the given. Husserl who preaches a world of noemata and also a world of 'natural things' parallel to the first and yet radically distinct from it through the ontological difference, has the spectre of duplication to fear no less than orthodox idealism which lets this *constitutum* be meant and 'apprehended', though it may never be adequately given nor may it arise in the data of consciousness without a remainder.

The σχάνδαλον of idealism, the fact that what is subjectively created is supposed to remain an *objectum* as well, opposed to the subject, is not eliminated by Husserl either. Kant himself spoke of a paradoxicality in his own philosophy which he hoped 'to explain'[68] through the Transcendental Deduction of pure concepts of the understanding. In the *Critique of Pure Reason*, the ego constitutes things by applying categories to the sensible (*Sinnliches*). The traditional concept of truth, however, that of the correspondence (*Angemessenheit*) of knowledge to its object, remains valid. Accordingly, what the subject knows is true, if it corresponds with what the subject itself has constituted. The subject's knowledge of the objective (*Objektivem*) leads – considering the radical indeterminacy of the 'material' – right back to the subject and is thus in a certain sense tautological. The fact that thought grew accustomed to that under the authority of Kant and all the idealists and positivists who followed him, changes nothing about the senselessness of the concept of truth as one of *adaequatio rei atque cogitationes*, as soon as the sphere of the *res* appears in that of the *cogitationes*.

Now Husserl did not want to let himself be terrorized by the thesis which had been worn down to bad self-evidence that mind prescribes the laws to nature, for that thesis undermines the concept of objectivity by grounding it. But he ensnares himself in his opposition to it. On the one hand, he accommodates the idealistic desideratum in the name of the 'phenomenological reduction', but, on the other, he would like to break up the philosophy of immanence with the help of the 'simply accepting' and so 'pre-critical' consciousness of objecthood. The divorce of the reduced from the unreduced thing, of 'the tree pure and simple' from 'the percept as such', assumes thingly transcendence within the philosophy of immanence.

[68] Ibid. B 152 ff.

The discovery (*Erfindung*) of the noema is supposed to mediate between a dogmatic concept of the thing-in-itself and the criteria of idealistic philosophy of consciousness.[69] The talk of the 'tree pure and simple' is equivocal. If it applied to Kant's 'unknown cause of appearances', then assuming it could neither be made compatible with Husserl's postulate that philosophy is a 'rigorous science', nor could that transcendent x be equated with the thoroughly determined and intentionally meant. If the tree, on the other hand, were the object of experience, the Kantian object, then it would not be protected from the possibility of abolition, not even by its apotheosis as act-sense. For we would be conscious of even the 'tree percept as such' as something identical, as 'this tree' and no other. And this consciousness includes, along with spatio-temporality which counts among the determinations of its object, the possibility of its transformation and annihilation.

Since all things are 'things of thought' for idealism, their annihilation would, according to its ground rules, be as categorial as their existence. At the core of his argument, wherein genuine phenomenological method resides, Husserl makes himself guilty of the same error, in the sense of immanent critique, as the butt of his polemics. He confuses the 'real' (*realen*) factual situation of consciousness, the single intentional 'lived experience', with what it refers to. Husserl concludes from the platitude that lived experience cannot burn out that what is meant in it is protected from the vicissitudes of facticity like a Platonic Idea.

Phenomenology, which arose as a reaction to psychologistic causal observation, persists in merely negating naturalistic representations of the casual relation, and thus forfeits any adequate concept of causality at all. Stopping epistemological analysis in this way at causality is re-assessed as something more, the conquest of an absolute region, purified of spatio-temporal conditioning. That concretion and plenitude of qualities, which is supposed to assure the superiority of phenomenology over epistemological formalism, is borrowed from the complete thing of experience, which is subject to causality.

Yet, on the other hand, the shadowy fetch of that thing, the a-causal noema, helps phenomenology reach the standing of a priority. This mechanism processes findings of experience as

[69] Cf. Adorno, Dissertation, pp. 51 ff.

insights into essence, as if experience vouchsafed essence without mediation. The power of attraction of this school, viz. the unity of concreteness and essentiality, derives from the equivocity of its central concept construction that takes from both meanings what suits it and jettisons what endangers it.

Critique Dismissed

Husserl's duplication of the object as thing and as meant content 'as such', was promoted from the very beginning of the phenomenological ἐποχή, which did not actually, like Hume and Kant, criticize the so-called naturalistic concepts of thing, ego and causality, but simply neutralized them. The 'thesis of the natural attitude' is supposed to be abrogated in the course of phenomenological research, but that should 'change nothing'. For in spite of the reduction to pure consciousness, the analysis should be able to propose as its object of research everything that holds for the 'natural attitude', with the sole difference that it renounces any judgement concerning the spatio-temporal existence of what 'appears'[70] to the natural attitude. Thanks to the twilight conception of the ἐποχή the method can refrain (whenever necessary and by means of the analysis of meaning) from reverting to naturalistic concepts, without first worrying over their constitution and the proof of their justification.

Thus Husserl feels free to bring up whenever he wants that tree which, as opposed to the noema, could burn down. The restoration of pre-critical doctrines by the phenomenological school lets it literally return, in the innermost recesses of its epistemological texts, to the disappearance of critique, which from the outside the historical hour seems to conceal. Husserl already capitulates before the excess power of what is, and the infinitization of being in essence and in the noema is at once the result and concealment of this capitulation. In Kant the critique of reason was supposed to prevent shaken dogma from entrenching itself behind the claim that it is knowledge. In Husserl even that power, along with the need for such a critique, has evaporated in the completely enlightened world.

[70] Cf. *Ideen* [53 ff]; and *Ideas*, p. 97.

The only thing that escapes idealism is the apologetic moment of securing the will, the ever one's own, as an absolute. The negative moment, on the other hand, the opposition to the pretension that the man-made is absolute, turns into simple precautions to remain untainted by any facticity and its terrifying power so that the self-implanted zone of mind may remain pure. The ἐποχή 'accepts' and exhibits deeds of possession, without committing itself, as if it suspected that what belongs to the subject already no longer belongs to it.

In this precaution, however, doom overtakes it. Suspension of judgement for the sake of absolute certainty opens the door to the dogma which cannot be made compatible with such certainty. The object, as an object of sheer subjective intention without *181* reference to the ground of its justification, simply melts into such a subjectivization with unquestioningly assumed objectivity. Husserl's declaration that the ἐποχή is not to be 'confused with that which Comtean positivism demands'.[71]* is like all similar ones of his school, a sheer protestation which indicts itself by exculpating itself. Freud's characterization of negation[72] applies to it. Husserl also wants to 'bring all grounding back to the immediately encountered'.[73] Husserl's reversion, however, out of vain respect for the state of the facts, no longer can test what is encountered and what not.

But he must pay for the chance he thus gains to put his hand on the non-encountered (as if the consciousness of that were secure), by renouncing the jurisdiction of reason, which was his concern since the final chapter of *Ideas*, though it destroyed step by step the *differentia specifica* of phenomenology from that idealism from which phenomenology promised an escape through idealistic means. The resolution of phenomenological antinomies is not a choice between either revoking phenomenology transcendentally or openly avowing its latent dogmatic aspect and, for the consistency of the science of pure truths of reason – as the new ontology had been inaugurated – slandering reason.

* [The qualification 'Comtean' is missing in Adorno. Trans.]

[71] Ibid. [57]; and ibid. p. 100.
[72] Cf. Sigmund Freud, *Gesammelte Werke, chronologisch geordnet*, eds. A. Freud, E. Kris, O. Isakower (Imago, London, 1948), vol. 14, 1925–31, pp. 11–15, 'Die Verneinung'; untranslated.
[73] *Ideen* [57]; and *Ideas*, p. 100.

Antagonism to System

Those antinomies find their highest expression in the highest concept to which pure phenomenology soared, a bit *contre coeur*, that of system. Husserl, of course, mostly avoided that expression, aside from the late qualification of formal logic as a deductive system.[74] The thing, however – since the problem of constitution was referred back to the transcendental subject – was just as unavoidable as the synthetic unity of apperception in Kant was indivisible from the system of pure reason.

Husserl shares his terminological timidity with other scholastic philosophers of his period, such as Rickert and his 'open system'. Academic thinkers entrenched themselves well behind their 182 official dignity against Nietzsche's derision of the dishonesty of systems. Even they, however, could not ignore the experience, irresistible since Hegel's death, that the totality of the contents of current consciousness – so brittle and antagonistic in itself as it is disparate in its disposition in the field of the sciences – can no longer evolve out of a unified principle. For otherwise, it would be diluted into triviality, or else sheer delusion would vindicate what is just once as the product of a mind harmonious in itself and identical with itself. On the other hand, however, epistemological deliberations, with which science strives to underpin its monopoly on cognition, themselves lead necessarily to the concept of system. Otherwise, the scientific claim would remain, in Kant's words, 'rhapsodical'.[75] This contradiction is crystallized in Husserl's philosophy without moral-historical (*geistesgeschichtlich*) reasoning, i.e. immanently, from the irreconcilability of the motifs of his thought. For even where he goes beyond the sheer description of structures of consciousness and, for the sake of the 'jurisdiction of reason', practises epistemology as a sort of critique of reason, by questioning the constitution of the thing or later other egos, he holds to the postulate of a practically passive attention to the 'things'. Even the unity of the 'I think' should for him collapse into something ultimately encountered in consciousness.

Although the concept of the infinitesimal plays its role in his

[74] Cf. Logik [93]; and Cairns ⟨78 ff⟩.
[75] Cf. Kant, *Kritik der reinen Vernunft*, A 81/B 106.

later writings, Husserl never turned to functionality, either as Kant in 'practice' or with the neo-Kantians in original creation. If that means a revision of his positivistic origins, it would be for the sake of the plausibility of his attempt to restore absoluteness of spirit, which had once been speculatively attained, on the basis of science, as itself a 'scientific' result, and to grasp Hegel's speculative concept (about which he clearly knew little) in the medium of the philosophy of reflection alone. But the system just guaranteed closed transcendental unity in which Husserl had to accept all reality in order to protect it against contingency. Hence the system itself cannot come out of facticity. It cannot be simply given, and yet Husserl must attempt to interpret it as such.

He does so in the 'Transition to the Phenomenology of Reason' in *Ideas* in the name of 'pre-figuredness', which as 'idea' compre- *183* hends the totality of the 'world', while the 'essential structure' as such which contains its infinity in itself is positively given. In this context, Husserl can no longer avoid the concept of system.

For the limitation to experiencing consciousness was intended only by way of illustration, as was also the restriction to the 'things' of the 'world'. Everything, however far we stretch the framework, and on whatever level of universality and particularity we may also be moving – even down to the lowest concretions – is esentially prefigured. As the sphere of lived experience is determined in accordance with its essential and transcendental structure as rigorously conforming to law, so is every possible construction on essential lines according to noesis and noema fixedly determined, just as every possible figure that can be constructed in space is somehow determined through the essential nature of space, according to unconditionally valid dispensations of lawfulness. What on both sides is here called possibility (eidetic exist-ence) is thus absolutely necessary possibility, an absolutely firm joint in the absolutely firm structure of an eidetic system. The goal of inquiry is this system's scientific knowledge. That is, it must be stamped into theoretical form and controlled systematically through concepts and formulations of laws which spring from pure essential insight. All the fundamental distinctions drawn by formal ontology and the theory of categories attached to it – the doctrine concerning the division of the regions of being and their categories of being, as also concerning the constitution of the material ontologies that fit them – are, as we shall understand in detail as we press farther forward, the main headings of phenomenological studies. And to these, there necessarily correspond noetic–noematic systems of essences which must permit of being systematically described and determined according to possibilities and necessities.[76]

The contradiction in a concept of eidetic existence tacitly marks the phenomenological antinomy. Husserl attests that essence, which should soar above all the frailty of existence, also has a being independent of thought that can be derived from nowhere else than from an existence with which Husserl's essences 184 (*Essenzen*) will not be contaminated at any price. He qualifies one and the same thing as ontological and ontical – a preliminary version of the later doctrine of being there (*Dasein*) as the ontical thing which has the priority of being ontological,[77] in which, moreover, no less than in Husserl, the constitutive primacy of subjectivity, the old idealism, lies concealed.

Since such an 'existence' (*Existenz*) must be included in the 'absolutely firm structure of an eidetic system', it remains incomprehensible, a second-order accident. For however spiritualized an enountered thing may be, one cannot anticipate what else will be encountered beyond it, unless the 'structure', in Kantian terms, is itself already fastened onto a highest point.[78] And Husserl must forego that as long as he takes 'pure intuition of essences', whose incorrigibility rests on the characteristic of being given, to be the source of justification for concepts.

Already, however, the drive to system preponderates, and the discreetly contrasted ontologies are reduced to instructions for a sort of phenomenological division of labour. The *Cartesian Meditations* ultimately speak bluntly of the ontologies as preceding the unity of the system. Yet the system itself, as a descriptive object, a fact of the highest order, is supposed to confront the subject. But its claim to completeness, absolute immanence and independence from anything which lies outside it, the idea that it *nulla re indiget ad existendum*,* postulates the transcendental subject.

* ['needs nothing to exist'. Trans.]

[76] *Ideen* [279 ff]; and *Ideas*, p. 346.
[77] Cf. Martin Heidegger, *Sein und Zeit*, (Niemeyer, Tübingen, 1972); and tr. John MacQuarrie and Edward Robinson, *Being and Time* (Harper and Row, New York and Evanston, 1962), p. 16.
[78] Cf. Kant, *Kritik der reinen Vernunft*, B 134.

Thus the system which is 'pre-figured' according to mathematical mores functions in Husserl, who does not gratuitously concern himself with space and geometry, as a concept of indifference. Objectively it is the unity of all formal and material regions encountered, and it also functions subjectively insofar as this unity is sought in that of subjectivity itself. This non-explicit conception of an indifference between subject and object became sedimented in the opalescent concept of *prima philosophia* as transcendental phenomenology from its late period. Investigation directed to the multitude of 'phenomena' of consciousness is phenomenological; and the necessity of its grounding in every experience of a pre-ordained structure of the subject is transcendental.

A chance assumption is made that the fact that the two ¹⁸⁵ converge is self-evident. The illusion of such self-evidence is possible because the subjective moment, the phenomenologically pure ego, and the objective moment, the eidetically reduced concept, are both equally sealed off against facticity and suffice unto themselves. Neither of them can venture outside or be impinged upon from the outside. But the only thing that guarantees this purity is the transcendental. Phenomenology's self-withdrawal is no act of cautious revision horrified of the consequences, such as, e.g. Scheler's ephemeral infinities. As the noema, subjectively meant, supposedly possesses more objectivity, all the more must the subject add on from itself in order to give the object its unity. But the subject demands as its aggregate the unity of consciousness and thus the system.

Husserl's Transition to Transcendental Idealism

Historically, the first time Husserl conditioned the concept of system was not in the justification of noematic sense as persistently identical objecthood. He already demanded 'Unity of Foundational Connections' at the beginning of the Prolegomena.

The realm of truth is, however, no disordered chaos, but is dominated and unified by law. The investigation and setting forth of truths must, therefore, likewise be systematic, it must reflect the systematic connections of those truths. . . .[79]

[79] *LU* I, p. 15; cf. Findlay, p. 62.

The system is certainly initially thought as an objectivity encountered by science, to some extent heuristically and without 'clues', such as in formulations of the sort 'We have thus exhausted the essential forms of universal normative propositions'.[80] But in the unity of logical reason, which should correspond to that of logic, the system is already nascent, in a way not so different from the relation between the completeness of the forms of judgement and that of the categories in Kant. Once unfolded, the doctrine of correlation hurtles fullblown into system.

The dualism of that doctrine, the banishment of being into consciousness and vice versa is a fraud. Once philosophy proceeds to search for the title deeds for being and entities in consciousness at all, then the principality of consciousness is thereby established, even when being is adjoined as the 'opposite pole' of consciousness. The following sentence from volume 2 of the *Logical Investigations* should, therefore, be interpreted as systematic. 'What we cannot think cannot be; what cannot be we cannot think.'[81]

The echo of Hegel's formula cannot be ignored. It is the avowal of a latent likeness. Husserl attempts to reconcile subject–object dualism, not by simply reducing objectivity to subjectivity, but rather by moving to embrace the opposition itself in something more comprehensive, like Hegel's 'spirit'. And yet both ultimately re-constitute the more comprehensive as subjective. Both, despite all their attempts to be different, are idealists. But, compared to Hegel, Husserl's attempt is so timid and weak that his desired reconciliation slips away. The idea of a system shrivels up into formulas. For Hegel the system was, according to the formulation of the *Encyclopedia*,[82] a concrete totality. In Husserl it acquiesces to pure structures of consciousness connected to the εἶδος ego.

All that remains of the system is that there is no being which cannot be thought, so all being, comprehensive and complete, must be measured by the unity of thought. The still bald assertion of a correlation between being and thinking proves to be powerless. It can no longer be tested by any determinate content. As if after a defeat, philosophy retreats behind the trenches of its

[80] Ibid. p. 43; and ibid. pp. 83 ff.
[81] *LU* II, i, p. 239; cf. ibid. pp. 445 ff.
[82] Cf. Hegel, *System der Philosophie*, vol. 8, p. 60; and Wallace, *Hegel's Logic*, p. 19.

stronghold, the doctrine of the categories of thought. The assertion of a thorough constitutive priority of consciousness is not what determines Husserl's idealistic character – for that is found only in the late transcendental phase. Rather, what is definitive is its permanent claim to identity. Whenever such an identity is affirmed, viz. a monistic principle of world explanation, which by its sheer form promotes the primacy of a spirit which dictates that principle, then philosophy is idealistic. Even where, as such a principle, being is dealt out against consciousness, the priority of spirit becomes evident in the claim to the totality of the principle, which comprehends everything. What does not arise in spirit is inconclusive (*unabschliessbar*) and escapes the principle itself. Idealism reigns even when the ὑποκείμενον is called being or matter or whatever, because of the idea of the ὑποκείμενον. Total conceiving from a principle establishes the total right of thinking.

187

The theoretical bounds of idealism lie not in the content of the determination of ontological substrata or primordial expressions, but rather primarily in awareness of the irreducibility of what clings to one pole, however fashioned, of the unsublatable difference. This awareness must unfold in concrete experience. If it adheres to the abstract asseveration of polarity, then it always remains imprisoned by idealism. Today the dialectical method cannot mean a 'project'. Husserl's turn to a 'correlative' concept of being, which prepared the later theologization of that concept, had precisely an extremely idealistic sense, which that concept never abandoned. Qualifications of thought, which include even the consciousness of the difference or 'otherness', are supposed to be wrested from the abstraction of facticity by a most external measure such that otherness may be extirpated.

Husserl's ontological drift is, like Hegel's, really idealistic. Since the most universal structures of consciousness are deprived of any relations to matter, and this relation itself just returns as a formal characteristic of the structure of consciousness, the purely spiritual is installed as an in-itself and ultimately being.

Certainly Husserl deals at an earlier point in *Ideas* – and indeed before it comes to the ἐποχή – with the 'alien', 'being-other' and speaks as if consciousness can be intertwined with this and 'with the whole world alien to consciousness'.[83] Immediately

[83] *Ideen* [70]; cf. *Ideas*, p. 114.

afterwards, however, he assumes without further ado the 'real unity of the whole world'. Thus the system is erected and the supremacy of consciousness (which had first been ontologically cut off from entities) over entities is finalized. Only if the totality of entities arises in determinations of thought without remainder, is talk of such a 'real unity of the world' motivated at all. References to being-other remain a mere methodological preamble to that move. It shows itself as such in the phenomenological method of reduction to 'absolute consciousness'.[84] For consciousness is only absolute as long as it ceases to tolerate any otherness which is not just proper to consciousness – and thus not otherness at all.

Fragility of the System

But the system which will not be speculative so much as a 188 scientific establishment of factual states drags the contradiction further. The legitimization of the systematic claims of *Ideas* founders. In the unity of the consciousness of things and only there does Husserl maintain his canon of systematically lawful cognition.

Among the essential necessities of an empirical consciousness of a self-same thing, which is a consciousness of 'all sides' and is continually confirming itself as unified in itself, is a multifarious system of continuous manifolds of appearance and adumbration in which . . . all the moments of objecthood occurring in perception, which have the character of bodily self-givenness, present (viz. adumbrate) themselves in definite continuities. Every determinacy has its own system of adumbrations; and for every determinacy, as for the thing as a whole, the following obtains, namely, that it remains one and the same for the comprehending consciousness that unites recollection and fresh perception synthetically together, despite interruption in the continuity of the course of current perception.[85]

That completely corresponds, aside from the unmistakable psychological concept of adumbration (*Abschattung*) to Kant's

---

[84] Cf. ibid. [91 ff]; and ibid. p. 136.
[85] Ibid. [74 ff]; and ibid. p. 118.

deduction of thingliness. What is missing, however, is the unity of consciousness, which is as such never 'given', and which in Kant renders possible the unity of the thing. Husserl glides over it as something which itself cannot be grasped descriptively. But without that unity the assertion that the 'adumbrations' and thus appearances of the thing are 'continuously ordered'[86] by the identity of the thing, would be dogmatic. After the phenomenological reduction, Husserl cannot derive this identity from things in themselves. As Kant stringently objected to empiricism, such a 'rule' does not present itself as an immediately given.

Husserl must forego deriving that identity, however, as long as he does not want to damage his 'principle of all principles'. The 'system' can just as well be different for sheer description. Its unity and thus the systematic claim is arbitrary. That, however, is incompatible with the idea of the system itself. In *Ideas* Husserl took that into account, by re-interpreting the indeterminacy of the consciousness of things and thus its incomplete character,[87] exposed to the arbitrariness of experience, as the 'determinability of a rigidly prescribed style',[88] and turning, in a neo-Kantian fashion, the thing as the system of its possible appearances into an endless task. 'To remain incomplete *in infinitum* after this 189 fashion is an unsublatable essence of the correlation, "thing" and thing perception.'[89]

Precisely where the neo-Kantian concept of law is due, the term 'style' turns up, just as late relativistic sociology of knowledge deals with styles of thought. It is avoided in practically aesthetic categories, which remove the unity of the object from the criterion of its objective binding force, and yet grant it the value of the encroachingly prescribed. Linguistic scars attest to the incompatibility of system and sheer encounterability.

[86] Ibid. [75]; and ibid. p. 119.
[87] Cf. ibid. [80]; and ibid. p. 124.
[88] Ibid.
[89] Ibid.

4

Essence and Pure Ego

Die Phantasie in meinem Sinn
Ist diesmal gar zu herrisch.
Fürwahr, wenn ich das alles bin,
So bin ich heute närrisch!

Fantasy in my sense has gone too far this time. Truly, if I
am all that, I'm really a fool.

Goethe*

Husserl and his Successors

Official academic discussion in Germany held even before Hitler that Husserl had been surpassed and had faded from importance. Although he may have been given credit for the method of the new ontological concreteness, which was supposed to overcome an idealism fallen into disrepute, his service seemed to the condescending estimation as fortuitous as the modest contributions of an empirical scientist to a metaphysical project. On the other hand, Husserl seemed to be very much a metaphysician to the representatives of philosophical scientism, such as Schlick in his *Allgemeine Erkenntnislehre*. He appeared a prophet of that 'insight' (*Schau*) as was depicted less by his own texts than by the poetry of George. He had to share with other theoreticians of reason, Hegel not excepted, the cheap predicate of 'mystic'.

The former reproached him as a formalist epistemologist, devoid of care for human existence as they interpreted it, viz. the

---

* [The Idealist in 'Walpurgisnachtstraum', *Faust*, erster Teil, *Gesamtausgabe*, vol. 9 (DTV, Munich, 1962), p. 128; cf. tr. Barker Fairley (University of Toronto Press, Toronto and Buffalo, 1970), p. 76. Trans.]

essence of man as existence *(existierenden)*. The latter assimilated the doctrine of ideation to vitalism and irrationalism, however obstinately Husserl may have bristled at such company since the appearance of the sixth Logical Investigation.

And yet for his part Husserl did nothing to deserve the fate that new objectivity *(neue Sachlichkeit)** and new non-objectivity reserved for him. He so conscientiously joined the game of 'discussion' with his colleagues, that, after Natorp's critique of *Ideas*, his difference from the apparently polar opposite neo-Kantianism of Marburg shrank to a nuance. He considered each *191* philosopher a 'researcher', and made his deliberations public for the sake of the 'rootedness in principles of the sciences',[1] but not for the management and function of what were 'radically' threatened in his view as well.

Husserl's ontological, anthropological and existential heirs are just as little justified in disowning the antecedent of their thought property. They are beholden to Husserlian method, and not to the method alone. This method was just so thoroughly covered over with bourgeois circumspection and critical responsibility that those disciples were simply unwilling to recall Husserl. That is true for Scheler as much as for Heidegger. It did seem in *Being and Time* that Kierkegaard's concept of existence had undone the posture on the part of the 'observer' in which the phenomenologist felt himself vindicated.

But one may count among the surprising results of more recent studies of Husserl that some principal themes of *Being and Time* are already assembled in the works of the teacher, though academically scored. Common to both, to begin with, is that no assertion is bound by 'the things themselves'. Just as the confrontation of any Husserlian concept with its object can be quashed by alluding to the fact that the concept obtains in the ἐποχή alone and not 'naively' in the world of facts *(Fakten)*, so any more drastic interpretation of Heideggerian theses about dread, care, curiosity and death were obviated even before the 'conversion' *(Kehre)*. For it is supposed to be a question of pure ways of being of being there *(Dasein)*. However striking and close to experience Heidegger's pronouncements may be, they simply do

* [Allusion to the *neue Sachlichkeit* movement in art. Trans.]

[1] *Logik* [7]; cf. Cairns ⟨3⟩.

not connect to the reality of society. Both Husserl and Heidegger let the breach between necessity and contingency disappear by beginning with the principle of the ego which Husserl called the transcendental ego and Heidegger being there (*Dasein*). In both philosophies there is an interplay of idea and fact. Heidegger's tendency to camouflage irresolvable contradictions, like those between timeless ontology and history, by ontologizing history itself as historicality and turning the contradiction as such into a 'structure of being' is prefigured in Husserl's epistemology. Husserl also sought to hypostatize irresolvability as a solution to the problem.

Husserl tried in his old age to get over the split between essence and existence (*Dasein*), with the same bold stroke as Heidegger who determines being there (*Dasein*) as a structure of being. In *Formal and Transcendental Logic*, Husserl says:

192

a life of consciousness is inconceivable, except as a life given originally in an essentially necessary form of facticity, the form of universal temporality.[2]

Fact is supposed to be sublated in essence, for facticity, viz. the discovery that facts with specific temporal loci make up the content of the 'pure ego', passes as a law of essence, as a thoroughly formal qualification of this very ego. The substructuring (*Substruktion*) of the form 'facticity' should be sufficient to master the fact itself by means of transcendental lawfulness of essence, without the theory conceding that the difference between formal 'facticity' and the particular fact with content, is identical with the old essence/fact difference. The name 'facticity', the universal concept which subsumes facts as facts, is magically transformed into an essence, which obstinate facts should no longer resent, even though the content of the 'essence' facticity may not be directly derived from pure necessities of essence. Drowning phenomenology seeks to pull itself out of the swamp of contemptible mere existence (*Dasein*) by its own essential bootstraps. Such a fraud provides the factual foundation for the linguistic correspondence with Heidegger. In both, concepts drawn from experience are repeatedly disguised with an antique

---

[2] Ibid. ⟨279⟩; not in German edition.

dignity by transplantation into the eidetic realm. This dignity should secure them from the clutches of the same raw life, to which they conversely owe the very palpability which corrupts those weary of abstraction. There appear repeatedly in both, on the other hand, purely formal determinations in a way which simulates their drastic perspicuity. In neither case are 'project', 'genuineness' and 'self-interpretation' gratuitous pet words.

Husserl occasionally calls the formation of a theory 'thorough-going work'[3] as if it were a question of blessed artisanship. Transcendental synthesis is not pondered through an honest foreign term, but rather translated into the term of art 'interiority of execution' (*Innerlichkeit des Leistens*). That is how formal *193* constatations reappear, such as arbitrary repeatability or critically unreflected cognizing, expressed in material particles such as 'ever' (*je*) or 'directly' (*geradehin*). In Husserl's pet discussions of the universal plague in which humanity dies off without the slightest danger threatening the phenomenological residuum, viz. the pure ego, one may even perhaps discern preliminary forms of that nihilism of the early Heidegger, which is both hostile to man and pointless, and indulged in being towards death and the negating nothingness.

Phenomenology Attempts to Break Out

The paradoxical complexes of both thoughts and language in late Husserl are the expression of a failure. But this failure is the measure of Husserl's philosophical importance, of an intransigence of thought which drives to absurdity its own attempt to turn the idealism of the epoch away from its presuppositions without impugning those presuppositions. In phenomenology, the bourgeois spirit strives mightily to break out of the prison of the immanence of consciousness, the sphere of constitutive subjectivity, with the help of the same categories as those implied by the idealistic analysis of the immanence of consciousness. Epistemology would like to penetrate the cells in which the world of self-made objects as an illusory image of 'nature' posits itself absolutely by means of its direct reducibility to subjective 'performance' (*Leistung*) – viz. labour.

---

[3] *Ideen* [314]; cf. *Ideas*, p. 385.

Much can be learned from both the attempt and the failure. The attempt indicates that advanced bourgeois self-consciousness can no longer be satisfied with that fetishizing of abstracted concepts in which the world of commodities is reflected for its observer. This consciousness would have to grasp the things themselves. The thing, however, is no fact. Husserl's promotion of the category of essence arises not just from his tendency to romantically resurrect the scholastic tradition. Essence does not just protect thinking from facts, it also opposes fact as sheer appearance whose validity is doubted and then posited in the ἐποχή, in order to bring the underlying lawfulness to consciousness.

The failure, however, objectively attests to what no bourgeois thinker after Hegel would have attested to of himself, viz. the
194 necessity of appearance itself. Against every one of his original intentions and from its ownmost, Husserl's philosophy produces all the categories of subjective appearance against which it was mobilized. At its end one understands that, as soon as the central concept of idealism, that of transcendental subjectivity, is assumed, nothing more is thinkable which is not subject to this subjectivity and in the strictest sense its property. Thus Husserl compromises the new, indeed equally apparent philosophy of reality of his successors so fundamentally as an idealism whose *ratio* he takes to be an *ultima ratio*. The work of the Platonic realists proves to be destructive.

Self-Revocation

Ratio in Husserl did indeed defy relativistic attacks which already in his time constituted a temptation to sacrifice reason and quickly turned cynicism, under total dominance, into good philosophical conscience. But, with rationalistic arrogance, Husserl also denied the power of the existing over self-mastering thought as recorded by relativism, as ever distorted and naive compared to accepted 'existence' (*Dasein*).

Now the motor of the Husserlian movement of thought is the will to establish existence rejected by *ratio* within the horizon of the autonomous *ratio* itself. Such a will determines the attempt to break out and the bounds of that attempt. Its antithetics is formulated in the two basic methodological demands of *Ideas*:

In the logical sphere, viz. that of assertions, 'to be real' (*wirklich*) or 'to be true' are correlated in principle with 'to be rationally provable'.[4]

In contrast we have that

. . . principle of all principles: that every originary dator intuition is a source of authority for knowledge, that whatever presents itself in 'intuition' originarily (as it were, in its bodily reality) is simply to be accepted as it gives itself out to be, though only within the limits within which it presents itself.[5]

The phenomenologist wants to fall directly in line with every 'originary dator intuition' without knowing beforehand to what extent its content may be 'rationally provable', universal and necessary. At the same time, however, he turns the possession of rationality itself, which in the final instance coincides with the unity of self-consciousness, into the measure of every 'reality', even of originary dator intuition and ultimately of givenness itself.

The clichés of the history of philosophy, would class phe- 195
nomenology, just like Kant's critique of reason, as a synthesis of rationalism and empiricism. The often observed overlapping of logical and psychological inclinations in Husserl is the manifest expression of that. Nothing makes one's comprehension of Husserl's fundamental concepts and their structure more difficult than the intersection of rationalistic and empiricistic tendencies.

This intersection is deciphered only by understanding Husserl's motive. Throughout Husserl wants to destroy merely 'fabricated' concepts, which camouflage their 'thing' by means of the critique of reason. He wants to dismantle 'theorizings' and unveil the real independently of stifling terminological apparatus. In *Ideas*, in the course of an apology for the *a priori* concept of essence, the surprising proposition appears:

If by 'positivism' we are to mean the absolute unbiased grounding of all science on what is 'positive', i.e. on what can be originarily apprehended, then it is we who are the genuine positivists.[6]

[4] Ibid. [282]; and ibid. p. 350.
[5] Ibid. [43 ff]; and ibid. p. 83.
[6] Ibid. [38]; and ibid. p. 78.

Of course, the concept of positivism switches thereby into the opposite of its original meaning. But this switch comes about under the compulsion to unveil the 'things'. Hence it inaugurates Husserlian rationalism. The method of proof of the Prolegomena, which is meant to demonstrate that fundamental principles are strict *a priori* propositions in themselves, remains throughout within the framework of positivistic encountering (*Vorfindlichkeit*). The causal law by which the act of thought operates is not identical in that act with the logical norm which guides it. In any given act of thought as a phenomenon, such as it presents itself to the reflective regard, the two do not coincide:

Causal laws, according to which thought must proceed in a manner which the ideal norms of logic might justify, are by no means identical with those norms. If a creature were so constituted as never to be able to frame contradictory judgements in a unified train of thought, as never to be able to perform inferences which defy the syllogistic moods, this would not mean that the law of contradiction, the *Modus Barbara* etc., were laws of nature explanatory of this creature's constitution.[7]

196   For Husserl, logical absolutism and anti-positivism are quite simply the result of more insistent positivistic research. Among the characteristics of the evidence of a logical assertion, according to his doctrine, no causal law of psychological association of thought may be included in originary dator intuition. The same inclination is effective in all the critical excurses of Husserlian phenomenology. Discovered 'feelings of evidence'; the equivocations of authoritarian terminology, against which the 'doctrine of meaning' was conceived, and especially the distinction between sensations and the contents of sensation; and finally the picture and sign theory in the interpretation of the consciousness of things; are all privileged points of attack. In each case Husserlian rationalism prevails at the behest of Husserlian empiricism. His propositions, pure meanings and, in the late phase, a pure ego oppose null changelings, concepts which cannot satisfy their claim to empirical, psychological justification, because they are not 'there'. Husserl would like to remove the walls of mirrors of thought products which suddenly pop up before thought as soon as it becomes incapable of recognizing itself in them. The goal of

[7] *LU* I, p. 68; cf. Findlay, p. 103.

logical and epistemological revelation is prescribed by what is 'as such', viz. propositions in themselves instead of psychological rules under which men simply reflect on them, pure meaning such as it is encountered and retained by the 'ray of vision of intention', the evidence of the 'things themselves' such as they are presented and not the subjective reflex, the 'feeling' of them, the perceived or otherwise meant object and not its mere consciousness-like substitute.

This is the sense in which phenomenology tries to break out of concept fetishism. It strips off the ornaments which assume the disguising and perishable expression of appearance in the realm of the abstract concept just like the sensuous ornament of the architecture and music of the same period. With Husserl the objective spirit of the bourgeoisie prepares to ask how idealism may remain possible without ideology. The answer returned objectively by the 'things' to that question, however, is negative. That dictates to Husserl the dialectical course of the movement of his thought. The empiricist analysis of what is encountered 197 always leads to rationalistic consequences, such as that of the absolute being of logical propositions as ideal unities.

But their being-in-itself is mediated through the 'pure consciousness' alone which, according to Husserl's doctrine, is prescribed to all entities. Hence phenomenology falls into the fundamental position of transcendental subjectivity, or as the late Husserl called it, the εἶδος ego. Transcendental subjectivity, however, is the origin and title deed of the very concept fetishes which the unbiased, accepting view of the 'things themselves' is supposed to undo. It defines the same idealism against which the historical tendency of the attempt to break out was turned. Hegel's definition of the dialectical movement of thought as a circle proves ironically true in Husserl. Phenomenology revokes itself.

Character of Immanence and the Fetishism of the Concept

Phenomenology resembles a circle because it arises out of idealism and reproduces idealism at every one of its stages, as usual as a sublated moment. Though all of Husserl's investigations are concerned with 'transcendents', with what is not proper to consciousness, yet none of them have left behind the level of traditional immanent analysis of consciousness.

The name 'phenomenology' spells out its concern with 'phenomena', trans-subjective 'things themselves' as simply appearing subjectively. That involves the specific contradiction of Husserl's thought. In struggling against concept fetishes it is thoroughly fetishistic, for the 'things themselves' which it abuts against are always merely images covering functions of consciousness, 'congealed labour'. The trans-subjective being of logical propositions, for the sake of whose apologetics phenomenology was initially cultivated, implies the reification of thought performances, the forgetting of synthesis, or, as the later Husserl in an entirely Marburg fashion calls it, 'creation'.

In the presence of reified products of thought, Husserl's thought deprives itself of the right to thought. It resigns itself to 'description' and generates the appearance of the appearanceless in-itself. Since Descartes, reification and subjectivism have not constituted absolute opposites, but rather reciprocally condition each other. The trans-subjective content of reality in the Husserlian concept of the object is just due to a higher degree of 198 dissection or reification. The phenomenologist was certainly incapable of thinking objects as other than subjectively constituted. But they thus remain so fundamentally foreign and torpid to him that he intuits and describes them as 'second nature', while they, once resuscitated, were immediately reduced to sheer subjective qualifications. As soon as the phenomenologist insists on the description of 'factual states of consciousness', there arises once again the dualism of thing and appearance in the pseudo-concrete terminology of adumbrated and adumbration.

Indeed, Husserl's things as abstract objects forfeited a great deal of the substantiality – despite their asserted incarnateness – which they still had as Kantian objects. By being plucked out of space, time and causality, and atomistically turned into sheer 'senses' of singular acts, they find themselves transplanted into a shadowy infinity in which no further mischief can befall them, but in which it is also no longer possible to reconstruct the substratum of the natural sciences out of them such as had remained the express result of the Kantian Transcendental Analytic.

'Attitude' (Einstellung)

But that makes the phenomenological posture itself ambiguous. If the attempt to break out gets trapped in the realm of δόξα, then the ἐποχή, on the other hand, which blocks the break out, comes to much too comfortable an understanding with empirical reality. It is characterized by Husserl as an 'attitude' which is to be distinguished in principle from the 'natural attitude' of the unreflective acceptance of the 'general thesis of the world' in its spatio-temporality.

But behind the Cartesian *dubitatio*, with which Husserl happily compares the phenomenological attitude, that thesis persists in the weakness of caprice. If Descartes undertakes the attempt at universal doubt in order to secure absolute conscience,* Husserl's posture in comparison is a mere methodological arrangement, which is recommended but in no sense itself deduced as necessary. It does without the intervening obligatoriness, because not so much changes with it, according to Husserl. It is conceived less as binding critique of reason than as the neutralization of a thing world whose power and right is not given serious doubt.   *199*

It is likewise clear that the attempt to doubt anything as present to consciousness conditions a certain sublation of the thesis [of the natural attitude]; and it is precisely this that interests us. It is not a transformation of the thesis into its antithesis, of positive into negative; it is also not a transformation into presumption, suggestion, indecision, doubt (in whatever sense of the word); such a transformation is not indeed a matter of free choice. Rather it is something quite unique. We do not abandon the thesis we have adopted, we make no change in our conviction, which remains in itself what it is as long as we do not introduce new motives of judgement, which we precisely refrain from doing. And yet the thesis undergoes a modification – while remaining in itself, what it is, we set it as it were 'out of action', we 'disconnect it', 'bracket it'. It still remains there like the bracketed in the bracket, like the disconnected outside the connectional system.[8]

It is not by chance that Husserl shares the expression 'attitude' with the bourgeois-private jape of relativism, which renders ways

---

* [*Gewissen*: root *gewiß*, which means 'certain'. Trans.]

[8] *Ideen* [54]; cf. *Ideas*, pp. 97 ff.

of procedure and meanings dependent less on binding knowledge than on the contingent state of the judging person. Both
may have borrowed the word* from the language of photography. The attempt has been made to take this as a model
underlying Husserlian epistemology in objective spirit. It claims
to take possession of reality intact, by isolating its objects and
fixing them with the Medusa's glance of a sudden 'ray of vision',
as if they were set up and exhibited in the studio before the
photographic lens. Like the photographer of old, the phenomenologist wraps himself with the black veil of his ἐποχή,
implores the objects to hold still and unchanging and ultimately
realizes passively and without spontaneity of the knowing
subject, family portraits of the sort of that mother 'who glances
lovingly at her little flock'.[9] Just as in photography the *camera
obscura* and the recorded pictorial object belong together, so in
phenomenology do the immanence of consciousness and naive
realism.

200   The philosophy of immanence goes so far that it leaves behind
'absolute consciousness as residuum after the nullifying of the
world'.[10]

> Immanent being is . . . without doubt absolute being in the sense that in
> principle it *nulla 're' indiget ad existendum*. On the other hand, the world
> of the transcendent *'res'* is related throughout to consciousness, not
> indeed to logical conceptions, but to what is 'actual'.[11]

But the claim to totality of sense-giving subjectivity directly
extinguishes itself. If the subject includes 'everything' in itself and
bestows meaning on everything, then it might just as well not be
there as an essential moment of cognition. It is a simple
framework for which no differences of any sort are posited, which
are the only things that could determine subjectivity.

Husserlian over-subjectivity also means under-subjectivity.
Since the ego as constituting or sense-providing condition
espouses and assumes itself as advanced before all objectivity, it

---

* [*einstellen* also means 'to focus'. Trans.]

[9] Ibid. [251]; and ibid. p. 313.
[10] Ibid. [91]; and ibid. p. 136.
[11] Ibid. [92]; and ibid.

renounces any interference from cognition and certainly praxis. Uncritically and in contemplative passivity it lays out an inventory of the thing world as that world is presented to it in the reigning order.

The phenomenologist correctly says of the ἐποχή: 'We have properly lost nothing',[12] even its rights over appearance and reality. He declares himself satisfied with a formal title of possession over the accepted 'world'. The powerless externality of the reduction, which leaves everything as it was, is indicated by the fact that no proper names are allotted to the reduced objects; the reduction, rather, merely renders visible as reduced a writing ritual, namely scare quotes. By using quotation marks, which is supposed to give notice of phenomenological purity, the rigorous researcher wields some of the fatal humour of the journalist who writes 'lady' when he means prostitute. The world in scare quotes is a tautology of the existing world. The phenomenological ἐποχή is fictitious.

Fantasy and Body

The ἐποχή interpolates absolute loneliness and yet avowedly relates in all its acts to the world – as the 'sense' of its acts – which it is supposed to swallow up. That reflects a fundamental contradiction of the state of society whose topography phenomenology records both faithfully and unconsciously. It turns the individual into a powerless receptive vessel, totally dependent on alleged reality, just concerned with adapting. But the 201 same mechanism renders him so unrelated, so much a thing among things that, in society which determines him down to his very existence, he feels indistinct, misunderstood and self-contained.

Phenomenology transfigures the contradiction of the two experiences. It passes off the merely assumed and intuited world as the possession of the absolute individual, the aggregate of all correlates of 'solitary speech'. It thereby confers the consecration and justification of the essential and necessary to the merely existing by means of that pure consciousness supposedly un-needful of things for existence.

[12] Ibid. [94]; and ibid. p. 140.

Husserl left no doubt about the fictional character of the solution. He owns up to fiction as the keystone of the method.

Hence, if anyone loves a paradox, he can really say, and say with strict truth if he will allow for ambiguity, that the element which makes up the life of phenomenology as of all eidetic science is 'fiction', that fiction is the source whence the knowledge of 'eternal truths' draws its sustenance.[13]

Indeed he seeks to guard against the fictional character of that sentence 'which should be particularly appropriate as a quotation for bringing ridicule from the naturalistic side on the eidetic way of knowledge'.[14]

But there is no need of such a provision. It is not the paradoxical boldness of the eideticist which provokes criticism. It expresses the best *agentem* of phenomenology: utopian excess over the accepted world of things; the latent drive in philosophy to highlight the possible in the actual and the actual in the possible, instead of confessing satisfaction with the surrogate of a truth distilled from the mere facts, their conceptual 'perimeter'.

Once avant-garde tendencies of expressionism could rightly appeal to Husserl. Yet Husserl's fiction itself swiftly betrays the possible to the actual. Though he suppresses the reference to experiential ransom situated in every fiction by defining it as 'pure possibility', he nevertheless did that by already transferring intuitability, such as only devolves on future experience, to 202 present fiction. Instead of thinking the possible as something which strictly surpasses the existing and which must first be actualized, he magically transforms it into something real *sui generis* which one should be able to perceive passively like accepted reality.

Elements of naturalism are directly associated with his a priorism. He demonstrates his fantasizings not by expressionistic figures, but by those of Böcklin, such as the Isle of the Dead, the flute-playing faun and the water spirits. Something naturalistic belongs to all these creatures.* They appear as unreal and yet as

* [Adorno plays on the two senses of *Wesen* throughout this passage: 'creature' and 'essence'. Trans.]

[13] Ibid. [132]; and ibid. p. 184.
[14] Ibid. footnote.

graphic copies of something practically real, as tractable imita-
tions of alleged fauns or elementary creatures, not as the
expression of thought which for its part determines the possible
as something new, and distinct from every existing thing. They
are not 'free'.

The possible in Husserl is analogous to fiction in the negative
sense, in that it presents itself as if it were something already real.
A *quid pro quo* governs Husserl's fantasizing. Naturalistically
intuited objects are raised to the level of being 'symbolical' and
essentially binding. In return what is thought is dealt with as if it
were preliminarily intuitive in a somehow modified experience.

The moment of unity of this *quid pro quo* is the concept of the
incarnate, in Böcklin's painted fantasies as well as Husserl's
thought 'things themselves'.

Those Boecklins! All the extraordinary pictures one had only seen on
postcards or hanging in coloured reproduction, on the walls of pensions
in Dresden. Mermaids and tritons caught as though by a camera;
centaurs in the stiff ungainly positions of race-horses in a pressman's
photograph.[15]

Though the body sets the limits of idealistic appearance, it
nevertheless dominates in Husserl's horizon as appearance. The
nude is the symbol of the unsymbolic. It abides in the recesses of
the neo-Romantic temple of essence. The purity of the almost
lust-less and passive phenomenological glance is as fitting to the
nude as the *à rebours* of phenomenological ascesis which is still
proclaimed in *Formal and Transcendental Logic*.

Before the body phenomenology conceives itself as an 'essential style',[16] and proceeds to the body by 'grades of clarity'.[17] If the
body is ultimately affected, then it is nothing but the regarding
consciousness itself which vanishes in it like in a mirror. The
merely existing world radiates like a world of subjective sense,
pure subjectivity as true being. The phenomenological attempt to   203
break out terminates in this delusion.

---

[15] Aldous Huxley, *Eyeless in Gaza* (Chatto and Windus, London, 1936), p. 457.
[16] *Logik* [253]; cf. Cairns ⟨217⟩.
[17] *Ideen* [127]; cf. *Ideas*, p. 179.

Categorial Intuition

The thesis of the perceptibility of the purely possible as a doctrine of essential insight, or as Husserl originally called it, categorial intuition, has become the motto of all philosophical approaches which evoke phenomenology. The fact that the new method should guarantee ideal states-of-affairs the same immediacy and infallibility as sense-data in the received view, explains the influence which Husserl exercised particularly over those who could no longer be satisfied with neo-Kantian systems and yet were unwilling to blindly hand themselves over to irrationalism. They felt that Fichtean and Schellingian intellectual intuition, though Husserl never referred to it, was raised by phenomenological management to the level of a 'rigorous science' whose programme Husserl claimed as his philosophy in the famous *Logos* article.*

The affinity of so many of his pupils to restorative tendencies suggests the suspicion which Troeltsch[18] already expressed, that the point of the method of essential insight from its inception was ideological machinations, under the unwarranted pretext of dressing up assertions of content of every sort as eternal truths, such that they refer only to 'being', viz. the existence of institutional powers. But those first attracted to Husserl felt themselves to be hardly just obscurantists. Rather they were enticed by the opportunity to cease dealing uniquely in philosophy with abstract empty forms which would later and contingently fill up with 'material' to which the forms were merely external. They hoped for a procedure which would disclose the material itself and extract its genuine concrete form.

The catchword 'concreteness' has long since become a cliché and itself entirely abstract. It appeared otherwise in the early days of phenomenology when Scheler attacked starchy ethics and the 204 'betrayal of happiness' and unmasked the mouldiness of official

---

* ['Philosophie als strenge Wissenschaft', *Logos* I (1910–11); tr. Quentin Lauer, 'Philosophy as a Rigorous Science', in *Phenomenology and the Crisis of Philosophy* (Harper and Row, New York, 1965), pp. 71–147. Trans.]

[18] Cf. Ernst Troeltsch, *Der Historismus und seine Probleme* (Mohr, Tübingen, 1912–25), pp. 59 ff.

ESSENCE AND PURE EGO

systems. Seeing into essences also meant dealing with the essential. Today phenomenological naiads just drive towards their own essence.

The Paradoxical Apex

Husserl himself took little interest in the investigations into content whose apparatus he helped to establish. It was not just that he distanced himself from most of his pupils and only very occasionally published material analyses. There is in fact very little room for the theory of essential insight in his *oeuvre* and it is in no way given the decisive accent which must have been expected from the effect of the concept. Except for the rather sibyllic opening chapter of *Ideas*, it is thoroughly discussed only in the sixth Logical Investigation. But the exposition even there remains cursory. Husserl immediately turns to protecting it from possible misinterpretations and revising it to such an extent that hardly anything more can be retained of the thesis than its name. The later writings tacitly eliminated the concept of essential insight and replaced it with a neo-Kantian functional interpretation of evidence.

The timid hesitation of the thinker is not responsible for that. Rather, categorial intuition is the paradoxical apex of his thought. It is the indifference into which the positivistic motif of intuitability and the rationalistic one of being-in-itself of ideal states-of-affairs should be sublated. The movement of Husserlian thought could not tarry at this apex. Categorial intuition is no newly discovered principle of philosophizing. It proves to be a sheer dialectical moment of transition: imaginary altitude.

The Provenance of Logical Absolutism

In a certain way categorial intuition was devised by the doctrine of propositions in themselves from the Prolegomena. If these are truly to be more than creations of thought, then they cannot really be products of thought but must simply be encountered (*vorgefunden*) by it. The paradoxical demand for a merely encountering thought arises from the claim to validity on the part of logical absolutism. The doctrine of categorial intuition is the result of this on the subject side.

If anyone likes to stay in a sphere of general discussions, he may allow the psychologistic arguments to deceive him. But a mere glance at any 205 logical principle, at its real meaning and the full insight with which it is seen as true in itself, must abolish such deceit.[19]

The sixth Investigation goes on to argue that 'truths in themselves', objectively advanced and yet ideal factual situations, are viewed by the insight of the 'simple regard'. It calls truths in themselves 'states-of-affairs'.

As the sense-object stands to sense-perception, so the state-of-affairs stands to the 'becoming aware' (*Gewahrwerdung*) in which it is (more or less adequately) given (We should like to say simply: so the state-of-affairs stands to the perception of it).[20]

Husserl the rationalist wants to confer the quality of immediate givenness to the *vérités de raison* of the Prolegomena through categorial intuition. For that quality is the sole source of justification for cognition to the positivist Husserl. The positivist assumes propositions in themselves, pure unities of validity; the rationalist assumes the immanence of consciousness which proves truth, the realm of givens and of lived experiences. The two are divided by the phenomenological line of demarcation. The former are 'essences' and the latter 'facts'. Between them reigns no other relation than ideality.

The *vérités de raison* are 'meant' in factical lived experiences. Intentions should lead to the *vérités* as such without in the slightest subjectivizing or relativizing them. The in-itself of the truths should appear. They are not supposed to be created in subjective reflection, but rather be self-given and intuitive. But they should not have to pay the tribute of the merely factical and contingent, which 'plain' sense-intuition owes. As a *deus ex machina* categorial intuition must reconcile Husserl's warring motifs. Its paradoxicality dissembles that dialectic to the philosopher which is completed well over his head.

[19] *LU* I, p. 64; cf. Findlay, p. 100.
[20] *LU* II, ii, p. 140; and ibid. p. 783.

Fulfilment of Unsensed Moments

Intentionality or 'thought' alone does not suffice to achieve paradox. Meaning (*Meinen*) a thing or even an ideal state-of-affairs in the way that arithmetical propositions do is not yet identical with their evidence. One can also mean a falsehood. That furnishes Husserl with the justification for exceeding the concept of mere intentionality by the construction of categorial intuition. He supplements it with the concept of its intuitive 206 'fulfilment'

where an expression first functions in merely symbolic fashion, and then is accompanied by a (more or less) corresponding intuition. Where this happens, we experience a descriptively peculiar consciousness of fulfilment: the act of pure meaning (*Bedeutens*), like a goal-seeking intention, finds its fulfilment in the act which renders intuitive.[21]

Intentionality asserts primacy over this concept of intuition. Intuition is not what determines intention. Intuition is oriented by intention, 'adapts' to it. The dependence of intuition on intention, which excludes from the beginning all of the moments of the material of intuition which are heterogeneous to subjectivity from the sphere of meaning (*Bedeuten*), leads Husserl to assume a thorough parallelism between intentions and their fulfilment. Fulfilment corresponds to intention in the moments in which it adapts itself to intention.

Husserl's assumption, however, lures him to the thesis that not only those moments of meaning which are directed to the factical, but also those which are 'categorial' and unsensed should find their own fulfilment. Husserl defines these fulfilments of the categorial moments of intention as categorial intuitions.

The paradoxicality of essential insight is concentrated in the theory of fulfilment. For Husserl cannot fail to notice that the specific moments of thought in judgements and propositions cannot be conceived as copies of a non-perceptible, trans-subjective being, since the non-perceptible moments themselves may not be determined otherwise than as moments of thinking.

Husserl did not attack the picture and sign theory just to restore

[21] Ibid. p. 32; and ibid. p. 694.

it carelessly in the 'phenomenology of cognition'. Hence he promptly rejected the picture theory in the sixth Logical Investigation and thereby introduced the revision of categorial intuition.

We started by assuming that, in the case of structured expressions, the idea of a more or less imageistic mode of expression was quite unavailing in describing the relation which obtains between expressive meanings (*Bedeutungen*), on the one hand, and expressed intuitions, on the other. This is doubtless correct and need now only be made more 207 precise. We need only earnestly ponder what things can be possible matter (*Sache*) for perception, and what things possible matter for meaning, to become aware that, in the mere form of a judgement, only certain antecedently specifiable parts of our statement can have something which corresponds to them in intuition, while to other parts of the statement nothing intuitive can possibly correspond.[22]

But the concept of categorial intuition cannot do without the picture theory. Only if categorial moments of meaning copy some objective-ideal being and 'correspond' to it instead of just producing it, can this objective-ideal being be intuited in any sense at all. Thus Husserl is forced, in spite of his own critical discernment, to plead positively for the 'object correlates' of categorial forms and thus for an intuition which fulfills them and is non-perceptible in principle, so that the fundamental thesis of propositions in themselves does not collapse.

The 'a' and the 'the', the 'and' and the 'or', the 'if' and the 'then', the 'all' and the 'none', the 'something' and the 'nothing', the forms of quantity and the determination of number etc. – all these are meaningful propositional elements, but we should look in vain for their object correlates (if such may be ascribed to them at all) in the sphere of real objects, which is in fact no other than the sphere of objects of possible sense-perception.[23]

In open contradiction to the restrictions of the theory of fulfilment, the concept of categorial intuition receives an extreme formulation:

---

[22] Ibid. p. 134 ff; and ibid. p. 778.
[23] Ibid. p. 139; and ibid. p. 782.

If we now ask: 'where do the categorial forms of meanings find their fulfilment, if not in the perception or intuition which we tried provisionally to delimit in talking of "sense-perception" ', our answer is plainly prefigured in the discussions just completed. We have taken it for granted that forms, too, can be genuinely fulfilled, or that the same applies to variously structured total meanings, and not merely to the 'material' elements of such meanings, and our assumption is put beyond doubt by the presentification of each case of faithful perceptual assertion. . . . But if the 'categorial forms' of the expression, present together with its material aspects, have no terminus in perception, if by the latter we understand merely perception of the senses then talk of expressing a percept must here rest on a different meaning: there must 208 be at least an act which renders identical services to the categorial elements of meaning that mere perception of the senses renders to the material elements.[24]

'Becoming Aware' (Gewahrwerdung)

Husserl construes categorial intuition as a mode of givenness on the analogy of sense-perception. But this analogy is of quite limited applicability. The *tertium comparationis* lies just in the negative fact that neither sense-intuition nor the modes of consciousness which Husserl calls categorial intuition, and which are in fact just grounded judgement, are absolute 'self-givings', but simply partial moments of the total process of cognition, or, as the later Husserl expressed it, they both remain subordinated to the 'possibility of disillusionment (*Enttäuschung*)'. But this in fact truncates the doctrine of categorial intuition.

The term 'becoming aware', which smooths the ground for that doctrine, is, like Husserl's concept of sense-perception, ambiguous. The quality of immediacy which he imputes to 'becoming aware of the state-of-affairs' is quite simply the immediacy of the performance of judgement. Traditional epistemology would express that in the form that judgement, according to its subjective constitution, is an act, and that the act of judgement is immediately given. Judging and becoming aware of a judged state-of-affairs are equivalent expressions, or rather the second disguises the first in metaphor. Nothing further, no 'perception of what is judged', is added to the act of judging, not even if the completed judgement is reflected upon.

[24] Ibid. p. 142; and ibid. pp. 784 ff.

This reflection surpasses in principle the 'immediacy' of any given performance of judgement by taking it as an object. That immediacy of the performance of judgement, meanwhile, lies in Husserl's concept of 'becoming aware'. Becoming aware for him means the original meaning of something judged, the performance of the judgement as act, the synthesis which befalls the judged state-of-affairs and turns it into a unit. At the same time, however, a critical achievement, the proof of the correctness of the judgement, is expected from 'becoming aware', and thus it transgressed the pure immediacy which alone legitimates the analogy with sense-intuition.

209

Becoming aware of the state-of-affairs also means for Husserl securing the truth of the judgement. The equivocation in the expression 'dator act of becoming aware' is exactly: becoming aware of a state-of-affairs, viz. performing the synthesis of the judgement; and, bringing the truth of this judgement to absolute evidence. Both, however, cannot be interpreted as categorial intuition. The synthesis of the performance of judgement is nothing of the sort, but rather that act of thought which, according to Husserl, should be directly 'fulfilled' only by categorial intuition. But reflection which constitutes the material necessary condition for the quality of evidence is as little intuitive as it is immediate. It relates the judged state-of-affairs to other states-of-affairs. Its proper result is a new categorization.

Even if reflection were ultimately to have recourse to sense-intuitive moments, it would retain non-intuitive conceptual forms in itself. Husserl shifts the first meaning of the term 'becoming aware', by which it signifies judging itself – and hence, if one insists, the 'fulfilment' of a previously empty and meant judgement through its performance at a time – to the second meaning, viz. reflection on founding (fundierende) states-of-affairs which produce evidence. This is 'fulfilment' in a completely different sense. It names the mediate immediately in the belief in 'data' in order to keep the possibility of disillusionment away from the mediate. It allots universality and necessity to the immediate such as comes only from the mediate, viz. progress in reflection.

If the total ἐποχή of epistemology turns into naive realism, it would follow then that the consequence of categorial intuition, as already in the Prolegomena, is naive realism of logic. As an escape from the immanence of thought, the paradoxical construction remains impotent. It also copies the Kantian spontaneity of thought in its sheer receptivity. In the later Husserl the hardly implausible concept of spontaneous receptivity expressly appears.

Motivation of Objectivism

The critique of categorial intuition brings down all of its con- 210 sequences. Autonomous essentialities, independent of man, his activity and his history, and yet to be grasped by man in their 'purity'; their exposition in a so-called material doctrine of value which owes its concreteness precisely to fictitious intuitability; the belief that one can by insight draw from a singular phenomenon its static essence, emancipated from space and time: All these were called to life by a simple methodological formula which does not present a new procedure of cognition so much as express the incompatibility of positivistic certainty and rationalistic truth. Categorial intuition is no 'seeing' of essentialities, but rather a blind spot in the process of cognition.

If the scientific claim of Husserl's philosophy feels itself superior to Hegelian speculation, still the doctrine of ideation itself nevertheless falls far behind Hegel for scientific circumspection. That is nowhere clearer than in the concept of being which took centre stage for Husserl's successors in existential philosophy. Hegel circumscribed the immediacy of the concept of being with which he lets the dialectic begin and conceives it as a sheer partial moment of his immanent movement. He says,

that there is nothing, nothing in heaven or in nature or mind or anywhere else which does not equally contain both immediacy and mediation, so that these two determinations reveal themselves to be unseparated and inseparable and the opposition between them to be a nullity.[25]

Hence,

---

[25] Cf. G.W.F. Hegel, *Sämtliche Werke*, ed. Hermann Glockner, vol. 4, *Wissenschaft der Logik*, part 1, 4th ed., Jubiläumsausgabe (Fromann, Stuttgart – Bad Canstatt, 1964), pp. 70 ff; and tr. A.V. Miller *Hegel's Science of Logic* (George Allen and Unwin, London, Humanities Press, New York, 1969), p. 68.

the beginning is made with being which is presented as having arisen through mediation, which is also a sublating of itself.[26]

For Husserl, on the other hand, being is immediately present in categorial intuition.

211   It is in fact obvious from the start that, just as any other concept (or idea, specific unity) can only 'arise', i.e. become self-given to us, if based on an act which at least sets some individual instance of it imaginatively before our eyes, so the concept of being can arise only when some being, actual or imaginary, is set before our eyes. If 'being' is taken to mean predicative being, some state-of-affairs must be given to us, and this by way of an act which gives it, an analogue of ordinary sense-intuition.[27]

The opposition between the moments of mediacy and immediacy which are sublated by Hegel in the concept of being, an opposition which already holds the dialectical movement of the concept itself within itself, is exorcised by Husserl in the magic formula of the categorial intuitability of being.

This equivocal usage steps in for the immanent movement of the concept. In Husserl's antecedent, 'being' is used in the most universal, abstract and mediated sense. The conclusion substitutes entities for being as the immediately intuitive moment of whatever sort which attains categorization.

The entirety of existential philosophy preys on this contamination. The being of existentialism is not that which as a sustaining, real moment of consciousness, no abstraction can neglect. It is rather a being which passes for ideal similarly to Husserl's pure consciousness, but which, as immediately intuitable, should be able to do without consciousness, and primarily epistemological reflection. It derived this intuitability precisely from the merely existing and factical which the ideality and a priority of the concept of being was supposed to fend off.

Hence Husserl prepares for the deceptive Eleatic metaphysics of being of the present day: pure being identical with pure thought. Hegel saw through this concept of being. Hegelian being is no turbid identification of mediacy and immediacy. It cannot be hypostatized and can only be violently misappropri-

[26] Ibid. p. 73; and ibid. p. 69.
[27] LU II, ii, p. 141; cf. Findlay, p. 784.

ated to contaminate being and entities. It is articulated according to its oppositions and turns suddenly back against itself. It is a critical concept in the eminent sense. It is identical with the nothingness which Eleatics disavow.

Withering Away of Argument

The original impulse of categorial intuition as one of escape may be detected beyond the bad identity of thinking and being. Behind the doctrine that one can have immediate 'insight' (*einsehen*) into 'states-of-affairs' like arithmetical propositions, stood the misgivings of a structure of objective lawfulness superposed in principle on every intellectual performance. For that structure should be removed from the arbitrariness of our meaning despite Husserl's assumption of our meaning as the basis of epistemological analysis.

Husserl is aware of the fact that the state-of-affairs 'seen into' is more than a mere subjective product of thought. Arithmetical 212 judgement does not simply consist in the subjective performance of the act of collecting whose synthesis it presents. It says that there must be something subjectively irreducible which demands this and no other collecting. The state-of-affairs is not produced purely, but is rather also 'encountered'. The non-arising of the logical state-of-affairs in its constitution by thought, the non-identity of subjectivity and truth, drives Husserl directly to the construction of categorial intuition. The 'intuited' ideal state-of-affairs is not supposed to be a sheer product of thought.

If, however, Husserl believes he can disclose the superposed law-likeness as a pure *quale* of the singular object without recourse to multiplicity, as he claims throughout the essence chapter in *Ideas*, then a reality may justify him unexpectedly. For as a 'system', it so thoroughly determines all ostensible individual objects, that in fact its 'essence' can be read off every singular trait of the system, while the unity of features of the numerical horizon of the concept offers no more than weak reflection of this essence.

We may perhaps surmise that this is one of the causes for Husserl's effect. His philosophy codifies an objectively historical experience without deciphering it, viz. the withering away of argument. Consciousness finds itself at a crossroads. Though the call to insight (*Schau*) and the scorn of discursive thought may furnish the pretext for a commandeered world view and blind subordination, it also exhibits the instant in which the correctness of argument and counter-argument disappears, and in which the activity of thought consists only in calling what is by its name. Namely, what everyone already knows, so no more arguments are needed, and what no one wants to know, so no counter-argument need be heard.

The bourgeois epoch has been called one of endlessly discussing classes. Phenomenology gives notice, provisionally and inadequately, of the end of the discussion. It remains inadequate by persisting with the categories of meaning (*Meinen*) and sheer subjectivity. It takes the non-identical state-of-affairs as the immediate givenness of consciousness, something purely mental. But the factical existence of that state-of-affairs becomes ideal being or thought.

Phenomenology as Philosophy of Reflection

This was perpetrated by the static initial approach to the subject–object relation. Husserl conceives of form and content

in this order of precedence: the object is regarded as something complete and finished for itself, something which can entirely dispense with thought for its reality, while thought on the other hand is regarded as defective because is has to complete itself with some matter and moreover, as a pliable and indeterminate form, has to adapt itself to its matter.[28]

Husserlian analyses, and even the paradoxical construction of categorial intuition, remain, in Hegelian terms, completely mired in mere reflection. Husserl believed that he could get hold of every individual concept in a 'theory-free' and thus contradiction-free way in the description of the life of consciousness without first examining the interdependence of epistemological principles.

In and against this reflectional thought, however, which is fully contrary to Hegelian thought, the dialectic nevertheless

[28] Hegel, *Wissenschaft der Logik*, vol. 4, p. 38; and Miller, *Hegel's Science of Logic*, p. 44.

triumphs, for the partial descriptions which it furnishes continually lead to contradictions. Propositions in themselves, fulfilment and categorial intuition are supposed to resolve these
contradictions. But they are inventions far more than the speculative concept which scientific thought renounces and which
completely sublates them already as its finite and restricted
moments. The dialectic restored *malgré elle* devours the inventions
of suddenly apologetic plain common sense.

While the descriptions of ideal factual states are disavowed by
recalcitrant facts, the postulate of encounterability destroys the
mechanism of idealistic concept formation. Traditional idealism
grandly rejected the question of the completion at a time of
subjective syntheses by calling them transcendental functions
which are in principle pre- and superscribed over all psychological 'doing' of individuals, although they are admittedly acquired
from precisely the abstractions of factical performances of cognitive activity, viz. those which are contained in contemporary
science. Husserl was not satisfied with that. He demanded *214*
justification of subjective syntheses as 'acts' and undertook to
save a second existent for their meanings. Accordingly these
meanings hardly seemed to him to be psychologically encountered facts as soon as he dared to establish them metaphysically.
His attempt is once again one of 'mediation', but no longer in the
speculative but rather in the reflective concept. This attempt
miscarried. Its abortion, however, affects idealism itself.

The System in Ruins

For the contradictions of Husserlian logic are no accidental and
corrigible errors. They are original and inherent to idealism. It is
impossible to correct a mistake of idealistic epistemology without
necessarily producing another error. One concept is evolved out
of another so that contradictions may be corrected in ordered
succession, but none would come closer to the 'thing' than the
first one. Indeed each falls deeper into the thicket of invention.

The deepest and most penetrating idealistic theorems, e.g. the
Kantian theorems of the schematism of pure reason and the
synthetic unity of apperception, lie furthest from the cognitive
activities of men performed and exhibitable at a time, whereas

they are most efficient at turning away theoretical contradictions. Simple concepts, untenable in harmonious foundation, such as Locke's sensation and reflection,* may more closely describe the procedural modes of thinking than the 'I think', which in truth already no longer expresses real acts of thought so much as an historical constellation of subject and object removed from individual activity.

The tenacity (*Geschlossenheit*) of the idealistic system consists in the forward movement of its contradictions. It transmits the debit structure of *prima philosophia*. However much Husserl remained concerned with *prima philosophia*, he did demand its objective liquidation. Only thus can his relation to Descartes be understood. In Descartes, bourgeois thought strives, though not yet fully autonomously, to reproduce out of itself the Christian cosmos. At its inception, the bourgeois spirit squats in the ruins of the feudal. With phenomenology bourgeois thought turns to its
215 end in dissociated, fragmentary determinations posited one after the other and resigns itself to the mere reproduction of what is.

Husserl's doctrine of ideas is the system in ruins, just as the first systems were clumsily heaped up out of the wreckage of the erstwhile *ordo*. If phenomenology ultimately seeks to restore totality and 'awaken' it out of the wreckage, the disparate 'substances', then its space soon shows itself as shrivelled to the point of the εἶδος ego, and in place of a unity posited in the manifold by autonomous reason, there enters passive genesis through association.[29] The formal unity of the world as constituted by transcendental subjectivity – that is all that remains from the system of Transcendental Idealism.

Advanced and Restorative Elements

One can thus drastically separate the advanced and the regressive elements of Husserl's philosophy. Those are advanced in which thought 'means beyond itself'[30] under the compulsion of its contradictions. This may occur by phenomenology turning,

* [In English in the text. Trans.]

[29] Cf. *CM*, p. 82; and Cairns ⟨113 ff⟩.
[30] Cf. *LU* II, ii, pp. 41 and 236; and Findlay, pp. 701 and 863.

however much in vain, to a reality not immanent to consciousness. Or by phenomenology bumping up against the primitive idealistic rock while pursuing its own contradictions, and falling into aporia which can no longer be avoided unless the idealistic beginning itself were abandoned. Husserl takes on regressive features as soon as he presents the aporia as positive determinations and hypostatizes the subjective stage (*Instanz*) as immanence to consciousness as well as the essentiality of the fact-free concept. – It is the dismantling motifs of phenomenology which in principle function progressively, particularly as they constitute the debate between the early Husserl and Brentano and the latter's closer followers. By attacking certain conceptual auxiliary apparati – such as the feeling of evidence, the 'object' of sensation, the ostensible psychological impossibility of the coexistence of contradictory judgements in the same consciousness at the same time, or the various picture and sign theories – Husserl destroyed theoretical inventions by confronting them with the cognitive activities from which concept fetishistic thought demanded the invented functions.

The disruptive force of Husserl's analyses, however, also serves to convulse his own fetishes. It initially freed the way for phenomenology to an extreme version of idealism, the transcen- 216 dental. But it did not stop with idealism's fundamental concept, that of pure subjectivity. Since critical progress transferred the power of all legality (*rechtssetzende Gewalt*) to that subject, it must ultimately repay the debts of the idealistic movement of the concept.

The impetus of such a movement had long since been established in his genuinely phenomenological phase when Husserl distinguished himself from positivism, viz. in the polemic against psychologism. This certainly also has its questionable components. Any recollection of real men and their drives which will not obey pure determinations of thought, should be banished afar by phenomenological exercises. But if phenomenology suppresses the human contribution to the propositions of pure logic, and then deifies the power of human thought by letting logical laws obtain beyond the circle of human judgement, even of those extra-terrestrial figures for which it has a predilection – still the polemic of the Prolegomena is directed against man's most insistent illusion, that of the individual.

The capital proof of the difference between logical and psychological laws has, at all events, simply shown that the norms by which individuals think do not coincide with the norms according to which the life of their own consciousness and unconscious proceeds. The individual himself does not belong in the very activity in which it fancies itself most at home, the 'free' activity of thought. Autonomy and isolation of the individual as a thinking individual are just as much an illusion (the illusion necessarily produced by bourgeois society) as relativism which, in contrast, hopes to escape the binding obligation for knowledge by recourse to the illusory individual. The Prolegomena just absolutized the stage on which the completion of logical operations depends. Husserl's later 'monadological' theories, such as are especially contained in the *Cartesian Meditations*, are supposed to remedy the deficiency. But if anywhere, it is here that Husserl's self-correction simply ruins a great fundamental insight.

A similar thing has certainly happened to another motif, the
217 anti-systematic theme which is in no way inferior to the anti-psychological theme in disillusioning power and also functions as its corrective. As the only German scholastic philosopher of the period, Husserl defended the critical rectitude of reason without inferring from it the claim that the world is to be deduced and totally 'comprehended' from the concept: The emphasis with which he contrasts pure reason and its objectifications from 'mundane' (*mundan*) being directly results in openly and ingloriously retaining the sacrificed empiricality. Empirical findings are not damned from the heights of the idea as long as they just remain empirical findings. Husserl's thought, of course, passively registers breaches and contradictions in his object, but his way to that was also seldom smooth. Indeed in its own realm phenomenology preserves a predilection for fragments, which it shares with scholars of the Dilthey and Max Weber sort. It juxtaposes 'investigations' and accomplished analyses without reasonably unifying them, indeed even without adjusting for inconsistencies which arise from the singular studies. Only after Husserl lost confidence in the phenomenological method did he find himself cautiously and unwillingly prepared for system.

His anti-systematic stance was rewarded by its discovery, in practically blind analysis guided by no higher concept 'from above', of what the construction of systematic idealists deductively posits and what, on the other hand, the posteriorly constructing thought of positivists forgets, viz. the dynamic moment of cognition, synthesis. This is for Husserl a factual state of description. The concept of judgement, as constitutive for formal logic, is designated by 'identical objecthood'.[31] And the analysis of the sense of this objecthood – without which any decision about truth and untruth, even the formal-logical sort, would be impossible – culminates in the question 'What assures us of this identity?'[32] But Husserl's answer is: Without subjective synthesis the objectivity of judgement would not be possible.

> . . . if the process of thinking progresses, and we, connecting synthetically, turn back to what was previously given as one, then this itself is no longer originally evident: We are conscious of it again in the medium of recollection and in a recollection that is not in the least intuitive. Recollection, succeeding as actual intuition proper, would indeed be restitution of each single moment or step of the original process. But, even if that takes place, even if a new evidence is thus brought about, is it sure that this evidence is restitution of the earlier evidence? And now let us remember that the judgements which, in *218* living evidence, were constituted originally as intentional unities – constituted in the mode, having itself – are supposed to have a continuing acceptance as objects existing for us at all times, available to us at all times – as convictions lasting for us from the time of their first constitution. Logic relates, not to what is given only in active evidence, but to the abiding formations that have been primally instituted in active evidence and can be reactivated and identified again and again; it relates to them as objecthood which is henceforth at hand, with which, taking hold of it again, one can operate in thinking, and which, as the same, one can further shape categorially into more and more new formations.[33]

Since the naive reification of logic appears in theoretical-critical consciousness by means of the concept of objecthood, its subjective synthetic moment is also called by name.

Uncovering the sense-genesis of judgements signifies, more precisely, an unravelling of the sense-moments that are implicit in and belong

[31] *Logik* [192]; cf. Cairns ⟨163⟩.
[32] Ibid.
[33] Ibid. [192 ff]; and ibid. ⟨163 ff⟩.

essentially to, the sense that has plainly come to light. Judgements, as the finished products of a 'constitution' or 'genesis', can and must be asked about this genesis. The essential peculiarity of such products is precisely that they are senses that bear within them, as a sense-implicate of their genesis, a sort of historicality; that in them, level by level, sense points back to original sense and to the corresponding noematic intentionality; that therefore each sense-formation can be asked about its essentially necessary sense-history.[34]

Husserl hardly ever went further than in this passage. Its content may seem lacking in novelty. Basing thingly identity on subjective synthesis comes from Kant and the proof of the 'inner historicity' of logic from Hegel.

But the significance of Husserl's insight is to be sought in the fact that he forced synthesis and history from the hardened thing 219 and indeed from the abstract form of judgement, whereas in classical idealists it belongs to precisely the 'systematic' interpretation of mind mentioned above which comprises the world of things without knowing the status of its own world in dialectical process otherwise than as one of reification and giving expression to this knowledge through the method. But Husserl, the retail scholar (*Detailforscher*) and converted positivist, persists before the solid foreign object of cognition till it submits to the Medusa's glance. The thing as identical object of cognition opens itself up and presents for an instant what its solidity should hide, viz. its historical accomplishment.

The assumption and analysis of reification through an intentionally uniquely descriptive philosophy hostile to speculation leads directly to the fact that history becomes manifest as its central 'finding'. Thus the concept of a descriptive finding certainly sublates itself. Husserl just had to go through the open gate in order to find that the 'inner historicity' which he conceded was not just inner.

[34] Ibid. [215]; and ibid. ⟨184⟩.

Natural History Museum

That is what phenomenology rejected: 'We are not talking here of any histories.'[35] With the discovery of genesis as a 'sense-implicate' it achieves its extreme but once. Otherwise the static interpretation of the subject–object relation remains dominant. *Formal and Transcendental Logic* and the *Cartesian Meditations* were the first to expressly supplement static phenomenology with genetic as constitutive phenomenology. He says about static phenomenology:

its descriptions are analogous to those of natural history, which concern particular types and, at best, arrange them in their systematic order.[36]

The concept of natural history does not appear in this passage gratuitously. Husserl believes he is giving a phenomenology of spirit by presenting and cataloguing its cabinet of natural history specimens. Just as in natural history museums, relics of vanished life are assembled into a collection and put on show, though 'nature' in these specimens just allegorically means past history, and their history is nothing other than a simple natural pastness (*Vergängnis*) – so there is also a phenomenological exhibit of its 'excursions',[37] which has to do with fossils and fossilized syntheses whose 'intentional life' faintly reflects the past-real.

The exhibition spaces of Husserlian demonstrations are always removed from the praxis of present society. As a melancholy 220 memorial, their inventory takes on a paltry aura of significance which Husserl interprets as essential. The obsolete expression 'inventory' (*Inventar*) belongs to the Secessionistic* inventory of vision (*Schau*), streams of lived experiences, and fulfilment, just as the upright piano belongs to the Isle of the Dead. Optical illusion and movable scenery meet in Husserl's texts.

Let us take an example which shows very complicated and yet easily

---

* [*Sezession*: German and Austrian avant-garde art movement of the late nineteenth and early twentieth century. Trans.]

[35] *Ideen* [7] footnote; cf. *Ideas*, p. 45 footnote.
[36] *CM*, p. 79; and Cairns ⟨110⟩.
[37] *Ideen* [265]; and *Ideas*, p. 331.

grasped representational constructions from representations at a higher level. A name on being mentioned reminds us of the Dresden Gallery and of our last visit there: We wander through the rooms, and stand before a picture of Teniers which represents a picture gallery. When we consider that pictures of the latter would in their turn portray pictures which on their part exhibited readable inscriptions and so forth, we can measure what interweaving of representations, and what links of connection between the discernible features in the series of pictures, can really be set up.[38]

The point of the example is not the disclosure of the bad infinity* which it describes. The absurd base line of the pictures along which phenomenology itself vainly pursues its objects from intention to intention, becomes for Husserl the canon of a world which rewards inspection, by holding still for the phenomenologist as a sparkling collection of well-founded noematic 'senses', aloof and odd, like pictures of pictures in a gallery. It is the world as a peep show stage.

Husserl came very close to an awareness of that in the very sentence where he denies it: 'experience is not an opening through which a world, existing prior to all experience, shines into a room of consciousness'.[39] He negates the peep hole notion simply because nothing so completely alien to the subject could be experienced. As someone would deny that he is in front of a peep show, if he can never leave the space in which it is played. The phenomenologist is disconcerted. That is how he appears in the wax figure museum which he also takes as a 'concrete example'.

Wandering about in the Panopticum Waxworks we meet on the stairs a charming lady whom we do not know and who seems to know us, and who is in fact the well-known joke of the place: we have for a moment been tricked by a waxwork figure.[40]

221 The strolling mind just reassures itself with the bit of wisdom,

* [Hegelian notion from *The Science of Logic*. Trans.]

[38] Ibid. [211]; and ibid. p. 270.
[39] *Logik* [239]; cf. Cairns ⟨206⟩.
[40] *LU* II, ii, pp. 442 ff; cf. Findlay, p. 609.

When the illusion vanishes, we see exactly the opposite, a waxwork figure that only represents a lady.[41]

He finds his peace in the world of things in intercourse not with women but with puppets. The embarrassment, however, is of one who does not know whether to take the internal as external or vice versa. And now he concedes himself the original wish to escape in no other way than in the distorted figure of dread.

Abstract Ideal of Security

Dread stamps the ideal of Husserlian philosophy as one of absolute security, on the model of private property. Its reductions aim at the secure: viz. the immanence to consciousness of lived experiences whose title deeds the philosophical self-consciousness to which they 'belong' should possess securely from the grasp of any force; and essences which, free from all factical existence, defy vexation from factical existence.

The two postulates contradict each other. The world of lived experiences is, according to Husserl, changeable and nothing but a 'stream'. But the transcendence of essences can itself never become lived experience. Husserl's development may be understood in the tendency to unite the two postulates of security in a final one which identifies essence and stream of consciousness.

His drive to security is so great that he mistakes with the beguiled naiveté of all propertied belief (*Besitzglauben*): how compulsively the ideal of absolute security drives to its own destruction; how the reduction of essences to the world of consciousness makes them dependent on the factical and the past; how, on the other hand, the essentiality of consciousness robs it of all specific content and sacrifices to chance everything that should be secured.

Security is left as an ultimate and lonely fetish like the number, one million, on a long deflated bank note. More overtly than anywhere else the late bourgeois resigned quality of phenomenology becomes evident. In it the idea of scientific critique shows its reactionary side: Without analysing the ideal of security as such,

[41] Ibid. p. 443; and ibid.

it wants to forbid any thought which cannot arise out of it – or best of all any thinking at all. Another trace of that can be found in the transformation of thought into 'seeing' (*Schau*) and the hatred of theorizing.

222   *Infinitization of the Temporal*

The tendency to infinitize the 'givens' encountered in consciousness as both unquestionably the property of the philosopher and as essential helps to justify the estate. With the infinitization of what is meant in the momentary act and thus ultimately of the purely temporal itself, phenomenological concepts have to pay for the illusion of their construction-free proximity to things and concreteness. Hence it immediately prepares the ideology of those who came after it. The more concrete phenomenology becomes, the readier it is to proclaim the conditioned as unconditioned.

Husserl more or less took over from the pragmatist William James the empirical thesis of 'fringes'* and expressed it eidetically in *Ideas*. For he then advocated a thorough parallelism between psychology as a pure science of laws and eidetic phenomenology which should have inclined him to be suspicious of its self-sufficiency. His conception of the 'court' of concurrent consciousness takes the form:

the stream of lived experience can never consist wholly of public current events (*Aktualitäten*).[42]

A Husserl inspired sociology has hastened to deduce from that the necessity of classes. They are supposed to be the expression of psychological consolidations which correspond to the current events of consciousness. A classless society presupposes universal currency of the life of consciousness of all of its members and just that is excluded by Husserl's understanding of essence. Husserl's theory must bear the responsibility for philosophemes of this sort. However harmless and formal it may appear, it can

---

* [In English in the text. Trans.]

[42] *Ideen* [63]; cf. *Ideas*, p. 107.

never sustain the claim of an unvarying 'structure of pure consciousness'. Since it arises out of psychological observations in specific persons in specific situations, it refers back to them. The 'non-currency' of men depends on the reification of the world in which they live. They congeal in the congealed, and if congelation is their own product, they are ultimately reproduced by it.

All reification is indeed a forgetting. But no phenomenologist could erect beforehand everlasting barriers established for the presentness of a world in which nothing else compels forgetting. The genuinely reactionary content of phenomenology is hatred of 'contemporaneity'. Though it seeks out the 'sphere of absolute   223 origins' in men, it would like best of all to expel them from the world that had arisen in them, similarly to the way deists treat their God, whom Husserl simply wishes to 'bracket out'. The human has value for phenomenology only in its inhumanity, viz. as something completely foreign to man in which he cannot recognize himself. Man becomes immortal through death. Phenomenology mercilessly sequesters meaning and intention (*Meinen und Meinung*) from those who mean and intend; it sequesters the given from the giver and feels its objectivity all the more fundamentally secured, the more it forgets existence.

The initial relation of synthesis to propositions in themselves and 'states-of-affairs', is also that of society, in the final 'genetic' analysis of cognition, to the real bearers and real objects of cognition. Husserl encounters social differences in his analysis of 'cultural milieus'. He records them as disparate stages of accessibility to objective culture for different human individuals and groupings. It is with reference to this that the French version of the *Cartesian Meditations* proceeds:

But this accessibility is indeed not absolute, and that is for essential reasons of its constitution which a more precise explanation of its sense easily clarifies.[43]*

If in fact objective culture is not as universally open to individual consciousness as, by Husserl's declaration, body and psychophysical being, it is not transcendental conditions, e.g.,

---

* [In French in the text. Trans.]

[43] *MC*, p. 112; cf. *CM*, p. 135; and Cairns ⟨160⟩.

which are responsible, but rather the historical conditions of class society. Husserl's transcendental interpretation, however, transplants time in space, exactly as did later totalitarian thought without transcendental circumstances. The differences between various contributions of different men to humane (*menschenwürdig*) life is founded on the fact that they live in spatially far distant 'cultures' from each other, which are primarily 'their own' and from which they may win access to 'human culture' only by stages.

But egology and phenomenological ἐποχή turn into a sort of transcendental xenophobia:

> It is I and my culture who form here the primordial sphere with respect to every 'foreign' culture.[44]*

224 The reality of lived experience of the 'purified' individual consciousness and plainly that of its nation as well is, in all its contingency and narrowness, turned into the foundation of social theory and society. As essential, they should also obtain as extratemporal. It is this spirit which induced Husserl to juxtapose in the sixth Investigation the three examples for 'non-objectifying acts as apparent meaning fulfilments': ' "May God protect the Kaiser." "Franz should have looked after himself." "The coachman should harness the horses." '[45]

Origin of the εἶδος Ego

The ultimate security at which the conceptual movement of phenomenology aims is that of the εἶδος ego. Essential subjectivity should be immediately certain and absolutely valid in its purity. The appeal to subjectivity causes all earlier contradictory concepts to vanish. The later Husserl can do without categorial intuition. Evidence itself may dissolve into a process[46] and renounce all thingly static givenness.[47] Yet nothing has been sacrificed of its security if 'absolute grounding of cognition is'

---

* [In French in the text. Trans.]

[44] Ibid. p. 114; and p. 137; and ⟨161⟩.
[45] LU II, ii, p. 215; cf. Findlay, p. 846.
[46] Cf. Logik [284]; and Cairns ⟨245 ff⟩.
[47] Cf. ibid. [290]; and ibid. ⟨251 ff⟩.

really 'possible only in the all-embracing science of transcendental subjectivity, as the one absolute entity',[48] even if it can be proved that evidence is a structure of transcendental subjectivity.

Because of the question of the εἶδος ego, phenomenology is more important than a simple shade of idealism. The labour of the scientific discipline of the foundation of pure logic, which fills Husserl's entire work, enabled him to continue to detect the factical, purely existing and ideationally non-derivable, where traditional idealism feels protected from all the accidents of the world, viz. in the thinking ego.

His critique of Descartes is directed against the naturalism of the cogito.

Even for Descartes, an absolute evidence makes sure of the ego . . . as a first, indubitably existing, bit of the world; and it is then only a matter of inferring the rest of the world . . . by using a logically valid deductive procedure.[49]

A realism like that of Descartes, which believes that, in the ego to which transcendental self-examination leads back in the first instance, it has apprehended the real psyche of the human being, a realism that then, 225 from this first real projects hypotheses and probability-inferences to carry it over into a realm of transcendent realities . . . such a realism misses the actual problem and does so in a countersensical manner, since everywhere it presupposes as a possibility that which, as a possibility, is itself everywhere in question.[50]

Dread over absolute security, even the original Cartesian postulate of indubitable certainty, leads Husserl to surpass the entire idealistic tradition. He points out the dependence on contingent fact in the Cartesian ego and establishes as a true and solely sufficient presupposition the ideal of the fact-free transcendental. But here he encounters the Archimedean point of idealism. If the critical analysis of the sense of transcendental subjectivity transcends his own, and if it is capable of attaining the moment of facticity and of the spatio-temporal 'world' in the εἶδος ego, then idealism cannot be saved. It has in fact ultimately brought its claim to validity to the form of all or nothing.

[48] Ibid. [278]; and ibid. ⟨240⟩.
[49] Ibid. [235]; and ibid. ⟨202⟩.
[50] Ibid. [236]; and ibid. ⟨203⟩.

Consciousness, Pure Essence, Time

The complete consequences of the conception of consciousness as
a pure essence are only drawn in the last two writings published
during Husserl's lifetime. *Formal and Transcendental Logic* asserts:
'The Necessity of Starting Each From His Own Subjectivity'.

To be correct, however, I must say expressly in the first place: I myself
am this subjectivity, I who carry on sense-investigation concerning what
exists for me and is accepted by me and who now, *qua* logician, am
carrying on sense-investigation with regard to the presupposed existing
world and the logical principles related to it. In the first place, then, it is
always I and I again: purely as ego of that life of consciousness by which
everything receives being-sense for me.[51]

But,

When, within the universality of my ego-cogito, I find myself as a
psychophysical entity, a unity constituted in my ego-cogito, and find
related to this unity, in the form 'others', psychophysical entities
opposite me, who, as such, are likewise constituted in multiplicities
belonging to my essential life, I become aware of great difficulties – in
the first place, even concerning myself. I, the 'transcendental ego', am
the ego who 'precedes' everything worldly: as the ego, that is to say, in
whose life of consciousness the world, as an intentional unity, is
226 constituted to begin with. Therefore I, the constituting ego, am not
identical with myself as a psychophysical reality; and my psychic
(*seelisches*) life, the psychophysical and worldly life of consciousness, is
not identical with my transcendental ego, in which the world, with
everything physical and psychic that belongs to it, is constituted for
me.[52]

What is decisive is how the two concepts of the ego relate to
each other: subjectivity, the 'I myself', which is unqualifiedly
equated by Huserl with the psychophysical person, and the
'transcendental ego'. For only when the latter is fully independent of the former, by its definition (*dem Sinn nach*), and
untarnished by facticity, does its structure attain the absoluteness

---

[51] Ibid. [243]; and ibid. ⟨208 ff⟩.
[52] Ibid. [245]; and ibid. ⟨210 ff⟩.

which should secure it priority before the subject of the Cartesian cogito. Husserl assumes that it is, 'thanks to transcendental clarification, already understandable that my soul' – the empirical 'I myself' – 'is a self-objectification of my transcendental ego',[53] and thus that the transcendental precedes the empirical by definition and as a constitutive condition.

Here lies the *nervus probandi*. The false transition, the 'surreptitiousness' of which Husserl himself once spoke,[54] can be detected in the consequence of this assertion: 'And I do not find . . . that my transcendental life and my psychic, my worldly life have, in each and every respect, a like content.'[55] The identity of the form of speech 'I' in the cases of the two ego-concepts says in the first instance nothing more than that the concept of the transcendental ego was derived from that of the empirical through abstraction, without clarifying as to why a single *a priori* principle should underlie both. But if the 'content' of both is in fact identical – why then the difference between them which Husserl so stresses? Why should distinct valence or transcendental originality be ascribed to each of them? Husserl gives no criterion for the difference. And he persists in maintaining the identity of content.[56] Nevertheless, he finds a 'falsifying dislocation, if one mistakes this psychological internal experience for the internal experience relied on transcendentally as an evidential experiencing of ego-cogito'.[57]

The assertion of a difference in principle between the two despite complete identity of their 'content' leaves no room but to turn to 'form' in a very Kantian and traditional manner and make the transcendental ego the abstract condition for the 'possibility in general' of the empirical without any content at all, even the accompanying content of the empirical ego. But what directly belongs to the 'transcendental' conditions of pure consciousness, 227 in the sense of the 'genetic' phenomenology of the late Husserl, is the constitution of the ego in itself which presupposes above all temporal and thus content-filled experience. It makes no sense to speak of a timeless consciousness, whether objective or subjec-

---

[53] Ibid. [246]; and ibid. ⟨212⟩.
[54] Ibid. [262]; and ibid. ⟨226⟩.
[55] Ibid. [245]; and ibid. ⟨211⟩.
[56] Cf. ibid. [261]; and ibid. ⟨224 ff⟩.
[57] Ibid. [260]; and ibid. ⟨224⟩.

tive, for a concrete structure of consciousness, such as the Husserlian reductions are supposed to dissect (*herauspräparieren*), cannot be thought as other than temporally determined in general. The structure of intentionality as retentionality and protentionality, which, according to Husserl, alone renders the life of consciousness possible, is the structure of time. The findings of all psychology, however, are for Husserl 'facts' (*Fakten*).[58] They become facts precisely by their temporal determinacy. But this also cannot be taken from a 'pure' life of consciousness, provided it may still be identified as the life of consciousness and be more than the abstract Kantian 'I think' from which Husserl so urgently wishes to distinguish it.

Transcendental Ego and Facticity

If the (or as Husserl ambiguously says 'my') transcendental ego were the sheer form of the manifold of empirical lived experiences, then it could not objectify 'itself'. It would become objective simply through the lived experiences as its factical content. Then the 'soul' or 'psyche' would not be a self-objectification of the transcendental. Transcendental unity remains, in order to make 'sense' at all, that is in order to be determinable as unity, referred to the factical. The factical belongs to the 'sense' of the transcendental, which may not be treated as having been granted autonomy or as an absolute foundation. . . .

Otherwise the transcendental ego would be 'my' ego in more than the formal sense. It would be the I with the fullness of its lived experiences. Then it would always have been the 'soul' itself and need not wait to be 'objectified' in a practically second layer. From the standpoint of the analysis of consciousness, the concept of the soul is equivalent to the concept of the structure of lived experience which is legally objectified in the forms of its relations. Husserl may twist the concepts however he wishes. The idealist may call the conditions of the possibility of the life of consciousness, which have been abstracted out of it, transcendental. They 228 still remain allotted to a determined and somehow 'factual' life of consciousness. They do not obtain 'in themselves'. They let

---

[58] Cf. ibid. [258]; and ibid. ⟨221 ff⟩.

themselves be determined. They assume meaning solely in relation to the factical I. They would be incomprehensible if hypostatized.

The most rigorous concept of the transcendental cannot get out of its interdependence with the fact. To that extent it remains what Husserl dislikes about the Cartesian ego: a bit of the world. Husserl correctly recognized that the worldliness of the substratum of psychology possesses no ontological primacy over the worldliness of psychophysical nature. If transcendental philosophy relies on the former, then it has no hope of grounding the latter. It collapses as *prima philosophia*.

Equivocation of 'I'

The *Cartesian Meditations* seek to pursue the general discussions of *Formal and Transcendental Logic* about the εἶδος ego. The transcendental 'I' should not be 'the man who, in natural self-experience, encounters himself as a man and who, with the abstractive restriction to the pure contents of internal or purely psychological self-experience, encounters his own pure *mens sive animus sive intellectus*'.[59]

Hegel had already criticized this thought in Fichte.

When pure knowing is determined as I, it acts as a perpetual reminder of the subjective I whose limitations should be forgotten, and it fosters the idea that the propositions and relations resulting from the further development of the I are present and can already be found in ordinary consciousness – for in fact it is this of which they are asserted.[60]

Accordingly the identity of the form of speech must plainly not be ontologically hypostatized. 'My' transcendental life is not contained in 'my' psychological life as its substrate. The moment of unity, however, which is expressed in the identity of the form of speech, should not be ignored either. If the transcendental 'I' were completely cut off from *animus* or *intellectus*, then the right to call it 'I' at all would become problematic. Critique can pursue that right into the syntax of Husserl's French version of the ἐποχή.

[59] *CM*, pp. 26 ff; cf. Cairns ⟨64⟩.
[60] Hegel, *Wissenschaft der Logik*, vol. 4, p. 82; cf. Miller, *Hegel's Science of Logic*, pp. 76 ff.

One may also say that the ἐποχη´ is the radical and universal method by which I grasp myself as pure self (*moi*) with the life of consciousness which is proper to myself, a life in and by which the entire objective
229 world exists for me, just *as* it exists for me.*[61]

Through the reflexive 'myself' the judging 'I' of psychological lived experience can be 'universally' (*je*) related to the pure self (*moi pur*), only if the individual reflecting on itself, as the grammatical subject of judgement, identifies itself with the pure self as grammatical object. Identity with the subject is expressed in the reflexive form, that with the object in the predicate qualification 'as pure self' (*comme moi pur*). Husserl directly challenges the relation of unity which Hegel invariably begins by characterizing as unavoidable. Yet the relation prevails against his will.

Solipsism

But the thesis of the *Cartesian Meditations* concerning the eidetic character of the transcendental subject as pure possibility depends on this equivocality of 'I'. It runs,

every constitution of an actually pure possibility among others carries with it implicitly, as its outer horizon, a purely possible ego, a pure possibility-variant of my factical ego.[62]

If the variant, 'pure ego', is always supposed to remain a variant of 'my ego' and draw its evidence from self-experience, then it is necessarily bound to a determinate life of consciousness, viz. that which is called 'I'. It is thus mundane or irrevocably referred back to the mundane. Otherwise, the loaded term 'my' which Husserl repeatedly employs, is strictly incomprehensible. Nevertheless, he asserts that the transcendental ego takes precedence through free fantasy variation as pure possibility even over 'my' ego in the logical sense.

* [In French in the text. Trans.]

[61] *MC*, p. 18; cf. *CM*, p. 27; and Cairns ⟨65⟩.
[62] Ibid. p. 73; and ibid. ⟨105⟩.

In this transition the relation of ostensibly absolute 'transcendental' being over facts disappears. Through variation the 'I' is no longer 'mine'; that is, it is no longer I. Certainly what is specific about the expression 'I' must not escape phenomenology dedicated to meaning analysis. It could not be replaced in a sentence whose subject is 'I' with any expression which presents the name of the speaking person. For the immediacy of the reference of the sentence back to the speaker, in contrast to a purely mediated sentence, itself constitutes a moment of the sense of the sentence.

Accordingly, one may lay hands on the ὕστερον πρότερον. For only 'my' ego is supposed to be doubt-free and certain as 230 immediately present. Husserl remains to that extent a Cartesian. If epistemology proceeds by variations from 'its own' to the eidetic ego, then for it the basis of correctness is the absoluteness of 'its' ego which acquires apodictic certainty by this abstract εἶδος ego. Hence the concept of 'transcendental experience' which devolves only on the position of 'one's own' consciousness. But then Husserl turns around and uses the hypostatized εἶδος ego to ground 'his' and every other ego through the a priority of the fact-free essential, which nevertheless, according to his doctrine, is itself grounded in the immediate certainty of factical personal consciousness.

Husserl is aware of the difficulty.

It should be noted that, in the transition from my ego to an ego as such, neither the actuality nor the possibility of other egos is presupposed. I fantasy only myself as if I were otherwise; I do not fantasy others.[63]

The phenomenological residuum is interpreted in the sense of solipsism and the construction of essential insight is once more applied in order to get out of solipsism. Since this construction, at least from the standpoint of *Ideas*, is meant to gain possession of its 'essence' in a singular individual object, the variation of the absolute singularity of 'my' life of consciousness, without regard to any others from which the essence could be abstracted, is supposed to produce the pure εἶδος ego.

But the construction collapses. If in fact 'his' ego were simply given to the epistemologist as a point of departure without any

[63] Ibid. p. 74; and ibid. ⟨106⟩.

more knowledge than that of 'his' ego, but with the full knowledge that each of his lived experiences qualifies as a moment of unified 'consciousness', then even variations could be at play only in the framework of 'his ego', provided they retain 'his ego'. All 'pure' possibilities, however they are accounted for, are 'his'; every variational ego is that of the speaker. The variation would lead, in any event, to changing content, but not to transcendental consciousness.

Whoever represents the pure ego as Husserl postulates it, viz.
231 without representing thereby in the least 'an other', not even as a sheer possibility, is always just himself the pure ego. Fantasy variation through pure possibility cannot break through the immanence of the monad. For the concept of unity which underlies the immanence and which in Husserl should ground the super-individual essence, 'ego', is itself monadological. 'My' ego is in truth already an abstraction and anything but the original experience that Husserl claims it is. The relation of possession determines it as very mediated indeed. 'Intersubjectivity' is posited along in it, only not as an arbitrary pure possibility, but rather as the real condition for being I, without which the limitation to 'my' ego cannot be understood.

Since Husserl's logic limits the ego as belonging to it, it expresses that the ego indeed does not belong to itself. But the impossibility of reaching 'essence' in the absolute monad, indicates the position of individuals in monadological society.

The Aporia of Transcendental Experience

Essence cannot do without the relation to existence. Monadological experience cannot become essential. Experience appears in Husserl within the transcendental conception itself and is christened with the paradoxical name of 'transcendental experience'.[64] The positivistic impulse prevails even in the εἶδος ego. The transposition of the pure ego into an 'essence' and its emancipation from anything 'wordly' satisfies Husserl as being prescribed simply by the course of 'research'. It is not posited in the sense of Fichtean Idealism. The transcendental ego should be accessible as an experientiable domain.

[64] Ibid. p. 24; and ibid. ⟨62⟩.

And indeed, instead of attempting to use the *ego cogito* as an apodictically evident premise for arguments supposedly implying a transcendental ['transcendent' in Husserl–TWA] subjectivity, we shall direct our attention to the fact that the phenomenological ἐποχή´ lays open (to me, the meditating philosopher) an infinite sphere of being of a new kind, as the sphere of a new kind of experience: transcendental experience.[65]

The 'existence' (*Existenz*) of the transcendental subject as an experientiable domain and its interpretation as pure possibility of fantasy variation, however, are incompatible. Husserl delimited 232 transcendental subjectivity against the ancestral concept of experience, that of the given, as much as against the abstract 'I think'. 'But, when descriptive theory of consciousness begins radically, it has before it no such data and wholes, except perhaps as prejudices.'[66] Then how should the structure (*Struktur*) of transcendental consciousness be understood at all? It should neither be posited nor deduced. It counts for more than just the content of consciousness. Its immediate intuitability is no longer advocated. But then it could simply be gained through abstraction. Yet no motive is adduced for discontinuing abstraction for categories such as 'my' ego (which can only be understood in their relation to the factical), or for the fact that abstraction does not go further to the Kantian 'I think' as the only 'pure' thing.

Both at peak and base the transcendental structure finds itself endangered. At the peak because it remains so long in relation to facts (*Faktum*) that it reduces to sheer identity. At the base because, aside from the relation to 'contents', it cannot be brought to transcendental 'experience', however construed. As soon as Husserl's theory ultimately examines the contents themselves, it openly concedes their contingency. But thus it reaches the position at which it must finally hypostatize the aporia, sublimate facts in ontology, and complete its Münchhausen* trick with systematic necessity – the position where idealism, instead of just giving up, turns into a metaphysics of tautology and projects its material (*sachlich*) failure on the ground of being.

* [Hero of *The Adventures of Baron Münchhausen* by Rudolph Raspe. The character pulls himself out of a swamp by his own pigtail. Trans.]

[65] Ibid. p. 29; and ibid. ⟨66⟩.
[66] Ibid. p. 40; and ibid. ⟨77⟩.

Husserl introduced the concept of the 'contingent* *a priori*' for particular material propositions of the form 'All tonal phenomena are extended in time'. He applies this concept to transcendental subjectivity itself and thus stamps it with the seal of paradox:

> To acquaint ourselves more closely with the concept of the contingent *a priori*, the following exposition will suffice within the bounds of our present, merely anticipatory observations: A subjectivity as such (whether solitary or in communication) is thinkable only as having an essential form, whose highly multifarious constituents (*Gehalten*) we
233 obtain with progressive evidence when we uncover to intuition our own concrete subjectivity and then, with the aid of a free changing of its actuality into 'other' possibilities of any concrete subjectivity as such, direct our regard to the invariable that can be seen throughout – that is to say: the essentially necessary. If we stipulate, from the beginning of this variation, that the subjectivity shall always have the capacity to be and remain a 'rational' and, in particular, a judicatively cognizing subjectivity, we encounter restrictive essential structures that fall under the heading of pure reason and, in particular, pure judicative reason. Such a subjectivity also involves as a presupposition a continual and essentially necessary relatedness to some hyletic components or other: as apperceptional foundations for the possible experiences that judging necessarily presupposes. Therefore, if we qualify the concept of form in principle by the essentially necessary components of any rational subjectivity whatever, the concept hyle (exemplified by every 'datum of sensation') is a form concept and not what we shall define as the opposite of this, a contingent concept. On the other hand, there is no essential requirement that a judicatively cognizing subjectivity (or rational subjectivity of any kind) be capable of sensing colours or sounds, that it be capable of sense-feelings having just such and such a difference (*Differenz*), or the like – though the concepts of such matters too can be framed as *a priori* (as freed from everything empirically factical).[67]

The distinction between 'necessary' and 'contingent' in these sentences is powerless. Since it is hardly a 'demand of essence' that subjectivity directly perceive 'colours or tones', then one can hardly conclude from pure thought that subjectivity makes

---

* [Husserl's term for 'contingent' is *kontingent*, Adorno's is the more colloquial *zufällig*. Trans.]

[67] *Logik* [33 ff]; and Cairns ⟨26 ff⟩.

experiences as such. The 'existence' of subjectivity is not to be deduced as necessary or a 'formal *a priori*'. And more. If the sentence, 'All tonal phenomena are extended in time', has a 'material core', then so does the purest formal *a priori* in Husserl's sense, the law of non-contradiction, as long as it is understood only as related to the whole of knowledge and its contents and not isolated and reified. In the sentence from acoustics, there is the moment of contingency, according to Husserl insofar as its validity depends on whether there is such a thing as 'tone in general', i.e. whether psychological factical consciousness constitutes factical lived experiences. What Husserl concedes for the 234 contingent *a priori* also applies to his formal *a priori*. Thus the concept of the contingent *a priori* logically acquires universal validity in Husserl's own theory. His absolute *a priori* included a moment of the non-*a priori*.

It should not be difficult to compute the meaninglessness of the thesis that the non-*a priori* fact has its *a priori* in being non-*a priori*. Certainly not too much is gained by that. Husserl's concept of contingency is, like that of accident in the entirety of bourgeois thought, the expression of the impossibility of reducing the real to its concept, the fact to its essence, or in the final instance the object to the subject. The talk of contingency, like that of the *a priori*, indicates an opaque and unplanned social process as the fate of the individual. The process is 'necessary', and the individual 'contingent', and not just the individual, but, to that extent, what could be possible.

The End of Idealism

The sublation of idealism, which is proclaimed at the end of Husserl's philosophy, cannot qualify as that philosophy's achievement. If the phenomenological method occasioned existential ontology and philosophical anthropology, then its 'shipwreck' (pet word of all διάδοχοι) certainly gives them free play. The fact that pure thought is not the absolutely first in the world, but has its origin in man and corporeal existence, has become a platitude for all those whose 'Anti-Cartesianism' is meant less to analyse concretely the relation between consciousness and being, than to calumniate consciousness itself by appealing to the solidity of the sheer existent. Husserl keeps his faith before them and in spite of everything in critical – 'judicial' – reason.

But if such reason gets entangled in irresolvable antimonies by attempting to prove itself the absolute and total ground of being, then the exhibition of those antimonies not only deprives it of its critical right but also obviously means it gives no absolute condition for being. It is one thing to irrationally decree the irreducibility of being as the ontological primacy of consciousness, and another to drive fundamental analysis of consciousness 235 so far that it turns into something improper to consciousness. Then such a counterpart is not just a counterpart; it is neither the unconscious, nor being removed from all assertion.

The demand for the primacy of consciousness over being is dishonoured. That does not mean that primacy is surrendered to existence (*Dasein*). The endless suit which Husserl brings against the absolutely first confutes the very concept of the absolutely first. Hence the old guard philosophy of consciousness is, by its objective function, more advanced than *arriviste* philosophy of being. The latter reverts to the thought of identity, whereas the former ultimately does not of course reach, but does extort the resolution of the philosophical drive to identity.

Idealism is not simply untruth. It is truth in its untruth. Idealistic illusion (*Schein*) is as necessary in its origin as in its passing. That consciousness assumes a monadological shape, that the individual feels knowledge of himself (*von sich selber*) is more immediate and certain than the same knowledge of all others – this is the correct appearance of a false world in which men are alien and uncertain to each other and every individual immediately relates only to his particular interests but in which, nevertheless, universal 'essential' laws are indeed realized: such as Husserl's transcendental εἶδος in the monad.

The intertwining of illusion and necessity in idealism has seldom become clearer in its history than with Husserl. An enemy of both the necessary illusoriness of induction and the illusory necessity of deduction, he strived to confine idealism in a paradoxical stand-off. The ground of the paradox, the monadological constitution of man, could only be sublated if consciousness were at some time finally to rule over being, which it constantly only with untruth asserts is grounded in consciousness.

Translator's Note

Translating *Against Epistemology* involves two distinct problem areas arising from Husserl's profusion of terminology and Adorno's conscious manipulation of German clausal order and sentence construction.

Husserl's penchant for inventing words, usually Hellenic or Anglo-Saxon neologisms, to correspond to regions of being he felt he discovered is well known. Moreover, he did not always use a single term consistently and he often invented new appellations for a single notion as his thoughts matured. The extensive tradition of Husserl translation into English has not really helped matters, since few of the major translators have paid much attention to what the others were doing. In many cases a single German term has a number of different English renderings. And the appeal to Ricoeur's French of those dissatisfied with the old English translation of *Ideas* has ultimately amounted to veritable verbal overkill.

The two principal English lexica of Husserl are those of Findlay and Cairns. In general I have followed one or the other of these systems, particularly Findlay for early Husserl and Cairns for more developed phenomenology. Where they conflict, I have had to choose one or the other, my principal desideratum being consistency. Another important source for Husserl translation is Adorno's own *Journal of Philosophy* article. I have tried wherever possible to conform to Adorno's usage, but deviated on one or two points. The reader will note that there is at least one mistake in Adorno's otherwise utterly limpid and masterful English. On p.13 Adorno obviously has in mind *nichts weniger als*, which he renders as 'nothing less than' rather than the more appropriate 'completely different from'. On one or two occasions I have also opted for terms from less reputable sources. I have chosen

Boyce-Gibson's 'essential insight' for *Wesensschau* as more elegant than Cairns' suggestions, and I would go even further to point out that *Schau*, while meaning 'sight' or 'view', is the root for *erschauen* and *Anschauung*, the latter meaning 'intuition'. So there is a grammatical relation to Kant's and Husserl's notions of intuition. I have also chosen 'factical' for *faktisch* from MacQuarrie and Robinson's *Being and Time*.

In some cases I have made independent choices. *Gegenständlichkeit* clearly means roughly 'what has to do with objects', while *Objektivität* means 'objectivity' in the sense of objective judgements. The single English term most appropriate to the first notion is 'objecthood' popularized in art criticism, instead of Cairns' barbarous 'objecticity'. The *meinen–bedeuten* problem is familiar from controversies surrounding Husserl and Frege. Adorno only refers at length to the distinction in isolated passages. Hence there was no need for over-subtlety about Husserl's inconsistent and changing definition of the distinction. Roughly, *meinen* is more personal and subject-oriented, and *bedeuten* is more objective, implying a relation between language and the world irrespective of individual minds. Where possible, I have rendered *Meinung* as 'our meaning' and *Bedeutung* as 'reference'. Where such practice clearly violated Adorno's sense, I have had to rely on 'meaning' with the German in parentheses.

It goes without saying that I doublechecked all quotations, particularly those from Husserl, Hegel and Nietzsche, and made revisions where the published translations contained errors and for the sake of consistency. I have also included a rudimentary lexicon so that scholars may know which German term is in question for persistent English usages.

Adorno himself poses different problems. It was one of the marks of his philosophical style to avoid technical jargon completely. But his approach to German style certainly retards immediate comprehension, even to the philosophically accomplished. Adorno's period is in fact somewhat shorter than that of traditional German stylists and even of some of his contemporaries. What characterizes Adorno, rather, is an odd and uneven sentential rhythm where the legato of complex philosophical arguments is broken unexpectedly by abrupt pronouncements and disjointed modifiers. It is a style infused with ellipsis, distortion of the order of modifying clauses, dense clusters of syncategorematic particles, and, after Hegel, the abandoned use of abstract nouns with anthropomorphic predicates, producing the effect of a deliberate category mistake, but expressing the very Hegelian persuasion that concepts have a life (for Adorno tied to society) independent both of any individual mind and of their logical status at a time. In this respect, Adorno's writing bears interesting comparison to Mallarmé's prose style, which, there is good evidence to believe, was also the product of a literary appreciation of Hegel. Adorno was indeed convinced that philosophy should take a cue from modernist literature, and that the linguistic experiments conducted by the avant-garde would, if adopted, have an impact on the content of philosophical doctrine and argument. Like Schoenberg, Adorno seemed to feel that the choice of one's language was practically a moral decision. And indeed, to this reader at least, the effect of Adorno's prose is to cut across the grain of the subject–predicate sentence as the unit of assertion. Unexpected modifiers and syntactical confusion give the impression that Adorno's argument lays down its pitch over the surface of and thoroughly out of synchrony with traditional punctuation. Like the Cubist ratchet plane or the Baroque shaft of light which do not respect the bounds of middle-sized dry goods, Adorno's style is certainly far from limpid, but only those who have trouble reading anything at all make clarity their highest value.

In this translation I have tried to make Adorno as accessible as possible without losing the literary flavour of the original. The ideal was to make each assertion definite and yet correspond as closely as possible to the letter of the original. The major obstacle was sorting out genuine Teutonisms from Adorno's inventions.

One aspect of Adorno's philosophical style is its terminological cosmopolitanism. I have tried to mirror this by imitating his liberal admixture of foreign terms – English, French, Latin and Greek – but could not do so always and only when Adorno did. Again, it was more important to retain the flavour of Adorno's style in this respect than absolute correspondence.

The effect of *Against Epistemology* is one of constant and unbroken flow. I have followed it in eliminating all italics from Husserl quotations, whose style is very nearly the contrary of Adorno's. I have, for the sake of the English reader, however, deviated from him on the following points: (1) I have occasionally introduced italics into Adorno's text where this would have the paradoxical effect of smoothing the flow. German has numerous stress particles which English does not possess, and it is best to accommodate this by indications of the stressed rhythm of English speech rather than rendering each individual particle. (2) I have added paragraphing and introduced Adorno's section titles into the body of the text. The reader should be aware that Adorno's only indentations occurred at the heads of sections. (3) I have introduced scare quotes for terms which are clearly mentioned and not used. This practice had not yet become common at the time of Adorno's composition.

My wife, Caroline Oliver Domingo, made substantive contributions to the translation, for which I am very grateful.

Bibliographical Note

Husserl's works cited in the text are listed below. The translations have in general been based on existing English versions, but all quotations have been revised in the interests of accuracy and consistency.

1 *Logische Untersuchungen*, Bänder I, II i and II ii, 3rd and 4th ed. (Niemeyer, Halle, 1922 and 1928); tr. *Logical Investigations* by J.N. Findlay, 2 vols (Humanities, New York, 1970). Abbr.: *LU* I, II i, II ii, p. 00 and Findlay p. 00.

2 *Husserliana, Edmund Husserl, Gesammelte Werke*, Bd. III, erstes Buch, ed. H.L. van Breda. *Ideen zu einer reinen Phänomenologie und phänomenologische Philosophie*, erstes Buch, *Allgemeine Einführung in die reine Phänomenologie*, ed. Walter Biemel (Nijhoff, The Hague, 1950); tr. *Ideas, General Introduction to Pure Phenomenology* by W.R. Boyce-Gibson (Collier-Macmillan, London, 1962). Abbr.: *Ideen* [00] and *Ideas*, p. 00.

3 *Formale und Transzendentale Logik, Versuch einer Kritik der logischen Vernunft*, Bänder I and II, ed. Paul Janssen (Nijhoff, The Hague, 1977); tr. *Formal and Transcendental Logic* by Dorion Cairns (Nijhoff, The Hague, 1969). Abbr.: *Logik* [00] and Cairns ⟨00⟩.

4 *Cartesianische Meditationen, eine Einleitung in die Phänomenologie*, ed. Elisabeth Stroker (Meiner, Hamburg, 1977); and *Méditations cartésiennes* (Paris, Armand Colin, 1931); tr. *Cartesian Meditations, an Introduction to Phenomenology* by Dorion Cairns (Nijhoff, The Hague, 1969). Abbr.: *CM*, p. 00, *MC*, p. 00 and Cairns ⟨00⟩.

Against Epistemology was originally published in German under the title *Zur Metakritik der Erkenntnistheorie, Studien über Husserl und die phänomenologischen Antinomien*. It first appeared in 1956

(Kohlhammer, Stuttgart), then later as vol. 5 of Adorno's collected works, eds. Adorno and Rolf Tiedemann (Suhrkamp, Frankfurt, 1971), and finally in paperback (Suhrkamp, Frankfurt, 1972). The marginal pagination in this translation follows that of the two Suhrkamp editions.

Other works by Adorno on the subject of Husserl and phenomenology are:

1 'Die Transzendenz des Dinglichen und Noematischen in Husserls Phänomenologie', Frankfurter Dissertation, 28 July 1924; projected for vol. 1 of *Gesammelte Schriften*.
2 'Husserl and the Problem of Idealism', *Journal of Philosophy*, vol. 37, no. 1, pp. 5–18, 4 January 1940; projected for vol. 20 of *Gesammelte Schriften*.

Adorno's Preface gives the further publication history of the chapters of *Against Epistemology*. Finally, this information is communicated in the Editorial Postscript to vol. 5 of *Gesammelte Schriften*:

Adorno's Oxford studies on Husserl of 1934–37 were preceded by an intensive treatment of phenomenology while Adorno was still a student. This led to the dissertation 'Die Transzendenz des Dinglichen und Noematischen in Husserls Phänomenologie' with which Adorno acquired his doctorate from the University of Frankfurt a.M. on 28 July 1924 at the age of twenty. The dissertation, which at the time was only printed in a two-page synopsis, will be published in the first volume of the *Collected Works*. – Whereas Adorno's first Husserl text criticized the concept of the thing-in-itself, as it is presented in Husserl's *Ideas*, from the immanence philosophy position of Hans Cornelius, the work on Husserl which Adorno took up ten years later applies especially to work on questions of materialistic logic. Initially undertaken to obtain the Oxford doctorate in philosophy, Adorno laid the manuscript aside in the spring of 1937 and wrote his 'Versuch über Wagner'. The following year, after moving to New York, he worked on a comprehensive presentation which was intended for publication in *Zeitschrift für Sozialforschung*, but never completed it . . . – The first, second and fourth chapters of the 1956 edition of *Against Epistemology* are based on portions of the Oxford manuscript. The Introduction and Chapter Three were written in 1955–56 especially for the book. The German title *Zur Metakritik der Erkenntnistheorie* represents a compromise with the first publisher; Adorno originally intended to call it *Die Phänomenologischen Antinomien*

(The Phenomenological Antinomies). In 1968 he still labelled it the most important of his books for him next to *Negative Dialectics.* He would allude to the Introduction above all as the work which, next to the article 'Der Essay als Form' (The Essay as Form) in *Noten zur Literatur I (Notes on Literature I),* came closest to encompassing a programme for his philosophy.

A more complete Adorno bibliography can be found at the end of *Theodor W. Adorno zum Gedächtnis,* ed. Hermann Schweppenhauser (Suhrkamp, Frankfurt, 1971).

German–English Lexicon

Abschattung: adumbration
Ausschaltung: suspension
   (in the sense of suspending
   judgement)
Bann: spell, jurisdiction,
   constraint
Bannkreis: jurisdiction
bedeuten: refer, mean
Bedeutung: reference,
   meaning
bewähren: verify, authentify
Dasein: existence, being
   there (in discussions of
   Heidegger)
dinghaft: reified
Entfaltung: development,
   unfolding
Erkenntnis: cognition,
   knowledge
Erlebnis: lived experience
das Erste: the first
faktisch: factical, factual*
Faktizität: facticity
Faktum: fact
gebend(e): dator, giving*
das Gegebene: the given
Gegebenheit: givenness
Gegebenheiten: givens

Gegenstand: object
Gegenständlichkeit: objecthood
hinnehmen: receive,
   accept
das Letzte: the last, ultimate
Meinung: meaning, our
   meaning
Objekt: object
Rechenmaschine: calculator,
   adding machine*
Sachverhalt: state-of-affairs,
   relatedness of things*
Satz: proposition, law (as in
   Satz vom Widerspruch)
Schuld: debit, debt
Sinnlichkeit: sense-
   perception, sensibility
   (where reference is to Kant)
Spezies: species
Tatbestand: factual state,
   reality*
tatsächlich: factual, in fact
Verdinglichung: reification
verifizieren: verify
vermeint: meant, thought
Vorfindlichkeit: encounter-
   ability, something
   encountered, finding*

* Adorno's English in 'Husserl and the Problem of Idealism'.

Vorgegebenheit: head-start,
  advance, pregivenness*
Wesensschau: essential
  insight, intuition of

essences*
Wissen: knowledge
Zusammenhang: structure,
  nexus, cohesion

* Adorno's English in 'Husserl and the Problem of Idealism'.

Index